RAY BY RAY

RAY BY RAY

*A Daughter's Take on
the Legend of Nicholas Ray*

A Memoir by
NICCA RAY

with an Introduction by
SAMANTHA FULLER

Three Rooms Press
New York

Ray by Ray: A Daughter's Take on the Legend of Nicholas Ray
by Nicca Ray

This is a work of creative nonfiction. Some parts of this book, including dialog, characters and their characteristics, locations and time, may not be entirely factual.

ISBN 978-1-941110-87-4 (trade paperback)
ISBN 978-1-941110-88-1 (ebook)
Library of Congress Control Number: 2019953546

TRP-080

First edition

COVER AND BOOK DESIGN:
KG Design International: www.katgeorges.com

FRONT COVER PHOTO:
"Nicholas Ray" © Photo by Mark Goldstein
"Nicca Ray" © Photo by Gary Leonard

DISTRIBUTED BY:
Publishers Group West / Ingram Content Group

Printed in the United States of America
Three Rooms Press
561 Hudson Street, #33, New York, NY 10014
threeroomspress.com. info@threeroomspress.com

Dedicated to my mother, the Fabulous Betty . . .

CONTENTS

Introduction

BY SAMANTHA FULLER

Film historians frequently talk about Nicholas Ray and my father, Sam Fuller, in the same breath. Jean-Luc Godard lovingly dedicated his noir film *Made in U.S.A. "To Nick and Samuel, who raised me to respect image and sound."* Both mavericks influenced a number of up and coming French directors as they created their own New Wave. They also fathered cinema sons like Wim Wenders, Jim Jarmusch, Curtis Hanson, Dennis Hopper, and many others. Wenders playfully cast both directors in *The American Friend,* and on the set Sam confessed to Nick that he never really liked these rebel-without-a-cause kids from upper middle class families, because he himself was a poor boy and had to make sure that his single mother with seven children had food on the table. Nick didn't take it personally and smiled understandingly, puffing his Gitanes while Sam offered him a Havana. Our fathers were two big souls who shunned competition and devoted most of their lives to the seventh art.

Nick embraced the Beat generation finding great fault in America's role in the world leading up to and following WWII. My father, the son of Russian immigrants, enlisted in the infantry and fought for the opportunities this country afforded him. The two artists embraced opposing philosophies yet from their very different vantage points, they searched for the truth about America. Both rebels rejected politics and authority as false gods. Their method was to tell hard-hitting stories paired with powerful imagery. Happy endings were not their concern. They embraced the new technology of CinemaScope during their years at Fox studios and their professional lives intersected as they employed the same cast and crew on multiple occasions. The title songs to both Ray's *Johnny Guitar* and Fuller's *China Gate* were composed by Victor Young and this is among my personal favorite connections.

Actors directed by both include Robert Ryan (Ray's *On Dangerous Ground* and Fuller's *House of Bamboo*) and the legendary James Dean who made his very first big-screen appearance in Fuller's *Fixed Bayonets!* in 1951.

Already the biography by Bernard Eisenschitz, *Nicholas Ray, An American Journey,* had left a deep impression on me, but this personal account by Nicca shines a new light on an unforgettable artist and father. Hopefully more generations will discover the great movies of Nick Ray thanks to Nicca's dedication. When I was asked to write an introduction to Nicca Ray's poignant and riveting book about her relationship with her father, I was very touched that she would think of me. Being the daughters of such independent spirits as Nicholas Ray or Samuel Fuller, I understand that honoring such a legacy could be daunting. Both Nicca and I lost our fathers at an early age so we were naturally curious about their body of work in order to know them better. Understanding their work was a way of understanding who we are. Nicca and I inherently carry on their legacy, and even though they had different life stories reflected in very different bodies of work, they both carried within them a deep empathy that modern society is losing. They were reminding us that humanity could not live without emotion.

—*Samantha Fuller*
Los Angeles
Director of *A Fuller Life*

RAY BY RAY

Please Allow Me to
Introduce Myself . . .

I am the youngest child of the film director, Nicholas Ray, best known for directing James Dean in *Rebel Without a Cause*. After his death in 1979, when I was seventeen, people who I met at the clubs around Hollywood called me a rebel with a cause. I didn't know what they were talking about. I hadn't seen my father's movie. The only cause I had at that time in my life was to get wasted.

I come from a long line of alcoholics and drug addicts. Aside from alcohol, speed was the drug of choice amongst us. Although I did dabble in heroin, I was squeamish with needles and blood, and so I never made it to full-on junkiedom. My father, Nick, was notorious for carrying a doctor's bag full of pharmaceuticals during the height of his career directing twenty movies (not including the films he doctored while under contract at RKO) in sixteen years. By the time I was born his illustrious career was on the skids, a doctor had prescribed methamphetamine to treat his alcoholism, and a nurse was coming to the house to shoot him up. At the same time my mother Betty, his third wife, was ingesting Preludin, an amphetamine that made her mind spin around in circles so quickly she could barely move. After Betty left Nick, she got off the Preludin, but continued popping the caffeine tablets, Vivarin and NoDoz, like candy.

I was five years old and standing in the small living room of the house my mother had called a shack when it became clear to me that I had to have a strong sense of self before achieving success. Otherwise, I'd become my parents. This is the first clear memory I have of childhood.

When Nick came to visit us ten years after my parent's separation, he brought along his drug dealer who always carried with him the best Bolivian and Peruvian flake. Not that I knew what cocaine was at the time. Hell, I didn't even know what the tiny silver spoon was that my father had dropped on our living room carpet. When I'd asked my older sister what it was, she looked at me like I was from Mars and said, "Coke, Nicca, coke."

I started my love affair with speed when I was twelve. First, I tried white crosses, pills that resemble an aspirin tablet but do much more than kill the pain. I graduated to their bigger sister, the time released black beauty, by the time I was fourteen. Two years later I was snorting cocaine practically every day. It was not a problem getting my hands on it. I'd started going to clubs on the Sunset Strip when I was fifteen. There were always men willing to give a pretty girl drugs.

I loved alcohol just as much as I loved speed and would put myself in the same precarious situations to get my hands on another drink that I would to get another line of coke. By the time I was of age I was sober, so I never took a legal drink and therefore had to scam for drinks just as I had to scam for drugs. Another family trait I shared was mixing alcohol and speed. The two just seemed to go hand in hand. Mixing cocaine and liquor really did the trick, though. The coke kept me from getting messy. Without it I was a falling down disaster.

Nick, once a Hollywood golden boy championed by the producer, John Houseman, and the director, Elia Kazan, became a fall down drunk in his later years. The doctor who had prescribed him the methamphetamine believed the speed would keep the alcohol from destroying Nick. It only added to his mania. I knew nothing about Nick's mania until I was in my forties and started on this search to find out about my father's career and life, the reason for my parent's separation and eventual divorce, and ultimately to learn what kind of a man Nicholas Ray was. In so doing I hoped to come to a better understanding of myself.

When I looked into the mirror, there was always a hole where my father was supposed to be. I could see my mother in me, because I had grown up with her, but I had not grown up with my father, in fact I'd only seen him a handful of times, and I was always left with an emptiness, a not knowing. And I needed to know what parts of me came from him because I was his namesake. I had been making attempts to shape my life in his image since I was a teenager running through my high school from cops with their guns drawn. The troublemaker, rebel, non-conformist. I'd gone to many bookstores and stood in the film book aisle reading about what a renegade Nicholas Ray was, reading how he understood the misunderstood, reading about his kinship with the troubled teen.

That was me! The troubled teen. He had been one, too. He'd been kicked out of high school sixteen times after his father died. After Nick died, I dove into a punk rock lifestyle that at first saved me. In the late 1970s it was the only place where it was okay to be an angry girl. The anger I had been feeling since Betty married a second time, putting my sister and I into danger and leaving us both the victim of violent rages and incest, amplified after my father's death. I met girls who were angry like me, girls who understood. I cut off all of my hair. I dressed in black with chains and spikes. I spent my nights slam dancing (we didn't call it moshing then) in the pit to bands like Black Flag, The Adolescents and The Circle Jerks. In the mornings my friends and I would count our bruises like they were badges of honor. We didn't live at home with our parents. We couldn't get jobs because of the way we looked or keep them because we couldn't wake up in time. We spent the money we earned panhandling on black beauties and Thunderbird wine or Olde English 40-ounces, instead of food, and eventually I got sick with hepatitis.

Nick's mother always came to his financial rescue and his three older sisters were always there to help him pick up the pieces. Nick would never risk actual homelessness, not even later in his drug-addled life. He had directed the masterpiece, *Rebel Without a Cause*, and that was the calling card that would always be his savior.

I had no such calling card to save me. Everyone in my family was always scrambling to save themselves. I have one full-blooded sister, Julie, and two half-brothers, Tony and Tim. Tony is Nick's son from his first marriage to the writer, Jean Evans. Tim is Nick's son with his second wife, the actress Gloria Grahame. If you're a film buff you may recognize her as Ginny Tremaine in *Crossfire*, Violet Bick in *It's a Wonderful Life*, or as Rosemary Bartlow in *The Bad and the Beautiful*. If you aren't a film buff but are big on Hollywood scandals of the 1950s you've probably heard about Gloria Grahame marrying Nick Ray's first son, Tony, eight years after she divorced Nick. And if you haven't heard, I am here to tell you.

For me, Tony and Gloria's marriage signified that relationship norms weren't upheld in our family.

The Rays had their own ethics. Navigating through them as a kid nearly killed me.

The acts of violence done against me as well as my alcohol and drug addiction took away whatever sense of self I had. By the time I was fourteen and fifteen and going to clubs I had a singleness of purpose. Not to feel anything at all. In adulthood I have learned that I am an emotionally driven person. I had purposefully wiped my core self out.

My father was an emotionally driven person, too. His movies are emotional canvases portraying what it means to be human.

Here, let me breathe and assure you that my sister and I are okay. In fact, we're both doing really well and, as a family, my mother, sister, and I have healed. It's important that you know that.

I got clean and sober two weeks after turning twenty. I had first tried getting sober when I was nineteen, but felt that I was too young, and could figure out how to control my alcoholism and addiction. One year later, in 1981, the year I got sober, there weren't a whole lot of people my age admitting their lives had become unmanageable because of alcohol and drugs. More than anything I wanted to continue fitting in with my misfit friends in spite of my not imbibing. And I did for a time, as well as you can when you're the only one in a room not shooting drugs. My first serious boyfriend, the first boy I ever lived with, became a full-fledged junkie right before my eyes. He was eighteen when we met and I was twenty and two months sober. We lived together for nearly three years. I never picked up, not once. Everyone I had been close to before I got sober was getting strung out. At first, I didn't see any reason why I should remove myself from their company. I was not threatened by their using. I knew I was done. I knew if I drank or did drugs again, I would die. I felt that I had come close to dying and never ever wanted to experience that kind of fear and compulsion again.

Nick got sober before the end of his life but was diagnosed with terminal cancer before he ever really had a chance to discover the riches of a sober life. However, I do believe he was at the threshold of attaining an artistic clarity he had lost in his drunken and drugged out years. Directors such as Miloš Forman and Wim Wenders were bringing him back into the fold, casting him in movies such as *Hair* and *The American Friend*.

Nick's sisters used to blame Hollywood for ruining Nick. Nick's son, Tim, felt that he was at his happiest when he was involved with the musicologist, Alan Lomax, and bringing the likes of Lead Belly, Pete Seeger, Josh White, and Woody Guthrie to the stage. Nick's first love as a boy had been music. He'd wanted to be a conductor. His second was poetry. He was in love with the poetry of Robinson Jeffers. When I first learned this, I rushed out to buy a book of his collected works and devoured his poem, "The Roan Stallion," in hopes of discovering something about Nick's personality. It didn't give me the definitive look into my father's psyche I'd hoped for, but it did shed light on how he found comfort in poetry that spoke of discomfort and unease.

I have found comfort in music that sang of discomfort and unease. My love of music and desire to be up close and personal with the bands on stage never left me. Newly sober, I continued going to see bands like TSOL, Youth Brigade, The Vandals, and Circle One at the Cathay de Grande in Hollywood and Godzilla's in the San Fernando Valley. I spent my twenty-first birthday watching the great D. Boon and Mike Watt play in their phenomenal band, The Minutemen, at The Anti-Club in East Hollywood. I sat on stage in front of the amps watching Motörhead play at The Country Club, a mid-sized club in Reseda, and shivered with excitement when Lemmy, the lead singer, wagged his tongue at me. When the Bad Brains played at the Whisky, I didn't steer clear of the madness in the center of the club floor. When the Ramones played The Palace in Hollywood, I moved through the pit and up to the front of the stage. I was as comfortable then as I had been when I'd been high. I had achieved a goal I'd set for myself when I first got sober: to be able to go into the pit without being drunk.

I know, some people would think a person getting sober at twenty would want to go to college and steer a more mainstream course for their life. Not me. I wanted to find comfort in my weirdness. I was weird. I'd always been. When I was ten,

I got the nickname Freaka Nicca because I wore hot pants to school, and that was before I ever did any drugs. It wasn't the drugs or the drinking that made me a misfit. It was me that made me one.

I would end up going to college in my thirties. Before I had the confidence to even apply, I had to attend to personal issues. I had to reconcile the abuse I'd endured as a child. Well, to tell you the truth, it wasn't like I woke up one day and said, "Hey. I think it's a good time to look into my past and see the damage that was done. Golly gee." No. I started having a recurring nightmare that I was being chased through my house by a rapist. That got me going to a therapist and for the first time in my life I started talking, really talking, not just telling someone what had happened to me as a way to get sympathy or a drink or a line of coke, no, I started really talking about the four years my mother was married to my stepfather and the abuse I endured. It unraveled me. I couldn't eat or sleep for days on end. I was in an emotionally dark place for a couple of years. I came close to shooting drugs again but before I did, I removed myself from that which was tempting me. I moved from Los Angeles to New York City and saw the darkness through without destroying my sobriety. Sometimes we need to unravel to find our true selves.

When I was twenty-eight, I fell in love with an artist, Jesse McCloskey. We met at Dojo's Restaurant on St. Marks Place where we were both working at the time, me as a server and he as a bartender. He had just graduated from the MFA program at Parsons where the artists Paul Resika and Leland Bell were his teachers. They passed along to him the teachings of Hans Hofmann, an abstract expressionist who was an important teacher in the New York School of Painting, famous for teaching the "push and pull" in painting.

Jesse and I were friends for a year before we ever kissed. He'd grown up on a horse farm in Massachusetts and would walk me home after our night shifts telling me about the harvest moon and sharing stories about the shenanigans that went on in the barn while tending to the horses. His stories of growing up in a small Massachusetts town at the beginning of the Cape were both unlike any I'd heard and strangely similar to mine. On many Sunday afternoons, Jesse would accompany his father on the drive back from the track. On the way home he'd pull into a bar's parking lot and tell Jesse to wait in the car. Hours would go by before his father staggered back to the car. There was a day to day uncertainty in both of our childhoods that shaped us and brought us together. Like my family, his had its problems with alcoholism. Like me, he wasn't paid much attention to when he was growing up.

Unlike me, Jesse was not an alcoholic. He wasn't self-destructive like I had been. He was focused and driven and saw art and college as his way out of his upbringing. He was the first one in his family to graduate from high school, let alone get his master's degree. He had the kind of inner strength that could withstand whatever storms blew his way. It was evident, just by the way he carried himself, he was not going to let anything stand in the way of his leading the kind of life he wanted. An artist's life.

I let him lead the way.

Since we were first together, I've known he is a man of his word. Before we had sex, he insisted I get tested for AIDS. He had just gotten his test results and was negative for HIV. I asked him what he would do if I tested positive. He said he wouldn't leave me and that we would figure it out together. Back then it took a few weeks to get your test results. I was so scared I'd be positive for HIV. I had so much shame about my sexual history. Jesse held my hand the entire wait time. He told me he loved me before we were ever sexually intimate. Even if my test results had come back positive (I tested negative) I knew without a doubt that Jesse would never leave my side.

I strongly believe that I would not have ever been able to find my way back to writing had it not been for my sobriety and Jesse's love. I have been sober thirty-eight years and with Jesse for thirty. This is not the kind of stability my family ever knew.

At ten years old I was writing stories and plays and had drawers filled with them. I would bring them to school and give them to my fifth-grade teacher, Mr. Harasick at Franklin Avenue Elementary. He would read my stories to the class. It embarrassed me but I craved the attention. I would try to share these stories with my mother, but she never had the time to listen. I ended up throwing away all of the stories and only writing if I had to for school. Then there came a time when I was so numb from drugs and alcohol, I couldn't even write a paragraph.

I was in my late twenties when I started writing again. I had been studying acting until then but when my focus and concentration returned and I was writing plays and publishing short stories I stopped studying acting and started going to The New School University where I hoped to (and did) attain an education that would make me a well-rounded person and therefore hone my skills as a writer. It was while I was an undergraduate that I began to broach the subject of Nicholas Ray. A friend of mine was working at the long defunct magazine, *Icon*, and mentioned how they were looking for my nephew, Tony's eldest son, in hopes that he would write about Nick for their legacy column. I said, "Let me write it."

I had just seen *Rebel Without a Cause* for the first time. I still knew very little about Nick's life. I wrote what I knew at the time, which mostly had to do with me finding a connection with him. I had just shot my first non-sync 16mm film and was editing it on a flatbed. It made me think back on watching him in an editing room in East Hollywood during the early 1970s, watching film go around and around like a hamster on a wheel. What had compelled him then, I thought was the same thing compelling me to sit in a dark room by myself trying to find the rhythm in the images and syncing them together. It gave me comfort.

Recently, I've been letting it sink in that I am my father's legacy; that is my birthright. It's been hard for me to accept that my birth gives me the right to anything, especially anything having to do with him. What comes from him to me isn't material. That's what stumps me every time I want to define what it means to be his legacy. Yet, I know there are those things inherent in me that come from him. I am of my father: not him, yet forever entwined. My legacy is not to take from him or to be him, it is to share and introduce his work so that he is not forgotten. I am Nicholas Ray's namesake, but it's taken me a lifetime to embrace who I am. I am the standard bearer of my family's history and carry the weight of their trespasses on my shoulders and the breadth of their artistry in my wings. I am the teller of their stories and the peacemaker of their turmoil. I am of them, not them, forever entwined with them. Allow me to introduce you to their stories and in sharing them I share myself.

Tinkerbell Betty

My mother, Betty, always held court telling her Hollywood stories. She would begin each story sitting with a perfectly straight back, feet flat on the floor, and holding an unlit Viceroy cigarette. She would make eye contact with everyone in the room, be it just my older sister and I or the roomful of friends she'd invited over for a dinner party. She would flick the Bic lighter she kept in the pocket of the brown leather cigarette case that never left her side. Once she had everyone's undivided attention, she would lift her feet off the ground so that just her toes touched the floor and with swift arm movements demonstrate one of a number of dance routines she'd performed throughout her career, dancing in a trio with the jazz dancer turned choreographer, Luigi, or on set with the goddess of movie musicals, Cyd Charisse, or dancing on a table like a cat in a bar in the Rock Hudson movie, *The Tarnished Angels.*

Betty used to brag to me how she'd never lost an audition. You can tell by the number of movies I've been in how my auditions went. My mother needed to be center stage. I did not.

It had been almost a year since she passed away from throat cancer on January 16, 2017, when I was looking through her personal belongings for the first time and opened a large manila envelope. Inside I found mementos from her Hollywood days: sales receipts from Capezio of Hollywood at 5619 Sunset Boulevard and Max Factor at 1666 North Highland Avenue, receipts for her Screen Actors Guild dues payments, and pay stubs from MGM. The envelope was addressed to 1208 N. Fuller Drive, where she lived with my grandmother, Joy, from 1956 to 1957. I knew where North Fuller Drive was. I knew the Hollywood streets that were a part of her weekly routine. These items gave me a window into her life that I'd never been able to see before. While they left acquaintances awestruck, her stories, like the one of being noticed by Cecil B. DeMille in the Paramount Studios commissary and then being cast as the Golden Calf in his epic masterpiece, *The Ten Commandments,* always kept me at a distance. What I heard was that I would never achieve time in the spotlight like she had.

I tried. In the spring of 1984, when I was twenty-three, I auditioned to study acting with Nina Foch, the most sought-out acting teacher in Los Angeles at the time. I sent her a hand-written note saying that I'd like to audition for her class, along with a Polaroid of myself and my golden retriever puppy. That's how much I knew about the business.

Nina Foch came up as a Shakespearean actor on Broadway and was nominated for the Oscar in 1954 for her role in *Executive Suite,* which, by the way, was produced by John Houseman, the actor and producer who, after a lifetime working in theater, radio, and film and founding the Mercury Theatre with Orson Welles, received an Academy Award in the 1970s for his supporting role in *The Paper Chase.*

Betty told me John Houseman was my godfather when I was in my forties, long after he had passed away. I always thought the reason Nina Foch had taken me into her class was because she had known my father, Nicholas Ray. I'd made the assumption she'd known my father because she was friends with Houseman and Houseman was lifelong friends with Nick. Imagine my surprise when decades later I discovered Nina Foch hadn't known my father at all. There was more of a chance of Betty knowing Nina Foch during the 1950s than Nick. They were in two movies together: *The Ten Commandments,* in which Foch played the beautiful Pharaoh's daughter, Bithiah, and in *Scaramouche* where she played the role of Marie Antoinette.

Scaramouche was Betty's first movie. "A choreographer saw me dancing and asked me if I wanted to do a movie. I said, 'Uh, well, when and for how long cause I have to go back to high school.'" Betty was discovered when she was fourteen. Who gets discovered? Lana Turner gets discovered. Charlize Theron gets discovered. My mother gets discovered.

My audition was held at the Coronet Theatre, which was where John Houseman produced Bertolt Brecht's play, *Galileo,* starring Charles Laughton, in 1947, the same year he produced my father's directorial debut, *They Live by Night.*

In his debut, Nick chose to film the opening sequence of a prison escape from a helicopter. There is no record of anyone shooting from a helicopter before this point. John Houseman, forever Nick's advocate, kept the studio heads at bay allowing Nick to listen to his intuition and take the risks he needed to create the mood and tension he wanted.

"Nick Ray emerged as an autonomous creator with a style and a work pattern that were entirely and almost fiercely his own," Houseman wrote in his autobiography, *Front and Center.*

The room at the Coronet Theater where I auditioned for Nina Foch's class was empty except for the small platform of a stage and the folding chair the famed teacher sat in. She was the most elegant woman I had ever encountered. Short, dark blonde hair, exquisite bone structure, and magnificent blue eyes. Her elegance intimidated me. I blanked out after the first sentence of my monologue from *The Glass Menagerie.*

"Oh fuck," I said.

She smiled and it was the sun.

"This is what we're going to do," she said. "You're going to take my assistant, James Bontempo's, scene study class for six months, and then you will study with me. Now, don't tell anyone I've promised you space in my class, because I never make that promise to anyone. Okay?"

The confidence with which Nina Foch carried herself made her look taller than her five feet, nine inches. She was Hollywood stature. Studying with her brought to mind the movie stills I had seen of my mother, an angelic dancer in MGM musicals with Fred Astaire. Betty had once been just as grand.

Betty fell in love with dance in 1942, at the age of seven, after seeing Nora Kaye, a dancer with the American Ballet under the direction of George Balanchine, in *Fall River Legend*, the story of Lizzie Borden.

"The curtain opened and there was this woman, Nora Kaye, in a gown sitting in a rocker holding an axe that was dripping blood. It was so viscerally dynamic. I followed her every move. I'd never seen anything like this."

From that point on there was no doubt in my mother's mind that she would become a ballerina. However, my grandparents, Joy and Karl Uitti, didn't have the money to pay for lessons. My grandfather, Karl, earned a living as a linotypist. He was also a boxer and a poet. I never met him. He died of a heart attack before I was born. My grandmother, Joy, had grown up wanting to be a fashion illustrator. When she was in her early twenties, she was stricken by syringomyelia, a rare disease where a cyst forms over the spine, eventually destroying the center of the spinal cord. Her fingers became like wilting flowers, they curled into her palms, and she spent the rest of her life a cripple.

Using his earnings from his newspaper route, Betty's older brother, David, gave her the money to buy greeting cards that she could then sell at a profit. Betty was able to pay for her own lessons with a teacher she called Miss Evelyn at a studio in downtown Detroit, twenty-five miles from her house. My mother was seven years old when she started taking two buses, by herself, into the city.

When I was in my thirties, Betty confided in me that when she was that young girl taking the bus to Miss Evelyn's in downtown Detroit, she would get scared. "But I wouldn't allow myself to be afraid," she'd say. "I'd tell myself I was excited."

She never let fear stop her from achieving her goals. By the time Betty was ten she knew who the premier dance teachers in this country were and found a way to take their classes. She spent a summer studying dance in Chicago with Berenice Holmes, who counted Gene Kelly as one of her students. It was while she was taking Holmes' class that she realized she was much further advanced than her peers back home in Detroit.

When summer ended, she returned to Michigan and her classes with Miss Evelyn, which she took for free in exchange for teaching preschoolers simple bar work and ballroom dancing.

Miss Evelyn lived with her girlfriend, Ruby, in an apartment above the studio, and Ruby would sometimes sit in and watch the classes. Betty felt both of their eyes on her. Throughout the day, Miss Evelyn would find reasons to touch Betty, pinch her cheek, that sort of thing. "You know, they couldn't come on to me straight, because I was a kid, but that's what it felt like they were doing. One Friday night after I'd been teaching ballroom dancing Miss Evelyn asked me to come upstairs to their apartment. She buzzed me up and I instinctively wouldn't go up. I sat at the bottom of the staircase. I didn't tell anyone that I felt their sexual advances. Miss Evelyn was the only resource I had so I dovetailed that."

She had to figure out how she was going to keep Miss Evelyn happy so that she wouldn't be kicked out of class. She would expose herself through dance but once she stepped off the dance floor or stage, she would close herself off, she would put out a sign, hands off.

This woman, who was supposed to be my mother's mentor, betrayed my mother's trust, and made my mother feel sexually objectified before she was even old enough to know what sexuality was. Without even knowing she was doing this, Miss Evelyn, was the first person to teach my mother how to maneuver around predatory people.

She learned how to "dovetail that."

"I was happier than hell when my dad said we were moving to California."

Karl got a job as a linotypist at a newspaper in California and moved the family to Bakersfield where Betty danced the lead in both *Swan Lake* and *Cinderella* with the Kern County Symphony and made the papers.

Karl was possessive of Betty her entire life, but it grew worse as she gained acclaim for her dancing. When my uncle David was accepted into UC Berkeley in 1948, the family moved from Bakersfield to San Francisco. David moved out on his own and Betty, then twelve, was left alone with her parents. For a short time, they lived in a flophouse in San Francisco's Haight district. "My mother, dad, and I shared the same bed. That's when my father started measuring my legs with a tape measure."

In my mind's eye I see my mother lying in the middle of her bed as stiff as a piece of plywood while her father hooks the cold metal tab of the tape measure on her baby toe and pulls the yellow tape all the way past her knee and up her thigh.

"I was deeply ashamed. It was like being raped. It wasn't a sexual assault, but it was. He wanted me to have the perfect body."

My grandfather measured my mother's legs with a measuring tape.

Betty had to get away from her father and knew dance was her escape.

The mention of Betty's performance in the newspaper got the attention of Miss Evelyn, who had moved to California with her girlfriend, Ruby, and the two drove up from Hollywood to watch Betty perform.

"Evelyn said, 'You've got to come to L.A. and study. You can stay with me and Ruby.' Well, I wanted to go because I'd heard Vaslav Nijinsky, the premier dancer with Ballets Russes, was teaching. I said to myself, 'Oh I can put up with Evelyn's advances. I'll be gone all of the time.'"

In the summer of 1949, at the age of fourteen, she fled to Hollywood to study with Theodore Kosloff. As a dancer he toured with Sergei Diaghilev's ballet company before coming to the United States and being cast in Cecil B. DeMille's 1917 film *The Woman God Forgot*. His successful acting career ended when sound came along, so he opened a ballet school in Los Angeles. It was through him that Betty began studying with Carmelita Maracci, known for creating her own style of dance which mixed ballet techniques with Spanish heel work and castanets. She was a respected teacher to many luminaries including Charlie Chaplin, Jerome Robbins, and Julie Newmar.

Betty was discovered by a choreographer while dancing in Maracci's class and asked if she'd like to do a movie. "The choreographer said the movie would start shooting in two weeks and it'll probably be about a three-week shoot. So, the movie was *Scaramouche*. I did a minuet and wore a big wig. But I had to call my mother because I couldn't work at MGM underage. She had to come and sit during the shoot. That was fun, walking through the gates of MGM and seeing Van Johnson and Tyrone Power, seeing all of these people I'd seen in movies was really such a trip. My mother wasn't excited. The first day she said, 'Betty, if you want to do any more movies you're going to have to lie about your age because I will not be a Hollywood mother.'"

As a child my grandmother, Joy, dreamed of being an artist and living in a big city. Joy had the most beautiful cat-like face.

It didn't match her crippled body. I thought she was amazing, because she could draw in spite of her fingers being dead. She wrapped them around the pencil like a toddler holds a shovel. When I was twenty-three, I became aware of how I held my fork like she held a pencil.

My mother was Joy's caretaker as she aged and made sure my sister and I understood that our grandmother's condition caused her extreme pain. For years, we believed Joy when she said she drank only to relieve the pain. I knew it was insurmountable; I was with her at her apartment when the man from Hillhurst Liquors would bring her weekly delivery of two cases of vodka to her door.

After *Scaramouche*, Betty was cast in a segment of *The Colgate Comedy Hour*, a variety show that aired on Sunday nights. Proposed to NBC by the comic Eddie Cantor, *The Colgate Comedy Hour* had a rotating slate of hosts such as Dean Martin and Jerry Lewis, Frank Sinatra, Peter Lawford, and Bob Hope. It ran from September 10, 1950 to December 25, 1955.

The first time Betty appeared on the show, Martin and Lewis were the hosts featuring the Marx Brothers.

"Martin and Lewis were great. You laughed from the time you started rehearsal. Nothing was straight. I was working my buns off and laughing all the way. I found out that we were going to be in rehearsal and shooting after it was time for me to go back to school, so I enrolled in Hollywood High. I never went. One day, the assistant director came over to me and said, 'The Board of Education is on the set. You're supposed to be in school.'

"I froze in my chair. Groucho Marx, who was one of the guests on the show, came over to me, acting a pantomime of the truant officer chasing after me. He grabbed me by the hand and brought me over to the script girl, and she said, 'Don't worry, we'll enroll you in the Hollywood Professional School.'

"I went to the Hollywood Professional School on a lunch break and found that it cost money that my parents would not be willing to pay. So, after the *Colgate Comedy Hour* job ended, I got myself a waitressing job at a drug store. I ended up working enough to pay for the Hollywood Professional School on my own. But I never went to class. I had a tutor on set. I was just going from film to film to film," Betty said.

No wonder Betty thought nothing of me getting my first waitressing job when I was fourteen, two months before graduating from junior high school, and one month after I was arrested for possession of marijuana in 1976.

My friend, Alice, and I were smoking pot in an apartment garage two blocks away from our school, Thomas Starr King Jr. High, when a police car cruised by, and knew we were up to no good. As soon as we saw them turning into the parking structure, we tossed the joint under a car and I tucked the quarter ounce I'd just scored into my brown corduroy jacket. We made a run for the exit at the other end of the garage. In their pursuit of us, the squad car hit a steel pole and started chasing us on foot.

Alice and I were running when guns were drawn and the cops were warning, "Stop or I'll shoot." We stopped. People came out of their houses and watched us get handcuffed. When we got to the Hollywood Police Station, we were taken for my mugshot and fingerprinted, then put into a holding cell while they called our parents. They reached my grandmother, who called Betty and the two came to get me. As we were walking out to the car my grandmother said, "It's a beautiful day, isn't it?" And as soon as we got in the car my mother started screaming at me, "How could you be so stupid?"

Betty got regular work on the *Colgate Comedy Hour.* In an episode I watched years later, Frank Sinatra was the guest star and my mother appeared dressed as one of the horses of the horse-driven carriage driving vaudeville star Jimmy Durante. She was dressed in a sequined bodysuit with feather balls attached to her hips and a feathered crown cascading like a fountain off of her head. She took my breath away.

After my arrest I had to meet with a narcotics officer at the Hollywood Police Station, where I'd been booked, and was told if I was arrested for any drug-related offenses before I turned eighteen, I would be sent to juvenile hall. I started doing drugs every day.

"I was fifteen and got a call from Paramount to audition for the Bing Crosby film, *Here Comes the Groom,*" Betty said. "The job lasted about a year. I danced many, many numbers. Bing would come in and sing and do some dancing with us. He was married at the time, but I saw his twinkling eyes following me across the set. I was so embarrassed because I was aware that he was watching me dance. It was scary, too. I don't recall having a conversation with him at that time. I didn't hook up with him until I did *White Christmas.*"

"Danny Kaye, Rosemary Clooney, Vera-Ellen, and Bing headlined, and I was dancing right behind them. I remember one number that went 'An-Dy there's a minister Han-Dy' and then there was a beat like a *bomp-bomp, bomp-bomp,* and it was so much fun. During that time all the stars had a dance-in, people who would come into the rehearsal hall and dance-in for the star, and then that dance-in would teach their star what to do in the scene. So, Les Clark was Bing's dance-in and he and I got to be friends. He told me, 'The old man really wants to take you to dinner. Why don't you go?'"

Bing Crosby was fifty-one years old and Betty was barely twenty. On their first date Bing Crosby took my mother to a party at an ex-Ziegfield girl's house in Bel Air. "He thought it would be fun for us to meet each other. We went to this beautiful house and everyone was smashed. Bing wasn't a drinker, and neither was I. He whispered, 'It's kinda boring isn't it?' It was only about 9:30 and we were driving around areas of Beverly Hills I'd never been to before. He pulled over to the side of the road. He had his hat on and he shoved it back and like a teenaged boy started making out with me. All of a sudden, a light came shining at us from behind. It was a cop car. And the cop came over to the window and Bing rolled down the window and the cop said, 'Mr. Crosby, for heaven's sake, take the lady home. You just live around the corner.'

"That was the first time I was in his home. He had this mansion and four kids. His son, Gary, was my age. His sons were playing some sort of card game on the dining room table and I really felt like a fool walking in with their dad. Their mother had died maybe three years prior to that. I felt weird, like why did the cop have to show up?"

On New Year's Eve, 1954, she went with Bing Crosby to a party at the Ambassador Club.

"Well, I didn't like going to nightclubs. But Bing really wanted me to go with him and promised we would come to my party afterward. I said okay. The show was good, but no one at the table was my kind of people. So, I got a headache, and I really wanted to go. On the way home, Bing stopped at Schwab's Pharmacy and got me some aspirin. The next day it was in all of the gossip rags: *"Who was that blonde that Bing was getting aspirin for?"*

When I was growing up the infamous Schwab's was the place on the Sunset Strip where Lana Turner had been discovered. It was Hollywood lore. Everyone knew the story. *"Who was that blonde that Bing was getting aspirin for?"*

"My house wasn't too far from Schwab's and when we got there, Bing parked the car, and put his hand on my knee, and said, 'I suppose you think I'm an old fool, but I'm in love with you, and I want to marry you.' Well, I went red from my toes to the top of my head. I told him I was in love with someone else."

Betty was in love with Nicholas Ray. She had met him three years earlier, in 1951, on the RKO set of *Androcles and the Lion*. Nick had been hired to add some sex appeal to what Howard Hughes thought was turning into a clunker under the direction of Chester Erskine. Nick thought adding a racy scene where Vestal Virgins, dressed in flesh-colored leotards frolicked in the Roman baths would be the perfect anecdote. When the studio censor board got wind of what he was planning on doing they were apprehensive, to say the least. "You propose to have a group of girls clad in tight-fitting, flesh-colored leotards over which are loosely fitted garments engaged in an intriguing ballet, which winds up with the girls divesting themselves of the outer garments before going into a pool enveloped in some sort of an effect of steam."

Nick assured them it would be done in good taste. He called his friend, the choreographer and famed dancer Carmelita Maracci, and asked her to send some dancers to the RKO lot for an audition. "She told us to show up at the studio the next day wearing bathing suits. She said whoever was hired would make a lot of money."

The next day Betty was ushered onto a soundstage and told to wait. Standing there in a swimsuit made her self-conscious about her body.

"I'd never felt like a bathing suit type of girl."

Of course she was self-conscious of her body. Her father put a tape measure to her legs!

When Nick walked onto the soundstage, she couldn't keep her eyes off of him. He was six foot, two inches and weighed just over two hundred pounds. His wavy brown hair wasn't brushed. His eyes were a piercing blue. He was wearing slacks and his polo shirt was not tucked in. He looked at each girl, up and down, walking slowly down the line. Betty was positive he was going to walk right by her and was more than a little bit surprised when he stopped in front of her, put his arm around her waist and walked her across the soundstage onto the Roman baths set.

"What's your favorite fruit?" he'd asked.

"Peaches," she blushed.

He called out to the prop master, "Get me some peaches."

The prop master arrived with a tray of fruit.

"Go in there and play," Nick told her. She bit into the peaches and the juice squirted out of her mouth, onto her lips, and down her chin.

"It tastes good?" he asked.

"Mmmm," she said, wiping the juice.

She danced in the water, showing him all of the different ways she could move her body, hiding some parts, revealing others. He never took his eyes off of her. He made her feel like she was the only girl in the world.

"He was the most magical human being I'd ever met. He cast this spell over me."

The next day on set, wardrobe transformed Betty into an ethereal princess using a long blonde hairpiece, falsies, and a tight-fitting flesh-colored leotard underneath a loose-fitting sheer dress. When she moved across the stage she was in full possession of her body. Her confidence made her stand out, but she was also shy, and it was that paradox that made her mesmerizing to watch.

A week after shooting the Roman bath scene Nick called Betty at home and asked her to meet with him in two days at his office on the RKO lot. She thought it was going to be a date. She was seventeen. A teenager who had never been on a date. In 1951, she hadn't dated Bing Crosby yet. When Nick called and asked her to meet him, she was so excited she bought a pink angora sweater especially for the occasion. "I've never been a frilly, pink, angora person. Totally out of character. I just felt I had to be pretty when I saw him again."

Instead of asking her out, Nick informed her that Howard Hughes liked the way she looked on film and wanted to put her under contract. He had arranged for the studio to pay for photographs and voice lessons with Hollywood's top coach, Nina Moise, who also happened to be the mistress of the playwright Eugene O'Neil.

Betty went home feeling so distraught she tore off her angora sweater and threw it on the closet floor.

Weeks later Nick called Betty and asked if he could take her to the ballet. She was living in Hollywood with her parents. They'd moved from Berkeley after she was cast in *Scaramouche.* She almost didn't tell her father that Nick had asked her out. When she was a sophomore at Berkeley High School the captain of the football team asked her to the prom. When he picked Betty up, Karl met him at the door and "knocked him out on the front lawn." Betty was afraid he would punch Nick too.

"What flipped me out was that my father said okay to my going with Nick, probably because he didn't feel like it was a date. I was going with a director."

After the ballet Nick took her to eat at a romantic Italian restaurant, Villa Nova, on the Sunset Strip, then home to the house he was renting in Beverly Hills. He had moved out of the house in Malibu he had shared with Gloria Grahame, who he was in the process of divorcing.

"I went as easily with him as I would go to the moon with somebody. I don't remember how we went to the bedroom. I do remember going to the bathroom and taking the hairpins out of my hair and setting them on his sink. And of course we get into bed and he discovers I'm a virgin, and afterwards wraps me up, feeds me a big cup of soup, calls a cab, and sends me home. I didn't hear from him again for a long time."

During his absence she met and started dating Bing Crosby.

The first time my mother told me about Bing Crosby's proposal we were driving to Will Rogers State Beach in her green Buick Skylark. At that time I was eight years old and hadn't seen my father for six years. I didn't know where he was. I thought I knew where Bing Crosby was. In Beverly Hills. All of the movie stars lived there.

"Bing Crosby wanted to marry me," she said.

"Why didn't you?"

"I wasn't in love with him," she said.

"But if you had married him, I'd know where my father was."

"If I had married him you would have never been born."

For Love and Theater

In 1933, Nick was living with a high school friend, Lonnie Hauser, and working as an artist's model making fifty cents an hour at the Arts Student League located on 57th Street between Broadway and Seventh Avenue. It was at work that he found out about a wealthy benefactress, Esther Merrill, who let struggling artists take baths at her Greenwich Village brownstone.

At the same time, Jean Evans, a poet, left Los Angeles for New York, traveling alone on a Greyhound bus. She was told by a mutual friend to contact Merrill upon her arrival. When Jean knocked on the door of the Greenwich Village brownstone, Esther Merrill answered the door absolutely naked. "She sort of kept an open house," Jean said.

Jean must not have been too uncomfortable. She stayed long enough that she and my father "fell madly in love." Tony, Nick and Jean's son, was suspicious of this claim. Neither Jean nor Nick struck him as the romantic type. Still, Nick moved out of Lonnie Hauser's apartment and into Jean's apartment on East 11th Street. Jean sure was a renegade, living with a man out of wedlock in 1933. They lived together for five months in a tenement apartment furnished with the bare necessities: a mattress on the floor, a card table, and apple crates used as chairs.

"We were rebelling against middle class respectability," Jean said.

I never met Jean. I didn't know what she looked like until 1993 when I saw a photograph of her in Bernard Eisenschitz's biography *Nicholas Ray: An American Journey.* Jean was dark and pensive, petite with short black hair, dark eyes, and a pronounced nose. She was beautiful in a boyish way.

They spent their nights sitting in the Greenwich Village coffee houses participating in heated discussions about changing the face of theater. They huddled close together with the participants of the downtown theater scene, and with their lips moving, arms flailing, foreheads perspiring, they raised their voices excitedly exclaiming that the theater must be used as a weapon. It could no longer be a place where only the wealthy could afford to go. The theatrical producers had to be less concerned with box office receipts. They had to stop putting all of their money into productions that entertained and catered to the wealthy. It was the height of the Great Depression and the masses who lost jobs and homes and spent their days struggling to find something to eat were feeling more and more marginalized and hopeless. What the theater could do and should do was become a place where the concerns of the people were heard. The theater had to focus on producing plays that tackled the problems that were inherent in present-day society. There had to be a place within the theatrical community where the stages could become a voice of the people. There needed to be a transformation where audiences connected to the material they saw performed.

My father might have jumped right into the movement, but the opportunity that arose for him was to become one of Frank Lloyd Wright's apprentices at Taliesin, Wright's school of architecture in Spring Green, Wisconsin. Wright launched the school in 1932 to infuse art with architecture. When Nick left Jean said, "We had a very young and tragic parting, with Nick saying, 'Wait for me,' and then he was gone."

Reading this quote, I thought theirs must have been a deeply romantic love and that their separation resembled the melodramatic breakups of the soap opera queen, Susan Lucci, who played Erica Kane on the daytime soap opera *All My Children*. Erica Kane was always breaking up with the men she was in love with. I thought that was the way real love should be. You know, to really know what love was, you had to lose it. You had to pine.

Nick asked Jean to wait for his return in two years and she did. He was the love of her life. Just like he was to become the love of my mother's life twenty years later.

In 1933, when Nick arrived at Taliesin, he was disappointed to learn that he was expected to help with daily chores. He boasted that he was brought to Taliesin by Frank Lloyd Wright to direct the theater but there were two problems with this tale. One was that the stage had yet to be built and two is that the only performance Nick had directed thus far was a radio adaptation of George Bernard Shaw's *Candida*. Instead of being treated like the big man on the Taliesin campus he was lumped together with his fellow apprentices who were expected to do hard labor and when they weren't they were expected to sit in hard back chairs and listen to Frank Lloyd Wright lecture about ways to assess space.

"What happens when the corners are removed from a building? In the first place the boxiness disappears. There is a new feeling of *continuous space*. Walls? They no longer serve as barriers, keeping the inside world out. They become screens, letting inside out and outside in. We apprentices must have heard this a thousand times," Edgar Tafel, a former apprentice and chronicler of Taliesin, said.

In a 1958 interview with the *Cahiers du Cinéma* writer, Charles Bitsch, Nick said that "the most obvious influence Wright had on me, apart from a kind of philosophical leaning . . . no, not philosophical leaning, rather a certain way of looking at things, is my liking for CinemaScope. I like the horizontal line, and the horizontal line was essential for Wright."

At Taliesin, Nick gained a reputation for being lazy and "tempestuous." He was more interested in getting drunk and picking fights than he was in digging ditches, driving tractors, or hammering nails into wood.

When I was in elementary school, every time Betty took us shopping at the Broadway on Hollywood and Vine, to eat at Musso and Frank, or to see a movie at Grauman's Chinese Theatre, she'd drive Franklin Avenue to Highland, hang a left, then a right onto Hollywood Boulevard. Before getting to Highland, we'd pass a muted pink house with an entrance that reminded me of something I'd seen in Bedrock, home of the cartoon family, the Flintstones. Every time we drove past it, my mother said, "The house was built by Frank Lloyd Wright," like I was supposed to know who he was, like he was a family friend or a relative.

The next time I heard about Frank Lloyd Wright, I was nineteen and living with Nick's third wife Susan. The biographer Bernard Eisenschitz, Susan, and I were standing over Susan's desk when Eisenschitz mentioned something about Wright's influence on Nick.

Betty said Nick thought all of the intellectual theories about his work were bullshit.

After several months at Taliesin, Nick was thrown out for reasons left unrecorded. Upon his dismissal, he wrote to Jean, "I have felt the hand of genius, and it's a heavy hand."

Nick returned to New York City, became a member of the leftist Theatre of Action, and he and Jean moved into the fifth-floor walk-up on East 12th Street where the Theatre of Action members slept four to a room on mattresses thrown across the floor.

The Theatre of Action along with the other radical collectives on the Lower East Side, was intent on becoming the voice of the people. The Theatre Collective founded by

Mordecai Gorelik, a former set designer for the infamous Group Theatre, abandoned Broadway in hopes of creating a more realistic theater where plays that reflected the times were given priority over plays that catered to entertainment. The Theatre Union, a proletarian theater organization started by Charles Walker and his wife Adelaide, two radicals who were influenced by Leon Trotsky, were committed to using the theater to make social changes. These theater groups, dubbed "workers theaters," were largely influenced by the transformation of Russian theater into a public forum. In a speech Konstantin Stanislavski gave to the Moscow Art Theatre company in 1898 he said, "What we are undertaking is not a simple private affair but a social task. Never forget that we are striving to brighten the dark existence of the poor classes, to afford them minutes of happiness and aesthetic uplift, to relieve the murk that envelops them. Our aim is to create the first intelligent, moral, popular theater, and to this end we are dedicating our lives."

While theater groups in America in the 1930s weren't fighting against state control, they were fighting against the bureaucrats who ran the Theatre Guild. Both the Theatre Guild and the Russian State-run theaters had a governing body who decided what plays would be produced, usually works that drew big box office and had no direct link to the struggles of the people.

According to Harold Clurman, who had worked for the Theatre Guild and was one of the founders of the Group Theatre along with Lee Strasberg and Cheryl Crawford, the Guild "had no blood relationship with the plays they dealt in. They set the plays out in a show window for as many customers as possible to buy. They didn't want to say anything through plays, and plays always said nothing to them, except that they were amusing in a graceful way, or, if they were tragic plays, they were art."

The Group Theatre founded in 1930 was touted in the trades as a revolutionary group. Their first production, *The House of Connelly*, which Clurman said was a play about the "basic struggle between any new and old order," premiered on September 23, 1931 to rave reviews, the same month Nick started his only semester as a non-matriculating student at the University of Chicago.

During its run at the Martin Beck Theatre on West 45th Street, Elia Kazan, then a student at the Yale Drama School sat in the audience with his soon-to-be wife Molly, a playwright and editor in chief of the Vassar *Miscellany*, who after hearing President Roosevelt give a speech over the radio in 1932 became involved with The Theatre Union.

In the spring of 1932 when Nick was hitchhiking from Chicago to California thinking he would work as an extra in movies until he sold his first screenplay, Elia Kazan was sitting in a dimly lit room in a theater on Forty-Eighth Street, interviewing with Lee Strasberg and Harold Clurman for an apprenticeship with the Group Theatre. When Strasburg asked Kazan what he wanted Kazan replied, "What I want is your job. I mean, I want to be a director."

Soon Kazan received a letter of acceptance to be an apprentice at the Group Theatre's second summer camp and on June 19, 1932 he arrived at the Sterling Farms in Dover Furnace, New York.

By 1934, Kazan adopted the Theatre of Action as his own and introduced them to the teachings of Stanislavski and Vsevolod Meyerhold, an actor and director who'd been a member of the Moscow Art Theatre under the direction of Stanislavski before breaking away from the theater and Stanislavski's teachings to form a method and style of theater all his own. Both Stanislavski and Meyerhold influenced the development of Method acting. Strasberg used to quote Meyerhold all of the time. "Words are decorations on the hem of the skirt of action."

"The Group Theatre brought Stanislavsky into cognizance in New York," said actor Norman Lloyd. "The great influence that changed acting in America for all time was the Group Theatre, and the Group Theatre's work, and how they approached the work. That was carried to the Theatre of Action by Kazan."

The Method consisted of, "recalling the circumstances, physical and personal, surrounding an intensely emotional experience in the actor's past. It is the same as when we accidentally hear a tune we may have heard at a stormy or an ecstatic moment in our lives, and find, to our surprise, that we are re-experiencing the emotion we felt then, feeling ecstasy again or rage and the impulse to kill. The actor becomes aware that he had emotional resources; that he can awaken, by this self-stimulation, a great number of very intense feelings; and that these emotions are the materials of his art," Kazan wrote.

"We believed every word he [Kazan] said," Perry Bruskin, the youngest member of the group, recalled. "Nick Ray and I idolized him. If Kazan had said, 'Nick, Perry, jump out of that window,' we'd have done it."

Kazan later wrote, "They did something that most professional actors could not—go the limit in improvisation. Scenes of anger had to be stopped short of bodily harm, love scenes cut off before they reached final intimacy. When the material was in their range of experience, their dialogue was absolutely true; they were the streets of New York incarnate."

Like the punk rock bands I started seeing play in 1979, the Theatre of Action wasn't interested in conforming, or appealing to a mass audience. In 1934, they were to the theater world, what, in 1979, the one-minute song blasts were to the mainstream radio that never played them. Their performances were raw expressions, just fifteen to twenty-minute docu-dramas, developed from improvisations, that were pure, truthful, rough, and jarring.

Instead of acting on theater stages, the members acted on street corners, picket lines, and in subways. Along with a small group of revolutionary theater troupes, they were committed to using the theater to bring upon the social changes necessary to improve the lives of those struggling to put food on the table. The Theatre of Action was labeled Communist, because of their endeavors to serve the poor. Jean once said, "The only people to take a family along to the welfare office and pound on the desk until they got something to eat were Communists."

Nick said, "The great thing about theater in the thirties was that everybody was involved. We all knew what everybody else was doing and we all cared. It didn't matter that we were poverty-ridden, that we had to burn bed bugs off our beds twice a week, that we didn't get paid for a performance. We survived and we survived with each other.

"We worked at learning our craft twenty hours a day," he added. "At nine in the morning we would take classes in body movement with Martha Graham or Anna Sokolow. At eleven we would take voice classes. At noon we would be given a dime for lunch, which we might use for subway fare to a museum or to buy a cream cheese sandwich. At one-thirty we had eurythmics; at two-thirty we began improvisations preliminary to rehearsals. At four we would rehearse until it was time to perform. We would perform on picket lines, at universities, union headquarters, in subways, wherever we could perform—because there is no actor unless there is a spectator."

Elia Kazan directed the Theatre of Action actors in a protest play against the Civilian Conservation Camps called *The Young Go First*. There wasn't a completed script when rehearsals started. Kazan created a third act by setting up a scenario and having the actors improvise their way through it while a stenographer jotted down what was happening. From those notes he wrote a final act. *The Young Go First* legitimized The Theatre of Action. Members received their Equity Cards.

"Kazan and I became friends because both of us wanted to be directors," Nick said. "And we knew in order to do so we had to learn the problems of the actor. How are you going to learn the problems of the actor unless you act? You can theorize a great deal, and it will keep you comfortable, and prevent you from doing anything. A director who hasn't had the experience of an actor is a cripple. I consider Gadge Kazan the best actor's director the theater training available in the United States has ever produced. His achievements as a director are immense."

"Kazan was made of iron," Perry Bruskin noted.

Nick spent his life measuring himself against Kazan. He once said that Kazan had a "more alert and ruthless mind," than he did. Perhaps Kazan was a storyteller and not a poet, more pragmatic, less a daydreamer than Nick. There was no one in his life that Nick held in such high esteem as Elia Kazan. No one.

When I was twenty-six Kazan published his autobiography, *A Life*. I knew of Elia Kazan's importance as a director. I had seen *On the Waterfront*, Kazan's classic film written by Budd Schulberg and starring Marlon Brando and Eva Marie Saint, but the movie of Kazan's I liked best was *Baby Doll* with Carroll Baker as the young bleached blonde wife of plantation owner Karl Malden, who sleeps in a crib and refuses to consummate her marriage. I wanted to wear baby doll pajamas every day all day, live in a crib, and have no responsibility. What could be better than that?

I didn't know how well my father knew Elia Kazan until 1988 when I stood in the aisle of the Strand Bookstore in New York City and read every page of *A Life* that mentioned Nick Ray.

"Nick and I were much alike," Kazan wrote. "We'd both started as actors and become directors. But he went 'all the way,' and I did not. I was more disciplined, more in control, more cautious, more bourgeois. Perhaps, I thought, he's been more of an artist, more of a gambler. But hadn't it been man's deepest desire all through history to have it all, heaven and hell? Faust sells his soul for that. Is this hunger applicable only to actors and directors? Hell, no. Is it specifically American? No. It is the question that life asks: How much do you want and how much will you give up for what you want? I recalled that Nick had always created an image of what he wanted to be perceived as—but it was always a different image.

"We'd once been very close. When I'd directed my first play for the Theatre of Action, he'd been a member of the cast. As the war was closing down, I went to Hollywood to make *A Tree Grows in Brooklyn* and got Nick a job as my assistant. He was studying filmmaking techniques and learning fast. Jack Houseman gave him his first job of direction in Hollywood, *They Live by Night*. It was immediately evident that Nick had a unique talent for directing actors."

Standing in the aisle of the Strand Bookstore with my eyes glued to the pages of *A Life* where my dad's name was printed, I couldn't get past myself and my feelings long enough to comprehend the major influence Kazan and the socio-political upheaval of the times had on Nick's life.

When the Theatre of Action disbanded in 1936 Nick went to work for the Federal Theatre Project. Created in 1935 and funded by the Works Progress Administration the project's director, Hallie Flanagan, made it her mission to build a national theater employing thousands of theater artists and making theater affordable to the mass public. Instead of charging $5.50 per seat they were able to charge as little as

50 cents. The project paid $23.86 a week to the theater artists. In its first year the Project employed fifteen-thousand people. In the four years of its existence the Project produced two-thousand-and-seven-hundred plays all over the U.S. More than thirty million people saw its productions.

Nick was hired as the stage manager on *Injunction Granted* (a phrase used by judges against workers who were trying to create unions), a "Living Newspaper" directed by Joseph Losey about the injustices of the courts. Losey had just returned to New York from Russia where he'd seen a production directed by Nikolay Okhlopkov, a protégé of Meyerhold. He was mesmerized by the way Okhlopkov broke away the proscenium of the theater by presenting it in the round, rectangle, and hexagonal.

"In other words, Losey had come back from Russia with all these modern ideas about theater—expressionism, for example—and all that was involved," Norman Lloyd, who played The Clown in the production, recalled.

Injunction Granted covered a two-hundred-year time span and was told in twenty-eight scenes. The multi-level stage used runways, platforms, and hatches to create individual areas that were highlighted at specific moments with dramatic uses of light, five hundred lighting cues to be exact, and at other times remained pitch black. Newspaper articles chronicling the injustice of the courts throughout time were projected and the sounds of sixteen snare drums and sixteen bass drums were used to emphasize the text.

"The show was quite complicated between the projections, the music, the movement, the number of people, etc. This required from the stage manager the ability to sit on top of it like a jockey and make it work every night, and Nick did that. It worked like a dream," Norman Lloyd said.

After *Injunction Granted* finished its run at the Biltmore Theatre, shortened by accusations of Federal Theatre funds being used to promote a Communist agenda, my father left the city to teach drama at the Brookwood Labor College in Katonah, New York. Nick was supposed to stay eight months and direct a show that would go on to tour the unions. Unsatisfied with time constraints on working with actors, he left after three. Earl Robinson, a fellow member of the Theatre of Action, was hired by the college to be its musical director. "We worked with improvisation—all the things [Nick had] learned during the Theatre of Action he was applying here as director."

For Love and Music

T he first time I ever heard of Alan Lomax was on the day
of my father's memorial, in June of 1979. He was tall and
burly and looked like a bear. He was in his sixties at the time;
his full head of hair was turning white-gray. I felt a quarter of
his size. My stepmother Susan introduced us minutes before
the ceremony started. He said hello, and shook my hand,
then took his place in front of the podium set near the front
of the stage at Alice Tully Hall. I sat in one of the folding
chairs on stage saved for those of us who had been asked by
Susan to say a few words about Nick. It was surreal watching
him move from one end to the other. Mostly, I had a view of
his backside. Alan Lomax didn't appear real. He was more
like a scene in a movie.

Alan Lomax was a folklorist largely responsible for bringing to life stories and music of countless musicians, such as
Lead Belly, who he first heard playing the twelve-string guitar, and singing "Goodnight Irene," at the Angola State Prison,
where the singer was doing time for murder. Or, that he, along
with Nick, created the first radio program to feature black and
white musicians performing on the same stage at the same
time. Due to his friendship with Alan Lomax, my father played
an important part in the folk-blues scene during the late 1930s
and early 1940s.

They met in Washington, D.C. in 1937. Lomax was running
the Archive of American Folk Song for the Library of Congress

and Nick had been working for the Works Progress Administration, and the Special Skills Division of the Resettlement Administration.

"Nick was certainly one of the most splendid young men in the whole world. He seemed to me to be the person I'd always dreamed of being. He was very powerful and gentle and wonderful to look at. He had a kind of grin and laughter that were the same thing. They were always playing on his face when he was discussing the most serious matters. And I think I represented something equally splendid for him, the whole America that he didn't know anything about, and I had already explored," Lomax said.

Alan Lomax grew up traveling through the South with his father, John Lomax, one of the originators of song collecting, loading a three hundred and fifty pound Edison recorder into the trunk of the family Ford station wagon, and setting out to places like the "ramshackle church" on a South Texas sharecropper plantation. But eventually, as Lomax told the CBS News journalist, Charles Kuralt, " . . . my father had the great idea that probably all the sinful people were in jail. And that's where we found this incredible body of music."

Right before newlyweds Nick and first wife Jean Evans arrived in Washington, D.C. with their new son, Tony (born November 24, 1937), they had been traveling across the country recording the stories of those living in rural communities, so poor that some didn't even know what a bathtub was for. Nick shared these recordings with Lomax, and Lomax shared some of his with Nick.

"Nick was a searcher. He searched all his life. In the theatrical world, in the entertainment world, in the world of government in Washington, in the folk backward of the United States, looking for the roots, the true roots of American culture and the American character, trying to unlock the human puzzle that has been lived out on the strange wild continent of ours."

In 1937, my father was a sparkly-eyed, curious adventurer who connected with his new best friend over records. "I had thousands of records, some of the first that were ever made," Lomax said.

I learned of his massive record collection from Pete Seeger, who worked for him at the Library of Congress. "Driving up to Connecticut and picking up boxes and boxes of old rpm records. I'd get back to Washington, D.C. and Alan would have me listen to them first. He'd say, 'Pete I can't listen to all of these. You listen first and put in one pile the ones you think are halfway good that I should listen to.' So, I did nothing from dawn to dark, but listen to hundreds after hundreds after hundreds of old records."

The closest I have ever come to being in a room with that many albums were in my favorite record stores: Platter Puss Records on Hollywood Boulevard near Vermont Avenue, then, as a teenager, Tower Records on the Sunset Strip, and Rhino Records on Westwood Boulevard.

I had always turned to music for solace and direction. By the time I was ten I couldn't wait to go to the clubs on the Sunset Strip. Whenever I passed the Whisky a Go-Go, the club Jim Morrison and Janis Joplin made famous, I recognized the names of some of the bands listed on the marquee from *The Real Don Steele*, a dance show hosted by local KHJ deejay, Don Steele. In an interview given after the show went off the air, Steele described his show as "Dick Clark on acid." Of course, Dick Clark's *American Bandstand* had wider appeal and introduced America to the musical icons of the twentieth century, like everyone who ever had a number one hit. But if I had been old enough to go on either show I would've chosen *The Real Don Steele*. It was wilder. Girls wore sequined halter jumpsuits and hot pants. The boys were real glammed out, with long shag haircuts, and stick thin bodies. Gary Glitter performed wearing an unbuttoned black sequined jacket that exposed his hairy and not so trim torso. Other performers included Dr. Hook, The Hues Corporation, Stories, and androgynous rockers The New York Dolls whose members dressed to the nines in leopard print platform boots, thick white tights and silvery glitter body suits, wore their hair in long teased masses reminiscent of the hair bands that would come along a decade later.

One of my favorite parts of the show was when Don Steele hung out in the faux backstage with the bands and introduced the Real Don Steelers, the swooning groupie girls, like Pamela Des Barres (former GTO, and best friend of bandmate Miss Mercy), the most famous groupie ever. I wanted to be a Real Don Steeler. The closest I got was making my mother buy me red velvet hot pants with a matching jacket at the Angel Youth Shop, an expensive boutique for adolescent girls that sold the hipper clothes you couldn't find at Sears.

The first time I realized that Nick loved music as much as me was when I was nineteen and living in the loft with Susan. There was a poster hanging on the wall featuring a photograph of the band, Television, and a quote from my father that read, "Four cats with a passion."

I knew of Richard Hell and the Voidoids before I ever listened to Television. My friend, Ray Gange, star of The Clash rocumentary, *Rude Boy*, played their *Blank Generation* album for me when we lived in the same apartment building on Highland Avenue. He was always playing me songs I'd never heard before. Anyway, I had written the words to one of Hell's songs in my journal. By the time I was living with Susan I knew that Richard Hell had once been a member of Television. So, when I saw that poster on the wall, and discovered that my father not only knew about the bands I listened to but loved them too, I felt like I was truly his daughter, in a way I hadn't felt before. It was one of those moments where I believed he understood me even though he hadn't really known me.

Nick's job working for the Special Skills Division of the Resettlement Administration afforded him the luxury of renting a house in Alexandria, Virginia. When Alan Lomax moved into the house with Nick and Jean he brought with him a revolving door of musicians, including Lead Belly. Nick, Jean, and Lomax spent nights at the house in Alexandria singing songs with various themes, like dogs, faithless women, or brown eyes, with a cast of characters that included Pete Seeger, Woody Guthrie, Lead Belly, Burl Ives (who gave Tony his first guitar), and Aunt Molly Jackson, a Kentucky coal miner's daughter and wife, who after losing both her father and husband in the mines, became a folksinger and political activist.

In a 1991 interview with CBS news journalist, Charles Kuralt, Alan Lomax nailed the reason someone like me turned to records (and drugs) for guidance and solace. He said, "Young people of the world had never been able to express their terrible need for parenting. This generation is a generation that came along where both parents work. And they were left alone in the house and what were they going to have to look after them? And they found that the record looked after them."

When I was nine or ten, and Betty brought home a promotional copy of David Bowie's record, *A Space Oddity*. Someone from KABC, the radio affiliate of ABC-TV, where Betty worked, gave it to her. I sat in my bedroom playing that album over and over again for hours. The song was like a prayer and a confession and a letter and the voice filled space, but also gave space, so I was able to think along and visualize what the song was about. He was bigger than me, otherworldly, and yet, he connected with me like a new friend. What my mother did that day was give me her replacement. Music kept me company. It told me stories. It rocked me to sleep. It embraced me.

Sometimes when I'm thinking about those first years of Nick's friendship with Lomax, the images that come to mind are like black and white film footage. I see them sitting in the living room, of what I presume was a two-story house, singing songs about the weather with Woody Guthrie. Jean sits next to the fireplace in a rocking chair with baby Tony falling asleep in her lap. The men are passing around a bottle of whiskey, getting drunk and singing at the top of their lungs. "Nick was a very bad singer. But he got to sing. And he was swimming in [song]. It was a very important part of his life," Lomax said.

I think that the years Nick spent with Alan Lomax working on the radio show *Back Where I Come From,* modeled after the sing-along nights at the house Nick, Jean, and Lomax shared, were the years he was most true to himself. There was no money to be made, so there was no power to seek. And the focus wasn't on his vision, it was on the musicians, and how their music brought people and communities together. He wasn't the center of attention. His ego couldn't get the best of him.

The pilot aired on August 19, 1940, with enough fanfare for CBS to give it a regular time slot. Starting in September 1940 it was broadcast on Mondays, Wednesdays, and Fridays at 10:30 pm. Each segment, written by Lomax and directed by Nick, lasted fifteen minutes and revolved around a given theme like the weather.

"*Back Where I Come From* was a rich folk-music show. That's when I first heard Woody Guthrie, Lead Belly, Burl Ives. There wasn't access to music in those days, because we didn't have much money. Think of a world without television, and only going to theater for music. The radio brought in that whole world of folk music, that my brother and I loved. My brother and I sat by the radio and listened to rebroadcasts of this show every Saturday morning. It was this Saturday morning treat," Betty said.

Working with Lomax, Guthrie, and CBS was not without conflict for Nick. Like when Woody Guthrie walked off the show because my father had taken airtime away from

Lead Belly. According to Woody Guthrie biographer, Joe Klein, Guthrie became "the avenging angel of *Back Where I Come From*, challenging Nick Ray on every artistic compromise. He was especially vehement on the subject of Lead Belly, who was given only an occasional subsidiary role on the program. CBS had received numerous complaints about listeners not being able to understand the singer's English. So, Nick had Josh White, a smoother, more accessible black singer, perform his songs so that white America could understand the words."

The first time I heard of Lead Belly I was thirteen. Nick had come home. It was 1974. I was sitting with him at the white dining room table Betty had bought at the Salvation Army after leaving Ward.

"You ever listen to Lead Belly?" Nick stared at me as he took a long drag off of his French Gitanes cigarette.

What I could have used right then was a long drag off a joint laced with some hash oil, followed by a Schlitz Malt Liquor chaser.

The long ash from Nick's cigarette fell on the tapestry Betty had thrown over the table.

Nick paused for a long time. No one had ever told me he was notorious for his long pauses.

I sure wasn't going to ask this man with the hawk eyes what a lead belly was.

It wasn't until after my father's death that I heard a recording of *Back Where I Come From*. Tom Farrell, one of Nick's students from the 1970s, gave me a recording of segment featuring the Golden Gate Quartet.

I listened to the spirituals of the Golden Gate Quartet crackle over my laptop speakers. They sang, *"The Lord told Noah there's gonna be a floody, floody/Get those animals out of the muddy, muddy/Children of the Lord/Oh rise and shout and give God your glory, glory."*

I knew this song! I sang it at a church camp when I was eleven.

My half-brother Tony said the only time he heard Nick talking about God was in 1958 when he was in Boston Hospital going through delirium tremors and ranting about Jesus. Another half-brother, Tim, said the only time he heard Nick mention God was when he was dying of cancer.

Music has always been my God. Music let me be a free bad-ass motherfucker in the fantasies songs allowed me to project. That's how I think of my father when he was hanging out with Leadbelly and Alan Lomax. I mean, Alan Lomax had real respect for the convicts he met when he and his father were collecting prison songs. They taught him about life. Lomax had the kind of guts that Nick lacked. As soon as the radio show came along, and the corporate CBS was calling the shots, Nick chose to please the people with the money.

It was strange listening to the crackly vocals of the Golden Gate Quartet through my laptop speakers. They sounded so long ago.

I'm sitting at my desk in my New York City apartment, listening to the radiator blow out the steam heat, and marveling at how Alan Lomax knew, so young, the power music had to connect us all. It connected my mother to my father, my mother to me, and me to my father.

The Darkness

I was in elementary school the first time I learned anything about my father's family. It was 1971. Betty had shown up at Joy's apartment out of the blue, demanding I leave with her before my grandmother, who was always drunk, passed out with a lit cigarette in her hand. The next day we were driving to Pasadena to visit one of my mother's friends, and she said, "Your father's sister, Ruth, died in a fire."

Ruth had gotten drunk and passed out in bed while smoking a cigarette. The fire was in full swing by the time she came to. She made her best effort to escape, but only got as far as the hallway. The firemen found her on the floor, dead from smoke inhalation.

I hadn't seen my father since 1964. After my parent's separation he stayed in Europe, where my sister and I were born, and my mother returned to Los Angeles, where they had met, and raised us. The last time I had spoken to my father was on the telephone a few days before Christmas 1966. He was crying because he wasn't going to be able to spend the holiday with us and I told him not to worry. Then, voom, he vanished, just like that, never to be seen or heard from or discussed. And then one day in 1971 my mother and I were driving along, and she blurted out, "Your father's sister, Ruth, died in a fire."

This statement sat dormant in my mind for years until it was awakened by my search to get to know who my father was, first by learning about his film career, and then by talking to what members of the Kienzle family were still living.

My father's grandparents fled Germany during the Revolution of 1848 and settled on the Western side of Milwaukee, where my grandfather Raymond Nicholas Kienzle was born during Abraham Lincoln's presidency. Raymond was twenty when his father collapsed and died of a heart attack while walking through town with a dead deer draped over his shoulders.

Lena, a devout Lutheran, was a Norwegian farmer's daughter, beautiful with blonde hair and high cheekbones. While it's believed she married Raymond more for his looks than his money, marrying him brought her into a higher socio-economic bracket than the one she was born into. She was ashamed of her farmer parents. She even had my aunt Helen convinced she was a mail order bride sent to Wisconsin from Oslo.

"Lena wanted nothing to do with her farmer relatives. She instilled that kind of snobbery in Helen and Nick," my cousin and Helen's daughter Gretchen said. "Helen used to say, 'They live out *there*.'"

In 1918, when Nick was seven, my grandfather sold his construction business and moved the family from Galesville, Wisconsin and into a twenty-two-room house on West Avenue in an upper middle-class neighborhood of La Crosse, Wisconsin. The two-story house had a neatly mowed lawn, a huge oak tree, and hedges. It reminded me of the big houses in Hancock Park, an affluent neighborhood in the center of Los Angeles, between Hollywood and the Mid-Wilshire district, not too far from Paramount Studios, where Betty had once been noticed by Cecil B. DeMille and cast in *The Ten Commandments*.

I dreamed of living in Hancock Park when I was a child. It's where the rat-loving Willard, from the early 1970s movies *Willard and Ben*, lived. Willard had made such a profound impact on me that after seeing the movie at Grauman's Chinese Theatre on Hollywood Boulevard, I rushed to the Woolworth in the Barnsdall Square and bought a white and brown rat I named Ms. Bigstuff. In the movie, the rats protected Willard. Ms. Bigstuff was going to protect me.

At the time my mother was married to her second husband, Ward, a special needs teacher who had been married four times before. He had two daughters and one son from his fourth marriage. The son, Mark, and his oldest daughter, Kristen, came to live with us, in a two-story Spanish Revival style house on Wanda Drive, a street with just five houses, tucked away in the hills off of Franklin Avenue, in the Los Feliz neighborhood of Los Angeles.

I was eight and Mark was fourteen when his father married my mother in 1970. Our bedrooms were connected by a wall. We shared a heating vent. If I left mine open, he opened his and watched me undress.

In the Kienzle's West Avenue house there was an entire section of the second story that had no windows at all. In total there were five windows on the second floor and thirteen on the first. I imagined the sun flooding in through the first story windows and filling the living room with light, while the upstairs bedrooms stayed dark.

Raymond Kienzle spent his days at any one of the twenty-one speakeasies that lined Main Street. Nick learned how to drive when he was thirteen so that he could pick his father up from the saloon and bring him home for supper. Nick and his three older sisters weren't allowed to eat until he was dressed and sitting at the dinner table. My grandmother Lena would take him up the back stairs off of the kitchen, give him a bath to sober him up, and get him dressed and presentable for the dinner table. On more than one occasion his daughters had to pick him up from the local jail where he was left to sober up in the drunk tank. When Nick was sixteen, he went looking for his father at the bar where he was a regular. There he found my grandfather's mistress.

"She led me to a hotel room where he was lying in sweat and puke with puke pans on the floor at the side of the bed. I took him home and nursed him through the night. In the morning the doctor came and, before I left for school, I watched him heat some substance in a spoon and draw it into a hypodermic. In Latin class I alternated between dozing off and hypertension. I asked to be excused and was. I went to the pool hall and practiced three cushion billiards. A phone call. My mother had trailed me—my father was dying. He was dead when I arrived."

After Raymond Nicholas Kienzle's burial it was as though he never existed. "I never saw any pictures of him in the house. Maybe Lena threw them away," Gretchen said.

Raymond Kienzle's own father had died of a heart attack when he was twenty. Nick's father died when he was sixteen. My father died when I was seventeen. My grandmother, Joy's, father died when she was two. My mother, Betty's, father died when she was eighteen. None of us talked about them.

My aunt Ruth's granddaughter, Barbara, contacted me after reading "Dangerous Talents," an article in the Hollywood issue of *Vanity Fair* written by Sam Kashner, who had interviewed me because of the research I'd done on Nick's films at the Museum of Modern Art Film Archive.

"I was reading the March edition of *Vanity Fair* about James Dean and Uncle Nick. It mentioned you. I did not know that he had a daughter."

Had Nick never spoken of me to his sisters, Alice, Ruth, or Helen? That would explain why none of my aunts ever reached out to my sister and I when we were growing up.

Alice was the only one of the sisters to escape the West Avenue house seemingly unscathed. She created a beautiful home in California where she lived with her three children and husband in an old cedar house surrounded by lush gardens, oak trees, and a swimming pool. Alice only returned to Wisconsin twice after moving to California: once, in 1951, for the hometown premiere of Nick's seventh film, *Flying Leathernecks*, in which Nick made a rare appearance, and the second time for Lena's funeral in 1959.

In the 1950s, at the height of Nick's career, he would show up at Alice's with the likes of the actor, Robert Mitchum, producer John Houseman, or star of musicals, Gene Kelly, in tow for one of Alice's scrumptious big breakfasts and afternoon horseback rides.

Helen never moved out of the West Avenue house, remaining even after marrying a widower, the local mailman, Ernie, and having a daughter, Gretchen. Gretchen attributes living there as the reason she became a psychiatric nurse as an adult.

Ruth's first marriage to a scientist named Gil deteriorated beyond repair after two years. When he found out she was pregnant, he begged her not to have the baby, so she left him and moved to be near her best friend, giving birth to Karen in 1932. Gil pleaded with Ruth to come back and join him in Chicago. She couldn't wait to introduce him to their daughter. When Ruth and Karen arrived in Union Station, however, Gil was nowhere in sight. Not knowing what to do or where to go, Ruth found a job in Chicago and arranged for Karen to stay at the West Avenue house with Lena, Helen, and Helen's family.

Helen showered Karen with warmth, but never resisted the opportunity to put her own daughter, Gretchen, down. Karen's admiration for Helen was just as great, nicknaming her Mama Hon. Whenever I see the words, "Mama Hon," I picture a large, cuddly, protective mama bear. The affection Helen was able to show Karen but not Gretchen reminded me of the tenderness Joy showed me but not my mother, Betty.

When Karen was five years old, Ruth married Stan Fairweather, and brought her daughter home to Chicago. Stan was the successful owner of an exhibit and display business and Ruth left her job as a legal secretary to work for him. When they brought Karen to live with them, they were living on Chicago's west side. As their business continued to prosper they were able to afford to buy the red brick brownstone with the black shutters and iron gate, where, in 1965, Ruth's scorched body was found lying on the second story landing, after passing out drunk on the couch in her study while smoking.

My aunt Ruth, like Nick, was described as building isolation around herself. "She slumped, legs bowed in front of her with one arm down the side clutching the whiskey bottle, the other loosely holding onto her cigarette that was dropping long ashes into the Venetian glass ashtray on the floor. On her face was the look of helplessness, shame, fear, and repulsion," according to Karen. There's a Rolling Stones song on the *Some Girls* album, "Far Away Eyes." A boyfriend I had in 1978, when that record came out, called me the girl with the faraway eyes. I'll never forget that when he said this to me, I turned away from him, because I felt he was seeing all of my secrets. I see my darkness in Ruth. In the photographs Barbara sent me I am struck by the faraway look in Ruth's eyes. She was restrained as if by straitjacket. "Ruth was totally bound up. She was all control," Gretchen said.

And when Ruth drank, she unwound, and let the venom spill out. After I got sober, at twenty, I asked someone who had known me during the last year I was drinking, what I was like when I was drunk. He said, "Well, when you weren't screaming at people you were passed out in the corner of the club."

In 2007, two years after first speaking to Barbara, she sent me a box of family heirlooms. Wrapped in bubble wrap were two Spanish tiles that had survived the fire in Ruth's Chicago brownstone, pieces of the wall still attached.

Barbara also sent me pictures of the Kienzle family I had never seen before. There were eighteen of Lena, nine of which were shot in the backyard of her West Avenue house. She was an avid gardener, like my sister Julie, born with a green thumb, is now.

In the photographs of Lena, her hair is white and wavy, cut short in layers that frame her face. She has a strong jawline, long arms, and excellent posture. She's wearing a striped linen dress that buttons down the front and white pumps. She has large calves like her daughters, Helen, Alice, and Ruth. And like my cousin, Karen, who, coincidentally looks like me. I got goosebumps. I saw myself in them in a way I didn't my mother or sister. I had their body type.

After finding her number in the Pennsylvania phone book, I called Gretchen and said, "This might be a really weird phone call. My name is Nicca Ray . . . "

"I know exactly who you are," she interrupted.

She spoke as if she had been waiting all these years for me to call. Her voice reminded me of the voices of Patty and Selma Bouvier, Marge Simpson's twin sisters on the animated series, *The Simpsons*. Like my mother, she was a self-proclaimed feminist. She was sassy and to-the-point and I liked and trusted her immediately.

Over the course of two days, and a couple of lengthy phone conversations, Gretchen compared being with the Kienzle family—Nick was born Raymond Nicholas Kienzle and changed his name to Nicholas Ray when he was twenty—to being in a room full of "porcupines. They were edgy. They kept everyone at a distance."

Similarly, when Betty went to Lena's funeral with Nick in 1959, she was immediately alarmed by the Kienzle family iciness. This was the first and only time Betty ever met the Kienzles. She "had never experienced anything as austere."

Lena wasn't the kind of woman who would smile and pretend she wasn't angry. She got quiet, stern. When I look at pictures of her I see a cold, unhappy woman. She has big eyes that blankly stare right back at me. Her lips are two thin parallel lines with no open space between them. No laughter. No light.

Nick's childhood was colored, in part, by the lack of affection between Lena and Raymond Kienzle. They slept in separate bedrooms. Raymond was a severe alcoholic. He had a mistress. Lena's devotion to Nick replaced the affection she should have shown Raymond. Lena loved my father. Alice, Ruth, and Helen were there to serve him. I wanted to think of Lena as a cold, heartless woman who pushed her husband into their daughter's beds, the same way I wanted to accuse my aunt Helen as being the instigator of her incestuous relationship with Nick.

Nick believed it was his birthright to have sex with his sisters and daughters. In a journal from 1968, a journal he intended to publish as his autobiography, he wrote, "I was born at 5am on August 7th. The astrologers will tell you that either my sun or moon was rising in or on my sun, which probably accounts for being bent towards incest with other people's children and wives, ex-wives, and daughters and such."

I had read this quote of Nick's years before ever knowing about Gretchen, let alone talking to her over the phone. So, when she told me that Nick's relationship with her mother, his sister, Helen, was incestuous, I had no trouble believing her.

Still, I'm reluctant to admit my father's complicity. I don't want to relinquish my childhood fantasy of his being my rescuer—my hero. I still catch myself wanting to forget that he had sexual relations with his sister so that I can believe that he would have taken me away from my mother and that Wanda house had he known what she was allowing to happen. I've learned this survival mechanism has a name, cognitive dissonance. It's like your mind can see the truth for a second but can't stay focused on it. It's like the memory fragments, breaks up into tiny pieces, and then disintegrates.

As teenagers, Helen and Nick snuck off to the Mississippi river and got drunk on liquor they stole from their father's cabinet. They recited Wordsworth, and Robinson Jeffers, and shared dreams of writing poetry and acting in the theater. They jumped into the river and floated on their backs, drifting to wherever the current took them.

I imagined them running away from home as if their escape was a scene right out of Tom Sawyer. When I was growing up, I loved going to Disneyland. Taking the raft from Frontierland across the rivers of America to Tom Sawyer's Island was like being transported into a favorite story. I lost myself in the woodsy world away from the rest of the amusement park. I'd walk on rickety bridges, climb on ladders into tree houses, discover buried treasures, and ogle at shipwrecks.

If only Nick and Helen's adventures on the Mississippi River were as innocent as Disneyland's Tom Sawyer Island. Theirs wasn't about discovering buried treasures and ship-wrecks. Their adventure was about sneaking away and kissing. It was about sex.

"I wanted to make it with her, because she was my sister."

He did it *because* she was his sister. I don't want to admit to myself how sick his thinking was, but I know that what he wanted to do with her reached into the darkest depths.

Be Free

B etty believed in nudism like born again Christians believe Jesus Christ is their savior. For Betty, nudism was about self-exploration. She had come to Sandstone, a membership only sex club, during the Thanksgiving weekend of 1974, after Nick had come back into our lives for the first time in ten years, after she discovered Nick had persuaded my fourteen-year-old sister to score him a gram of cocaine, after she had caught her second husband, Ward Schwab, beating my sister with a vacuum cleaner, after she left Ward, after she kicked Nick out. Arriving at Sandstone, fifteen acres on Saddle Peak Road atop Topanga Canyon, was "like coming from hell and going into heaven. No one was around. They took me into what was called the Ball Room. Wall to wall beds that curved around like a horseshoe. You could see the trees through the windows. I was exhausted. I'd never been on a waterbed before. I said, 'Gosh, let me lay down. Wake me up before any activities start.' I fell into a deep sleep and awakened to this guy kissing my feet. I was there from morning until midnight. Never made it to the cabin. That's how I met Rod."

Rod was Betty's first boyfriend after her marriage to Ward. At first I was wary of Rod's appearance in our lives. When my mother brought him home the first time I was dumbfounded. Not even a year had passed since Ward. Later, I grew to love Rod, dearly. When I was arrested at the age of fourteen and my mother was screaming at me for being so stupid to have been caught smoking a joint, he let me know I wasn't and that I would always have his ear. Whenever I felt like my mother and sister were ganging up on me, he made me feel like he was my ally.

"Before I could go back to Sandstone," Betty said, "I had to attend a weekend seminar that was given by a renowned therapist, a woman. It was for all people who were interested in joining or participating in some way at Sandstone. It was the first time I got naked. We all worked in the nude. We did body self-imaging in the mirror. Being so much in my body as a dancer it was a natural thing to evolve to. Without Rod I would never have gone back. He was my educator."

On Sunday nights Rod and Betty disappeared into her bed. Hours later, when my sister and I were turning off our bedroom light to go to sleep, our mother would emerge from her bedroom with a sheet wrapped around her body. She would float into our bedroom and give us each a kiss goodnight, and I would cringe, because she was like sex leaning into me.

When I was fourteen, I saw my mother making out with another woman. I had woken up, thirsty, in the middle of the night, and gone into the kitchen to get a glass of diet soda. I heard someone moaning and peeked into the living room. What I saw was my mother lying on a mattress. Her naked body was entangled with the naked bodies of two men and a woman, who had come over for dinner earlier that night. This was not a scene out of the free love 1970s. This was having an orgy while your teenage daughters are sleeping in the other room. She didn't know boundaries. She didn't know what was inappropriate sexual behavior. Her father had measured her legs with a tape measure and stood in her bedroom doorway watching her practice ballet routines. He had showed up in her hotel room bed naked, professing his love.

In 1975 most, if not all, basic psychiatry textbooks stated that incest only occurred in approximately one in a million households. One in a million! I knew three off the top of my head: the Kienzle's, my mother's, and my own. The deception began with Sigmund Freud, who knew from his interviews with young women, that incest was occurring, rather frequently, in households headed by prominent men. Men, like Raymond Kienzle, Nick Ray, Karl Uitti, Ward Schwab, men who didn't fit the bill of the stereotypical degenerate sex offender.

More concerned with protecting the reputation of the "respectable family man," Freud covered up his findings, and joined the overwhelmingly popular male consensus that children, primarily girls, *lie.* Thus, the stage was set for how incest victims were ignored throughout most of the twentieth century. In fact, it wasn't until 1975, that women started breaking their silence, which the renowned psychiatrist, Judith Lewis Herman, whose research made the connection between incest and post-traumatic stress disorder, attributed to the Women's Movement.

Women like Betty and my aunt Helen, who was seventy in 1975, never had the chance to change their sexual behavior. Gretchen shared with me that in Helen's older age she had a tendency to disrobe in front of a roomful of guests. Gretchen also told me that when Helen did wear clothes, she dressed provocatively for La Crosse, Wisconsin in her day. I once had a sheer gold dress that I wore without a bra, and sometimes without underwear. Gretchen described her mother as overly sexualized, an exhibitionist, whose husband repeatedly caught her in over-the-top public displays of affection with other men, including Nick. Gretchen's description of Helen reminded me of how my mother would run down the driveway, stark raving naked, to greet me whenever I visited her at Elysium.

Sandstone had closed in 1976 and by 1982, Betty was living at Elysium, where she lived from the time I was twenty-one until I was in my forties. Founded by *Life* magazine photographer Ed

Lange, the nudist retreat was located just off Topanga Canyon Boulevard at the end of Robinson Road, a secluded residential street. Neighbors fought for years to shut Elysium down. It was my mother, by representing Elysium on the Topanga Canyon Community Board, who improved relations between the club and its neighbors. She was able to help people understand that Elysium wasn't a playground for perverts by opening the fields, with their tennis courts, Jacuzzi, swimming pool, and sprawling lawns, to the community one day per week. On this day, members and those who lived on the grounds, like Betty, agreed to wear clothes.

In 1982, Betty moved into one of four pool houses surrounding the Olympic-sized swimming pool. So, I had no choice but to go there. I mean, I wanted to see my mother. In my early twenties I even had to live there for a couple of months when my living situation was in flux. Her apartment consisted of two small rooms, with a double bed and a couch in one room, and a double loft bed in the other. No more than a dozen people lived there full time. On weeknights you'd only see Betty and a few other people naked, as opposed to the weekends, when the grassy lawns were crowded with unclothed people of all shapes and sizes. Lots of sagging boobs and jiggling asses strolling across the grass. For many it was the only place where they didn't feel self-conscious or judged about their bodies. My mother always told me that living without attachment to clothing was equivalent to letting go of pretenses. You couldn't hide from yourself behind the image your clothing projected.

In my early twenties, whenever I visited her at Elysium, I literally clung to my black leather jacket and combat boots. There was no way I was going to take part in that hippie nudity bullshit. Okay, I did once. But it was because I wanted to go swimming and there was a rule that no one wearing a bathing suit was allowed in the pool. I was nervous about baring my twenty-year-old body in front of strange men, but my mother swore none of them would even notice me. "They aren't looking at your body, darling," she'd say.

Throughout my childhood, Betty never left the house without putting on her face. Every morning she'd sit in the bathroom on the edge of the bathroom sink. With unbreakable focus she would apply false eyelashes, liquid black liner, eye shadow, blush, and lipstick. When I was in elementary school, she wore her dyed blonde hair in a three-inch bouffant that she had styled every Saturday morning at the beauty shop on Vermont Avenue, near the car wash and the Orange Julius stand. However, by the mid-80s she had literally stripped herself of any of the exteriors linking her to her show biz past, becoming Nick Ray's bride, and having to appear by his side in the latest Chanel fashions. When I was in high school and whined about not being able to afford Fiorrucci or Pierre Cardin she would tell me wearing designer clothing didn't mean a thing. They were just clothes.

I am lucky because I can look at the beauty my parents created and wonder in all that they contributed to the twentieth century. It doesn't make me forget that they were fucked up. But I get to embrace them for all that they were. I don't just have parents who were fucked up. I have parents who were involved and engaged and contributing and thinking and doing and sacrificing and dying and living lives most people just dream of.

States of Mind

Nick Ray would not have become Nicholas Ray without John Houseman. In 1941, when John Houseman was working with David O. Selznick Productions, he got a call from the Office of War Information to produce a radio broadcast called *Voice of America* following the bombing of Pearl Harbor on December 7th. The radio broadcasts were designed to keep the soldiers overseas informed about the state of things back home as well as to help form a common bond between the European and American communities so that their united forces could win the war. Houseman, deciding that music would be the connection, hired Nick to be in charge of the folk music division.

"We discovered that folk music is international," Houseman wrote, "and more and more, we used a lot of folk music in order to convince everybody—our allies, our enemies—that we were brothers under the skin; that Americans were not remote barbarians. We needed somebody to organize all that and to bring in people to execute these things and Nick Ray was in charge of that department."

Then, in 1945, when Houseman was working as an associate producer at Paramount Studios, the West Coast branch of the Office of War Information asked him to make a propaganda film intended to inform foreign countries about the democratic electoral process called *Tuesdays in November*. He hired Nick Ray, who had just finished working with Kazan on *A Tree Grows in Brooklyn,* to be his assistant. On the set of *Tuesdays in November*, my father participated in all phases of the production but his contribution to the sound and editing of the documentary made it the success it was. "There was a good deal of music and sound, and Nick was very, very good at it. He was an absolutely brilliant sound editor in all those montages and things we used to do at the OWI," Houseman said.

He considered the film, distributed in twenty-four countries, Nick's first. From there, the two teamed up to adapt the radio play *Sorry Wrong Number*, a suspenseful one-woman show that had starred Agnes Moorehead, into a teleplay for the fledgling CBS television studio. John Houseman signed Nick on to direct. *Variety* gave Houseman and Nick high praise, saying, "the most successful instance of blending of top-drawer film artistry with a live video performance. The show was tops."

Next up for John Houseman was directing the Broadway production of *Lute Song*, based on the Chinese play *PI-PA-KI*, starring Mary Martin and Yul Brynner. Houseman hadn't directed anything for seven years. Terrified of failing, he hired Nick to be his assistant. He credited Nick's "unselfish collaboration" with getting the play off on solid ground.

After *Lute Song's* successful opening, Houseman returned to Hollywood and his office on the RKO studio lot. There, in the slush pile on his desk, he came across the dime store novel, *Thieves Like Us*, which Nick and the screenwriter Charles Schnee adapted into the screenplay for Nick's first film. It became *They Live by Night*.

The second and last film John Houseman and Nick worked on together was *On Dangerous Ground*. One of my favorite movies directed by my father, it is the quirky and beautiful love story of Jim Wilson (Robert Ryan), a city cop on the verge of homicide, and Mary Malden (Ida Lupino), the blind older sister of a murder suspect.

The film is based on a novel, *Mad with Much Heart*, that Nick read while filming *In a Lonely Place*. He sent it to Houseman hoping it could be their next project. "I saw what drew him to the story but not how he proposed to turn it into a viable movie."

RKO's story department shared Houseman's reservations. An inter-office memo stated that the book, while a powerful story, "is likely to emerge as an 'art' production which may receive critical acclaim but no sizeable box office returns" and voted no on adapting it for the screen.

Houseman sought the opinion of his friend, Raymond Chandler, with whom he had worked at Paramount on *The Blue Dahlia*. Chandler thought the story was humorless. "The cop is ridiculous. . . . The blind girl is obviously an idiot. And there's hardly a line of dialogue which would not be pure slop on the screen."

Houseman went ahead with getting the movie into production in spite of the reservations. To honor his contract with the studio he had to make one more film. He also wanted to see Nick get what he wanted. Houseman never mentioned his doubts about the film's viability to Nick. He wrote in his autobiography *Front and Center* that *On Dangerous Ground* was made with love.

As he had done with *They Live by Night*, Houseman wanted a writer he could trust to not interfere with Nick's vision of the book. Following the recommendation of William Fadiman, a story editor turned head of the literary department at RKO, John Houseman asked A. I. Bezzerides to write the screenplay. "He and Nick seemed to understand each other, though I was never quite sure how closely they agreed on the nature of the film we were about to make."

On December 14, 1949, Nick signed the contract, which stipulated the studio's right to "revoke the assignment at any time at our discretion."

Nick modeled Robert Ryan's character after a policeman he had met while riding in a patrol car with officers from the Boston Violence Squad. He'd become a policeman in order to pay for his younger brother to go to college and become a priest. The man seethed with anger. He was a lifelong bachelor having given his life to police work.

Upon Nick's return to Los Angeles he and Bezzerides rode in patrol cars with the Los Angeles Police Department, furthering the research Nick had begun doing with the Boston Violence Squad. They wrote a one-hundred-page treatment and on February 14, 1950 turned in a completed first draft of the script. Houseman wasn't convinced the storyline worked. He felt it consisted of two halves of a story that never really came together.

"We had two pictures. We had the business of the good cop given to violence and then we had the perfectly ridiculous plot about the blind girl and the boy, and all that. I always rather disliked it," Houseman said.

Critics weren't too kind when the movie was released two years later. A. I. Bezzerides, who Nick had known during his years with the WPA, described it as "a treadmill of stumbling, fumbling, smooching, hurtling movement," and as a story "told with the camera" which "is often late to the scene and not sure of what is about to happen." *The New York Times* review said, "For all of Nick Ray's sincere and shrewd direction and the striking outdoor photography this RKO melodrama fails to traverse its chosen ground."

Nick considered *On Dangerous Ground* a failure, to which the critic Mike Wilmington replied, "But it is the kind of failure only a great director can make. For most of its length *On Dangerous Ground* functions effectively on three different levels: as an exciting genre thriller, as a 'heightened' but basically serious study of the police, and as an intense symbolic drama of the conflict between love and violence."

Jeanine Basinger, a film scholar and head of Wesleyan University's Film Studies program, called it a masterpiece. She wrote:

"What happens in *On Dangerous Ground* is you start out with the dark, dark city. The traditional world of film noir. The first shot is a close up of a gun in a holster on a bed. Then you see three cops and you see their different lives and in the leading character Robert Ryan's life you see the incredibly intelligent layering. You learn from plot and dialogue how he is. He talks about garbage. You learn in visual and in symbolic meaning how he is. He's alone. He eats with his gun on while studying mugshots. But you also learn in formal terms. In forward tracking shots that take you into an urban world of neon and darkness, seeing his hand in the foreground of the frame struggling to keep from beating up on someone. Seeing him always in isolated frame away from other more normal people. Then finally what you see is the change of landscape and in one of the best sequences in any movie Robert Ryan drives out of the city into the country and you see him leaving behind the dark urban setting. It moves incredibly economically. You see a sign that says something like County Sheriff's Office and then you're there. I mean it's incredible economy but then what happens is he brings the noir ugliness out into the white landscape. He comes out into a world of white and light and purity and allegedly small town or country values but he brings the ugliness with him. What happens is you have a flow of movement out of the darkness into the light and in the light he finds a woman who's actually blind. She's living in total darkness but her home is more decorated than his. Her life is more human, warmer, than his. You have this incredibly wonderful

contrast and you move forward in time and space
through these short dissolves and so he comes out
there and has to accept light and whiteness and some
kind of purity into his own life. He loses ugliness
there. He learns to be human."

Nick knew he wasn't like other people. He was isolated even in a crowd. He was always asking himself what it meant to be human. Searching for answers that might bring him peace. *On Dangerous Ground* ends on a hopeful note. Love saves Robert Ryan's Jim from himself.

For Love and Hollywood

In 1954, Nick was having a boozy love affair with Hanna Axmann, the wife of the failed actor Ed Tierney, brother of the actors Lawrence Tierney and Scott Brady. She was a German Jew and survivor of the Nazi occupation. She wrote a script called *An Ordinary Spring* for Howard Koch based on her experiences living in hiding during WWII. She met Nick at a Hollywood party and moved into his bungalow at the Chateau Marmont shortly thereafter. "It was like two magnets at that party. The way we just didn't leave each other anymore," she said.

The way Hanna Axmann described him during their time together sounds like he was manic. "At four or five in the morning he'd start talking nonsense; by seven he'd be more or less fresh, contemplating his feet a bit, to get back to earth. Then he would go off every morning to his psychoanalyst, Dr. Vanderhyde, come back and start drinking. The maid pre-pared meals for us; sometimes I did the cooking, badly. Then we would go and play cards—Nick played a lot of gin rummy. This famous Dr. Vanderhyde insisted on meeting me, looking like the perfect devil. He talked about drinking, and said, 'Do you think Nicholas Ray is the solution to your life?' I don't know whether he helped Nick very much."

Nick's agent, Lew Wasserman, orchestrated a deal with Republic Pictures for Nick to produce and direct the western *Johnny Guitar*, with a script written by Philip Yordan and starring Joan Crawford. It was Nick's first time working as an independent contractor.

Wasserman had emerged as the ever-powerful agent credited for taking the power away from the studios and giving it to the talent. His implementation of talent-as-independent-contractor further dismantled the studio system changing the studios from production factories into distributors of independent productions. The studio moguls were slowly forced to relinquish their control over talent beginning on May 3, 1948 with the Supreme Court ruling taking away the studio's right to own the theater chains where their movies played. By law the studios could no longer control what movies played in theaters across the country. Owning the theater chains had provided studios with the cash flow to pay their contract players. With the loss of ownership came the loss of capital needed to keep the factory model of production going.

"You must remember, when all the things happened, L.B. Mayer, the Warner brothers, Harry Cohn, the Paramount group were all older men. . . ." said Dore Schary, the head of production of RKO at the time *They Live by Night* got the green light. "They wanted to be left alone, leave things as they are. Twenty years before, those same men would have made arrangements with stars, given them a piece of the picture, done this and that, and prevented agents from taking over the entire operation."

Nick was caught between the old and the new Hollywood. He was riddled with anxiety going into production on *Johnny Guitar*. He asked Hanna Axmann to go back to Germany and promised to meet her there once the production wrapped.

Westerns had lost their big box office draw. Joan Crawford's star was fading. Crawford demanded script changes so that she would take on the masculine lead role. If her demands weren't met, she threatened to walk off the picture. Phil Yordan and

Nick had to oblige. If Crawford wasn't accommodated, Herbert Yates, the owner of Republic Pictures, would stop production. Nick would lose the $75,000 he was being paid to make the picture. Money he needed to pay off gambling debts in Vegas. Begrudgingly, Nick did what was asked of him. Phil Yordan made the changes Joan Crawford wanted without hesitation.

Nick asked Yordan, "Jesus, how the hell am I going to direct her?"

Yordan replied, "Well, why don't you do this, Nick? It'll only be another six weeks. Get up every morning, look in the mirror, and when you shave, say, 'Look, I've only got five more weeks and I'll never have to see Joan Crawford again.' Each day, just keep telling yourself you'll never have to see her again, till the six weeks are over."

Nick stared at him, and after a few minutes, said, "You know, never is a long time."

As soon as filming was over Nick wrote to Hanna Axmann, "The atrocity *Johnny Guitar* is finished and released, to dreadful reviews and great financial success. Nausea was my reward, and I'm glad for you that you were not there to share the suffering."

Nick's next film, *Run for Cover*, wasn't a critical or financial success. Produced by William H. Pine and William C. Thomas, best known for their B-movies, the film starred Ernest Borgnine, Viveca Lindfors, John Derek, and James Cagney. "I did the film," Nick said in an interview, "because I got a call that Cagney would come out of retirement if I directed it. I love this guy, so I did it . . . it's a terrible story for chrissake! It's an awful story. There's no conflict, none. You try to breathe it in there, but you can't. You don't have any bones to work with."

My father's next project was directing *High Green Wall*, a half-hour CBS television drama starring Joseph Cotten, which aired on October 3, 1954. Cotten liked working with Nick but "thought he needed time to prepare; time to form a concept."

Nick hoped the experience would bring "something new, accidental, or unplanned to happen, but it didn't."

He wanted more. He wanted his cast and crew to care more. He was disillusioned. He dreamed about moving to Europe where the writers of the *Cahiers du Cinema* understood that he was a poet. What kept him in Hollywood was his addiction to money, property, and prestige. And then Nick found the answer to how he was going to make the big box office movies without compromising his artistic integrity.

James Dean.

"Like Nicholas Ray, James Dean was suspect within the industry," *Rebel Without a Cause* screenwriter Stewart Stern said. "Actors trained in the studio system paid attention to hitting their marks and saying their lines as written. Dean scoffed at conventions. On stage he improvised his lines constantly altering them from one performance to the next. Dean was oblivious to Hollywood as a going concern, oblivious to budgets and shooting schedules. He was openly contemptuous of authority, including powerful men like Jack Warner. Like Nicholas Ray, Dean's radical style did not mesh with Hollywood's corporate gears."

Nick and James Dean were brooders, moody, at times insolent and uncooperative, both had reputations of being emotionally unstable. Nick was a force, but so was Dean. Dennis Hopper insisted there wasn't a power struggle between them. Rather Nick gave into Dean.

"Nick felt Jimmy was his possession," Stern said. "I felt that Nick emotionally saw himself as—that Jimmy was his boy and nobody better touch him. I wasn't thinking about a sex act but I think he was deeply in love with Jimmy."

Is it too much to say that when James Dean died my father lost the love of his life?

"He was wary and hard to catch," Nick wrote. "In the minds of many people their relationship with Jimmy was complex, even obsessive. For him it was simple and probably much less important. He was still intensely determined not to love, not to be loved. He could be absorbed, fascinated, attracted by something new or beautiful but he would never surrender himself. There were girls convinced they were the only one in his life when they were no more than occasions. Involvement was out of the question because the pain that lies waiting in human relationships was a risk he was not prepared to take." Nick could've been talking about himself.

I'm beginning to think that everything concerning my father's state of mind from 1954 on had to do with finding and losing James Dean.

After Dean's death on September 30, 1955, just days before *Rebel's* theatrical release, Nick stopped caring. They say at some point in an alcoholic's drinking career they cross an invisible line. It's the point of no return where you resign yourself to the fact that you live to drink no matter the cost.

I stopped caring about what happened to me when Nick died just as I was graduating high school. But I really crossed that invisible line in 1980. It was after a screening of The Clash movie *Rude Boy* at the Tiffany Theater on the Sunset Strip. I was dressed in my armor: ripped black tights held together with safety pins, a red and black plaid kilt, and a t-shirt with a newspaper headline reading, "Justice for Sid Vicious." I stood amongst twenty-five punks in the middle of the boulevard drinking from a forty-ounce Olde English. I was angry about everything that had happened in my life from the time I was eight and my mother married Ward Schwab, a man who threatened to kill my sister every afternoon after school and whose teenaged son snuck into my bedroom at night.

I was angry that the day my mother left him, four years after they were married, that both she and Julie were able to move on with their lives. Because after Betty left Ward, I became emotionally paralyzed, and the only thing that could get me out of bed was knowing that I could get drunk and do drugs. I was angry that my father had died before I got the chance to know him and that after his memorial services both my mother and sister were able to move on with their lives as if they had lost nothing. By the time I was eighteen I felt like I had lost *everything*.

That night in 1980 when I crossed the invisible line, I was standing on the corner of Miller Drive and Sunset Boulevard. I was standing next to my best friend, Anndoll, with her jet black shoulder length spiked hair, plaid bondage pants with the straps from one leg buckled into the other, a chain locked around her neck, and her sleeveless green and black leopard print t-shirt exposing the fresh track marks in the crux of her right arm. I knew that night there was never going to be a chance of my returning to the person I had been before my father died. I might have been a mess when he was alive but whenever things would get too out of hand with my partying, I would force myself to gain some control. But after he died? If living included dying, so be it.

Bigger Than Life

Nick Ray said goodbye to 1955 at a New Year's Eve party in London given by the producer Leon Clore and his wife Miriam. He was there to attend the premiere of *Rebel*. He knew the young film critic, Gavin Lambert, was also invited to be the party and went specifically to meet him. He was waiting in the corner of the living room when Lambert, who had written favorably about *They Live by Night* in *Sequence Magazine*, the British film journal, arrived.

It was just before midnight when Lambert entered the foyer and was greeted by Miriam Clore. "Thank God you're here. There's someone waiting to see you," she said.

Gavin Lambert looked to where Miriam gestured and "saw this tall figure, who seemed to create isolation around himself."

"I knew at once who it was," Lambert said.

Introducing himself to Lambert, Nick quoted a line from the film critic's favorable review: "I'm a new director of very remarkable talent."

They rang in the New Year at the Clore's party and then Nick took Lambert back to his room at the Hyde Hotel. Lambert watched as Nick poured himself one vodka after another. He was aware that James Dean had been dead just three months and it was obvious that Nick was still shaken. They spoke a little about *Rebel* and when the subject of Dean came up Nick looked at Lambert and said, "You can imagine how I felt," then poured himself another vodka.

"So, how did you like *In a Lonely Place*?" Nick asked.

"Very much."

"I had to fight to get the ending I wanted."

"I liked the very open ending. That you don't know what is going to happen to the Bogart character. How he's going to spend the rest of his life," Lambert said.

"You don't know whether the man is going to go out, to get drunk, have an accident in his car or whether he is going to go to a psychiatrist for help. And that's what it should be; either one or two things could happen to him because now the pressure is off. But now there is an internal pressure. He has a problem about himself. The man has three alternatives, to be psychoanalyzed, become an alcoholic, or to kill himself. Just like me," Nick told him.

"A lot of people thought the movie was about Bogart. It wasn't. It was about Nick," Gavin Lambert told me in 2002 while we were sitting in the living room of his West Hollywood apartment.

I called the Authors Guild in hopes of acquiring Gavin Lambert's contact information. I was given the name and number of his agent. I called, reading from a script I'd written for myself. I'm extremely shy and fearful of getting tongue-tied when calling anybody. Anybody. A friend. A colleague. A relative. I just always feel like I'm imposing and whoever answers the phone is going to get mad at me for bothering them.

I dialed the number for Lambert's agent and said, "Hi. My name is Nicca Ray. I'm the daughter of Nicholas Ray and I was hoping to talk to Gavin Lambert about my father for a book I'm writing."

Two hours later I received a call from Lambert. I scheduled an interview with him later in the week. I had come from New York City, where I've lived since 1987, to Los Angeles for a few weeks. I was staying with Betty and her fourth husband, Sandy Meltzer, at their house in Sherman Oaks.

I knew little about Gavin Lambert other than he had known Nick. Over the years Betty had mentioned Lambert's book, *The Slide Area*, his 1959 collection of connected short stories based on the Hollywood characters he'd mostly met through my father. Betty claimed that the pretty blonde character, Tina, was based on her. Gavin Lambert said it was based on Shelley Winters. A few days after my initial conversation with Lambert, I was sitting in the living room of his elegantly furnished landmark courtyard apartment building at 1337 North Laurel Avenue, between Sunset and Fountain in the historical district of West Hollywood. It was across the street from the Villa D'Este, the famous courtyard building where Nick actually lived and modeled where the character Dix Steele of *In a Lonely Place* lived, and where Lambert lived throughout the 1990s.

Lambert was in the kitchen getting me a glass of water. I was nervous, but he made me feel welcome right way. I don't know if seeing a painting hanging on the wall that was done by a friend of mine helped but it sure did give me something to talk about besides Nick. And that was a godsend.

"Oh, I know this artist," I said.

Lambert's eyes lit up. The ice was broken. There was something connecting us that had nothing to do with Nick. I was beginning to feel assured that this interview experience would be nothing like the last.

"I think I saw you as a baby." Lambert spoke softly. "I was in Rome working on a movie and Nick called me. We hadn't seen each other in quite a while. I stayed at your house for two or three nights. I'm pretty sure there was a baby around."

Lambert was thin. I would guess not quite six feet. He was dressed casually expensive, in a navy blue sweater and tan trousers. His hair was white and perfectly combed. His complexion was smooth. There was hardly a wrinkle. He was aging well. He set a tall glass of water on the coffee table in front of me before taking a seat in the armchair across from me.

"Now, this I hope won't come as a surprise to you. Or at least a disturbing surprise. Over a period of about one year to eighteen months Nick and I were in a very casual way, lovers."

"Oh. I figured," I said.

I had come to the conclusion that Nick and Lambert had been lovers from reading the Bernard Eisenschitz biography about my father and from insinuations my mother had made in the rare moments when she'd mentioned Nick's friend, Gavin.

On that New Year's Eve night, 1955, Nick was on his way to the bathroom and asked Lambert how old he was.

"Thirty-one."

"I'm forty-one," Nick said. "Not quite old enough to be your father."

Lambert thought Nick was being flirtatious. When Nick came out of the bathroom he was in his underwear.

"He put his arms around me and kissed me on the mouth," Gavin wrote. "An hour or so later he said that he wasn't really homosexual, not really even bisexual, as he'd been to bed with a great many women in his life, but only two or three men."

The next day, after a screening of Lambert's film, *Another Sky*, Nick asked him to come back to Los Angeles with him. Nick handed him a copy of a *New Yorker* article entitled, "Ten Feet Tall," about the miracle drug, Cortisone. Nick had a two-picture deal with Twentieth Century Fox and was thinking of basing the first one on the article. He wanted Lambert to be his assistant on the picture.

"He gave me twenty seconds to get over my astonishment and accept," Gavin said.

Nick hugged Gavin goodbye.

Nick flew to Paris for the *Rebel Without a Cause* premiere. One week later he returned to London. The studio was making arrangements to get Lambert a green card. Once Gavin arrived in Hollywood he was hired as dialogue director on *Bigger than Life*. Nick cautioned him to hide his homosexuality and emphasized the importance of a "butch handshake. Then demonstrated a bone-crushing one and gave his startling smile."

Gavin Lambert believed Nick "was scared about his career. It was not quite as bad for a director as it was for an actor, such as Rock Hudson. But, within the industry it was never very acceptable. It was okay if you were a tremendously commercially successful director. Nick was not that. He was a very talented director, but he never made a film that made a good deal of money. So, he wasn't invulnerable."

Bigger than Life was scheduled to start production during the last week of March 1956. The first film for James Mason's production company, starred Mason as Ed Avery, an underpaid schoolteacher moonlighting as a cab driver who suffers from severe arthritis. He's prescribed Cortisone, a new miracle drug, which he becomes addicted to, and suffers manic episodes that include fits of paranoia, megalomania, and rage culminating in an attempt to kill his son.

Lambert arrived in Los Angeles on March 1, 1955 and moved into Nick's bungalow at the Chateau Marmont. They lived together and were lovers for the next eighteen months. Nick told him, "Officially you belong to Fox as a dialogue director. Unofficially, you belong to me."

Lambert took a submissive seat beside Nick. That night in London it was Nick who initiated sex—and immediately after distanced himself by telling Lambert that this sex with men thing was rare, he'd only been with two or three, but he'd been with many women. Gavin Lambert fell deeply in love with Nick even though he admitted being with someone whose best companion was loneliness proved difficult.

It didn't take Lambert long before he realized Nick not only had a drinking problem but was doing a lot of drugs, too. He told me, "Nick expected me to take him on trust because he had taken me on trust. I waited for him to tell me what he wanted me to know. I also discovered very early on that if I asked him, chances were he'd shut me up. So, I let him come to me in his own way. And anyway, what could I have really said? Except I know you're taking a lot of drugs? Occasionally it affected him on the set. He was never a falling down drunk, but his responses got slow when he'd had a bit too much."

Released in August 1956, *Bigger than Life* was a financial and critical disaster. Pharmaceutical companies were fervently against it, film critics dismissed it, and American audiences ignored it.

I first saw *Bigger than Life* when it was shown in Museum of Modern Art retrospective of Nick's films that were screened at the Gramercy Theatre on 23rd Street in 2003. I lived three blocks away. I couldn't wait to see the movie on the big screen. I had done research at the Museum of Modern Art's film library where I got to know the curators, Charles Silver and Joshua Siegel. They left four tickets for me at the box office. The Gramercy was filled to more than half its four-hundred-and-ninety-nine seating capacity. This retrospective of Nick's, which had kicked off with the restored print of *In a Lonely Place*, was an event. I passed Siegel on the way to my seat. He asked me if I wanted to say anything. I declined. I was thrilled to be an anonymous member of the audience. The attention Nick was getting made me proud to be his daughter.

I was swept up in the melodrama of the movie, the bright colors, and the over-the-top acting. I could feel his mania oozing out of the screen. It was exhilarating. Watching it was like walking through Greenwich Village with a manic friend. Drama, drama, drama, every step of the way. You can't stop to take a breath. I used to love being around that kind of energy.

Bigger than Life is one of Nick's personal films, like *In a Lonely Place* and *The Lusty Men*. When you come down to it this is a movie about a drug addict who sets out to destroy his son. It is also a story about Nick's drug dependence and how he blamed the doctors who prescribed the drugs for his addictions and manic outbursts. He doesn't take responsibility for the damage he causes. He doesn't apologize to anyone.

Watching the movie, I couldn't help but compare Nick's style with David Lynch. Especially the painterly splotches of color used to express danger, fear, paranoia. I kept flashing back on the more abstract visuals from *Blue Velvet, Twin Peaks: Fire Walk with Me,* and *Lost Highway,* analyzing. It's one of the ways I have kept myself from devastating feelings of discovering that my father, the man I fantasized would and could make my life better had he known what my stepbrother was doing to me, was, at times, insane.

His mental and physical disintegration was evident even before James Dean's death. When Stewart Stern, the screenwriter of *Rebel*, met Nick he was surprised to find out Nick wasn't thirty years his senior. His hair was gray and his skin wrinkled. He was loose, smelled of cigarettes, and would fasten you with his eyes.

Gavin Lambert said, "There were times when Nick seemed like a visitor from another planet and I felt like someone hallucinating a romantic encounter with an alien."

James Mason described Nick as having a handsome but dilapidated face. Like Gavin Lambert he felt Nick had a black cloud hovering around him. He compared him to the comic strip character L'il Abner with his "small cloud of bad luck" above his head.

Lambert said watching Nick gambling away huge sums of money was the first time he saw what it was in Nick that gave him the insight into Ed Avery's mania in *Bigger than Life*.

As far as the cast and crew on *Bigger than Life* could tell Nick never showed up on set intoxicated. However, he was known to visit the Twentieth Century Fox studio doctor to get his daily Vitamin B12 shot. "Doctor Siegal. He gave everybody shots," said Barbara Rush, who played James Mason's wife in the film.

"Nick was this lovely, tall, graceful hawk of a man," Barbara Rush said. "He had this wonderful kind of lined intellectual face. Wonderful blue eyes and that lovely gray hair. He spoke very carefully. He was not excitable. He was purposeful. He could explain. He was very polite. I liked working with him. He made things quite clear. That's all you want in a director. He would say things like move closer to the boy or stay at the bottom of the stairs and don't get emotional so quickly."

James Mason, on the other hand, found Nick terribly difficult to understand. "He was the kind of person who was rather mysterious, rather inarticulate, and really not an easy communicator. We did not communicate very well, Nick and I. He was a great one for lengthy pauses."

Walter Matthau, who played Wally Gibbs, a fellow teacher and James Mason's good friend, would do impressions of Nick standing there about to give the actor direction but leaving before the words came out of his mouth. Norman Lloyd said Matthau used to imitate Nick for him and his wife Peggy. Barbara Rush told me that Walter imitated everyone. "He was a mimic. He'd not just do Nick Ray. You should've heard his James Mason!"

Nick was drinking heavily throughout the production of his next movie, *The True Story of Jesse James*, his second one for Fox. The week before production began, he fell down the stairs of his bungalow at the Chateau Marmont and had to use a cane. Lambert chauffeured him to and from the studio. He didn't care about pulling himself together. He told Lambert, "Why bother?"

Just after completing *The True Story of Jesse James*, Paul Graetz, a well-known German-born French producer, sent Nick the English translation of the French novel, *Amere Victoire* (*Bitter Victory*) by René Hardy, in hopes that he would direct the film adaptation. Lambert described *Bitter Victory* as "a story of betrayal during World War II. After an attack on Rommel's North African headquarters, the mission commander wins a decoration. But he's a false hero, a coward and liar who left a younger officer, the true hero, to die in the desert."

Nick and Lambert arrived in Paris in November 1956. Shortly after arriving, Nick met Manon, a young Algerian woman, who Lambert described as, "a heroin addict with dyed blonde hair, pale skin, manic eyes, and a violent temper." It was this affair that ended Nick and Lambert's relationship, and this production that ended their working relationship. It was also Manon who introduced Nick to shooting heroin.

Nick brought Manon with him when he returned to the States and met with Budd and Stuart Schulberg about directing the first film for their production deal with Warner Bros.

Budd Schulberg and his brother Stuart were sitting with Nick in Nick's suite at the Plaza Hotel in New York City discussing *Wind Across the Everglades*, the film written by Schulberg about the poachers who descend on the Everglades and kill the rare birds to sell the feathers to hat makers at the turn of the century. They had contacted my father while he was in Paris. There was brief correspondence via phone and telegram, but nothing prepared them for the condition Nick was in during their business meeting in this hotel room, for which they were footing the bill. They were there five minutes when Manon, dressed in panties and bra, trolloped out of the bedroom and onto Nick's lap cooing, "I love you Nick."

Budd Schulberg was shocked. "What is this? What's going on?"

Nick looked him straight in the eye. "We're very much in love."

Right away the Schulbergs suspected drugs. Budd's instincts were to not go through with bringing my father on to direct. But Stuart was worried that Jack Warner would call off the production if they fired Nick because he'd had success with *Rebel Without a Cause*. He convinced Budd they should go forward as planned.

Schulberg, looking Nick straight in the eye, laid down some ground rules. He said, "Nick, the Everglades is a very primitive, backward, old-fashioned kind of place. You weren't thinking of . . . You're not thinking of taking her down to the Everglades, are you?"

"Yes," Nick said. "I thought I would."

"Well, look, Nick, that will really upset people there. They're very redneck, primitive people, not used to seeing anything like a Manon, and it will really affect our relationship with the locals who are already somewhat suspicious of Hollywood people."

Leaving the hotel Budd and Stuart Schulberg believed Nick had agreed to their suggestion of putting Manon up in a motel in Naples, thirty miles away from Everglades City. But on the day cast and crew started showing up, so did Manon, with Nick, and to make matters even worse, they were staying in the same motel as Budd Schulberg, in the room right next door.

In the mornings Manon would run out of their room and chase his car, banging it, "Nick. Nick don't leave me. I love you."

"Jesus Christ," Budd Schulberg said. "She would come out in her negligee and finally she jumped into the canals to commit suicide and one of the crew members jumped in to save her and the other crew members came up to me and said, 'Budd, we think you should fire him for saving her.' She would pick fights with Nick. She never stopped."

Everyone knew they were on drugs, but it was Doris Lilly, the society writer and author of *How to Marry a Millionaire*, who said to Budd, "Where's Nick getting heroin? I know those eyes."

"The trouble with Nick happened after lunch," Budd Schulberg said. Instead of going to the buffet with the rest of the cast and crew Nick would join Manon in his room. "He would come out late and obviously be on something. His pupils were pinned. It was very noticeable. His eyes were different."

Everyone, cast and crew, reporters covering the shoot, were whispering about Nick's behavior and his suicidal druggy girlfriend. He was showing up late, not fully connected with reality, he set himself apart, didn't eat with everyone, talked down to the crew, kept emphasizing that it was *his* set, forgetting continuity, going on at length about Stanislavski to locals who were just extras excited to be in the background of a scene and had never heard of Strasberg or Method. He wasn't in sync with the actors, didn't have the respect of his crew, and even Christopher Plummer, whose first film it was, pulled Budd Schulberg aside and asked him, "You do realize your director is mad, don't you?"

"It is the story of a really obviously talented man who had come back in bad shape," Budd Schulberg said. "He was just in a cloud. He wasn't clear. He was out of control. I don't think he knew what the story was. He really didn't know what he was doing. He was gone."

My Keechie to His Bowie

The first time I saw Nick's film, *They Live by Night,* was in 2000, on video. I was resistant because it was made in the 1940s and I have attention deficit disorder when it comes to watching movies made before 1950. Usually, I find the language dated, the pace too slow, and the sound stilted. I was watching *They Live by Night* for reasons other than entertainment, though. I was watching it in anticipation of receiving some sort of message from my father. I got one right away.

There's a close up shot of Keechie (Cathy O'Donnell) and Bowie (Farley Granger) with titles at the bottom of the screen that read: "This boy . . . and this girl . . . were never properly introduced to the world we live in." *Bingo. I* was never properly introduced to the world. The sexual abuse I'd endured made me feel the perpetual outsider. It was my biggest secret. The stain keeping me from ever being a part of.

When I met Ray at Al's Bar in downtown Los Angeles on New Year's Eve 1981, I found the person I was meant to be with. He was the Bowie to my Keechie. I was clean and sober a little more than two months. I had never had a legal drink, and, yet, I'd almost died from drinking the way Lee Remick drank in the classic 1950s movie about alcoholism, *Days of Wine and Rose*s. When I was a child, I would watch that movie with Joy and secretly wish to grow up to be just like Remick's character. She got to stay drunk all of the time and wear pretty dresses. The night of my last drunk I'd picked up a guy at the Ritz nightclub in New York City, blacked out, and come to taking a pee in a parking lot in Queens. After peeing I blacked out again and came to having sex with him in my bedroom. At the time I was renting a room in the Soho loft where Susan lived. In the morning when I'd woken up the guy was gone along with two hundred dollars that had belonged to Susan.

The night I met Ray I'd been back in Los Angeles for one week. I'd left L.A. for New York City seven months earlier and had every intention of going back to New York after the holidays passed, but I met Ray, the person I was meant to be with for the rest of my life. That New Year's Eve night in 1981 I was standing outside of Al's Bar and Ray, this boy with brown bedroom eyes and freckles, spiked dark brown hair, and wearing a mod-style suit and white creepers, asked me what my name was. I was so shy I couldn't even tell him. I nudged my friend, who did. That night I had sex with him on the floor of my friend's kitchen. A month later he told me I had given him gonorrhea. I'd caught it from the guy I'd picked up at the Ritz. Instead of telling me I was a whore, Ray took me to the Free Clinic in San Pedro, where I was treated for the sexually transmitted disease. That he didn't treat me like I was a dirty piece of shit that should be discarded made me think the world of him.

Ray was like Bowie from *They Live by Night*. He planned robberies with his friends in the living room of our one-bedroom house on Venice Way, three blocks from the Venice Beach Boardwalk, while I looked the other way. Bowie was a bank robber who had escaped prison where he was serving time for a murder he committed when he was sixteen. Raymond escaped from a juvenile detention-prison when he was sixteen. He was sent there after his mother found baggies of pot hidden in the cover sleeve of his records. In juvie they wanted to keep him dosed on Thorazine and instead of complying he figured out how to escape and in the middle of the night broke free.

From there he landed on couches in crash pads in Hollywood. When I met him, he was on probation for robbery.

At the top of his treatment for *They Live by Night,* Nick wrote about the characters, Bowie and Keechie, "Their need for each other is as deep and ill-starred as was the love of Romeo and Juliet, and their span of happiness reins just about as long."

The first year Ray and I were living in Venice—which at the time was such a sketchy neighborhood you couldn't even get a pizza delivered to your house after dark—Ray's friends came over night after night and sat around the coffee table shooting dope. He'd tie my fuzzy pink bathrobe belt around his arm and clench and unclench his fist. When the vein popped out, he'd stick the needle in. The ritual would then proceed around the room, skipping me, because I was staying clean and sober.

We were together eight months when we got into an accident that left me unconscious for three days and in the brain damage ward at Los Angeles County Hospital. It was just before my twenty-first birthday and I was on the back of Ray's white Vespa when a car turned right into us. I wasn't wearing a helmet. I blacked out the moment Ray said, "Oh shit. A car." After regaining consciousness, I was moved into the motorcycle ward where I shared a room with five other casualties, some who had been there for six months. I stayed ten days. I split open my left knee. My face was one big scab. I wore a full-length cast.

Interns crowded around my bed and watched as the doctor tried picking the scabs off my face with tweezers. I wouldn't let him. I covered my face with my hands. I didn't want to know what was happening underneath the scabs. Nothing he said, none of his warnings about possible scarring, or needing to see how the wounds were healing got me to move my hands away from my face. By allowing the scabs to fall off naturally I was protecting myself from having to face the possibility of disfigurement. I didn't cry. I didn't tell anyone I was afraid that my face had been destroyed. I didn't look in the mirror for three weeks.

I finally looked at myself and saw a deep red two-inch jagged line running alongside my left cheek. There was also a piece of black gravel from National Boulevard underneath the skin that the emergency room surgeon had forgotten to remove. I went to a plastic surgeon who said he could significantly soften the appearance of the scar. The money I got from suing the driver of the car wasn't enough to cover the plastic surgeon's fees. My lawyer had wanted me to sue Ray's insurance company, but I refused. Ray was on probation for burglary and I didn't want his parents to cut him off financially or emotionally. I was naïve. For years the scar made me feel like I would never be able to escape my past. The scar has faded and is hardly noticeable now. I'm probably the only person who sees it. Eight weeks after the accident the doctors took the cast off my leg. There was a four-inch red scar running lengthwise across my knee. The scar is still visible, and my kneecap has remained numb. After the cast was taken off, I had to walk with a cane for a few months. I would walk through the Santa Monica Mall, feeling ravaged. Feeling like I was living life in reverse. Like I knew of death and dying before ever experience living.

Ray said that he couldn't look at me, because looking at me reminded him of nearly killing me. He couldn't live with the guilt, so he got high, and it was my fault he had to. You know, because I decided to fly into the air and do a nosedive onto National Boulevard.

Ray disappeared for days at a time. I was spending hours staring at the ceiling. My mind raced so fast. I was trying to make sense of my life. I wrote in my journal: "I've got to know all of what's inside of me and not be afraid of any part of me. I've got to become used to myself. Around people I'm really uncomfortable. If I were comfortable, I wouldn't need to fit in. See, I want to be Nicca, fit in or misfit. People will like me if they like me. I tell you, this time alone hasn't been so bad. I needed time alone. There've been the bad parts of feeling lonely and isolated, but I feel isolated in a crowd as well. Then there have been times of pure satisfaction inside. I sort of feel like I'm coming alive. I want to go out and dance and listen to bands and be nutty minus the drugs and alcohol. But the problem is I keep waiting for Ray to come home."

Like I waited for Nick to come home those years my mother was married to Ward.

In *They Live by Night,* Bowie and Keechie run away to New Mexico where they dream of being free from T-Dub (Jay C. Flippen) and Chickamaw (Howard Da Silva), the ex-convicts who broke Bowie out of prison and bring him further into a life of crime. Bowie struggles to free himself from his dependency on them.

Ray was getting high at least three times a day. There was not an unbent and unburnt spoon in the house. Needles were hidden behind books and forgotten in the pockets of the leather jacket we shared—the leather jacket that had supposedly belonged to Darby Crash, the Germs singer who died from an overdose the same weekend John Lennon was murdered. I bought the jacket off of Ray's friend with the money I earned waitressing at the IHOP. Ray's friend was the boyfriend of the girl who had been with Darby the night he died. I bought the jacket for the price of a bag of dope and bus fare downtown.

Heroin never let Ray go, just like the menacing and manipulating Chickamaw in *They Live by Night* never let Bowie go. He makes Bowie join him and T-Dub in a bank heist that gets T-Dub killed. Bowie and Keechie hide out in a motel that is off the beaten track. But, when Bowie's picture is all over the news, he is recognized by the plumber who comes to fix a broken water pipe in their motel room bathroom. Fearing that their dream of living a normal life, especially now that Keechie is pregnant, forces Bowie and Keechie to make a run for it. They think they find cover when they stay at a motel run by Mattie, the wife of T-Dub's brother. When the police go to Mattie looking for Bowie, she doesn't hesitate to make a deal. She'll hand over Bowie if they release Chickamaw from prison. He had been caught and arrested after the bank heist that got T-Dub killed.

Ray had grown up in an upper middle-class gated community in Palos Verdes, near San Pedro, and swore to me he would be able to kick dope if we moved to Pedro from Venice. It didn't occur to me until several years after I left him that San Pedro was a harbor town. There was a ton of heroin there. Twenty-nine years later, when I was fifty, I was driving through the neighborhood with a friend who had once done drugs with Ray. That was how we'd met. This friend had gotten clean and was instrumental in my leaving Ray. Now we were driving past the apartment in Pedro where Ray and I had lived. It was five blocks from Cabrillo beach and a five-minute drive from Point Fermin Park and the Korean Bell. I said to my friend, "This wasn't such a bad neighborhood."

My friend said, "Well, it has always been called the felony flats."

He would know. His father had been a longshoreman and he'd grown up nearby. Of course there was heroin.

When it finally dawned on me that Ray had no intention of kicking, I had been clean and sober two-and-a-half years. It was insane for me to stay as long as I did, but there were reasons I did. I had fallen deeply in love with him before he had gotten strung out. He rode a skateboard. He dressed in thrift shop suits and white Creepers, the shoes with the two-inch thick black platform rubber soles. He had freckles and eyes like Paul McCartney. He played bass. He was a thief. He wasn't good, so I didn't have to be good, although I wanted to be a good girlfriend, and was when it came to promiscuity. I was faithful to the end. Something I had never been to any of the boyfriends I'd had.

The worst thing I ever did to Ray was throw out his new syringes in a Denny's bathroom. I had found them on the bookshelf behind the *Big Book* of Alcoholics Anonymous. He tore the apartment apart, screaming at me that I was a murderer.

By the end of the two-and-a-half-years I was with him, we fought constantly. Sometimes violently. Our telephone, a rotary landline, was frequently in pieces on the hardwood floor, from throwing it at each other. Instead of punching me he smacked whatever object was in close vicinity. Like, the windshield of my first car, a blue Volkswagon Squareback that I never drove. I bought it with the money I'd gotten from suing the driver of the car who hit us when we were on the Vespa. I bought it before I even knew how to drive. I didn't know then that my mother had also bought her first car before she learned how to drive. Ray had gotten furious when I complained that he was two hours late picking me up after my shift at the International House of Pancakes and smashed it with his fist while he was driving. I never drove that car. Never. Not even after I got my license.

I was afraid of leaving Ray because I could think of no place to go. I didn't want to live with my mother at Elysium. I had cut myself off from friends and was afraid because I knew I only had two choices: to get high with Ray and ruin two-and-a-half years of sobriety or leave him.

He called one morning, after being gone for three days, to say he was going to San Francisco for a while. I gave him an ultimatum. San Francisco or me. He chose San Francisco. I told him I wouldn't be here when he returned and hung up the phone. I waited a few minutes for him to call back. He didn't. I walked five blocks to the local donut shop, bought a dozen bear claws, walked back home, sat on the rust couch, and ate all twelve donuts in one sitting. I then called a friend of Ray's who had gotten sober and said I needed to leave. She offered me her couch. I packed all of my belongings into the yellow Ford coupe Ray's father had given me for a Christmas present to replace the damaged VW Squareback. By then, I'd gotten my driver's license. I left the Squareback, with its flat tire, parked on the street in front of our apartment and left San Pedro for Hollywood.

Nicca love,

you write the most interesting letters I ever get and I wish you'd write more often. Since it is really my fault that you don't spell so very good I think it's easier for me to understand your writing.

When we moved from Italy, where you were born, you spoke Italian more than you spoke English. Then I had to go to Spain to work and you began to speak Spanish better than Italian and at the same time you were with people who were almost always speaking English. So someday soon you should realize, I mean, not worry about having to talk or write in any language except the one which is most useful to you and I think that is American, isn't it?

And please, Nicca—you have never to worry about being loved, or buying love or trading for love or to fear giving or taking love. You can and should feel it more naturally than any of us.

Nick, 1966

In a Lonely Place

In a Lonely Place was the first Nicholas Ray film I saw. That is, if you count watching the opening credits a complete viewing. Seeing the words "Directed by Nicholas Ray" on the television screen was all I was looking for—his name like a wave hello. I watched it on the *Late Night Movie* after Nick had appeared in our lives again and vanished. I was fourteen. Alone in the two-bedroom apartment we'd moved into after leaving Ward. Over the years the mere mention of *In a Lonely Place* made me think about Nick, Tony, and Gloria. Gloria wasn't anything real. That's what I told the writer David Thomson when he asked me if I'd known her. I said, "Someone as beautiful as she was who was married to my father and my brother? There's just something unreal."

I saw it in its entirety on the big screen in 2003. The director Curtis Hanson was introducing a newly restored print at the Gramercy Theatre on 23rd Street in New York City, where the Museum of Modern Art was screening movies during the renovation of their 53rd Street space. *In a Lonely Place* was the first film in their series celebrating film preservation; the screening would also kick off a Nicholas Ray retrospective.

Hanson saw the film the first time when he was fourteen years old, living in the San Fernando Valley where his father was a teacher. "This movie was so incredibly vivid in the world that it created, the picture of that world, it was almost like walking into a dream. It's somebody else's dream but you're seeing it too. And there was this yearning in me to get closer and to understand it more."

"I don't know how this film was developed but I do know that somehow Nicholas Ray and Humphrey Bogart found themselves consumed by it," Hanson said. "Ray found himself in this character. I know it because I can feel it."

"I hate a script," Nick said. "I resent a script. It's inevitable that I'm going to have a fight with the script no matter how I choose it. It represents authority. I resent authority. It's a flaw in my character."

Nick's personality clashed with the screenwriter, Andrew Solt, but it was also old Hollywood clashing with the new. Solt wasn't used to directors taking his scripts and personalizing them in the way Nick did. Arriving in Hollywood from Budapest shortly before the war, Solt had written the screenplay adaptation for *The Jolson Story* (1946), the screenplay for Victor Fleming's *Joan of Arc* (1948) starring Ingrid Bergman, and the script for Mervyn LeRoy's *Little Women* (1949) starring June Allyson, Elizabeth Taylor, Janet Leigh, and Peter Lawford. Solt was used to working with directors of classical cinema, not directors like Nick whose films were breaking new ground. They were intimate. They got under your skin.

"Intimacy [in film] started in the aftermath of the war," Bernard Eisenschitz, a Ray biographer, said. "I don't think getting close to people in this way going under the surface in this or many other ways, although other filmmakers were doing that at the time, was something that was really happening before 1945. Of course, we can always find examples, but I think the great filmmakers were not really working on that. It was not getting under the skin. If you look at *Citizen Kane* it has nothing to do with intimacy."

My father called *In a Lonely Place* his most personal film.

Four years after the Museum of Modern Art screening I met with Curtis Hanson in the bungalow of his Deuce Three

Production office on the grounds of what was known as The Lot. Located on the corner of Santa Monica and Formosa these eighteen acres of offices and sound stages were originally the Pickford-Fairbanks Studio, where Samuel Goldwyn and Joseph Schenck rented space. Pickford-Fairbanks gave way to United Artists in the early 1920s and was known as the United Artists Studio until 1940 when it became the Samuel Goldwyn Studio.

Warner Bros. bought the property in 1980 and sold it in 1999 at which time it became known as The Lot. When I was a child and Betty and I would drive by it in her green Buick Skylark I'd press my nose against the passenger window wanting to go inside. Now I was in and it felt good. It made the bad things that had happened when I was a kid feel further away than they'd ever felt before.

When Hanson made *L.A. Confidential* in 1996–97, he had his actors Guy Pearce and Russell Crowe watch *In a Lonely Place* so they could get a feel for what Los Angeles was like in the early 1950s and for what the people looked and talked like. It was important to Hanson not to make a big deal out of his screening my dad's film prior to filming his own. "I was having them look at a lot of things to understand the period and the place. It was also a perfect movie in terms of Russell's character to see this guy who's tortured, for Guy's as well, but Russell's? There's a stronger connection in a way because of the way his psychological difficulties become physical in their expression. You know the rage."

It's night as the opening credits roll and you see Dix Steele (Humphrey Bogart) driving, a close up of his face in the rear-view mirror, his intensity exposed. We follow his car to the traffic light turning red his car stops next to a convertible. The fancily dressed woman sitting in the passenger seat says, "Hi Dix. Remember me? I was in the last picture you wrote?" He doesn't. Her husband, who is driving, throws Dix an empty threat, and without missing a beat Dix is getting out of his car to meet the challenge. The light changes to green and the husband drives off.

"You think about *In a Lonely Place* and the struggle between the artist and the business and it's never been expressed better than that," Curtis Hanson said. "When it's good, even in the world of the so-called independent movies today, there is such a desire to be successful that that scene in the bar where he's sitting there with the director and the dialogue about being the popcorn salesman and so forth, that's the same deal today. As much as things have changed, it's not been expressed better than that. And it never will [be]. I mean, as much as it changes it never will change completely because if you don't sell the popcorn then you don't get to make another movie. And the directors who have a body of work manage to have a successful movie often enough to keep going or else they don't keep going."

Like most of Nick's best films, *In a Lonely Place* was a critical rather than a financial success. He followed it up with the box office hit *Flying Leathernecks* starring John Wayne. However, *In a Lonely Place* is the one that stands the test of time. On December 27, 2007 the Library of Congress announced its list of twenty-five National Film Registry selections, including *In a Lonely Place*.

At the time *In a Lonely Place* was released *The Hollywood Reporter* called Nicholas Ray "a director with plenty of imagination in rounding out a scene and getting laughs from the flip dialogue." *Motion Picture Daily* wrote, "Bogart is perverse and unmanageable and lacks sympathy unless audiences determine to line up in his corner in an understanding of his never clarified mental roadblocks. Unquestionably, however, he sinks his teeth into the part and does very well with it as unsavory as the characterization is. By underplaying, Miss Grahame strikes conviction. Others in the small cast do well under Nicholas Ray's direction, which is tight and competent."

When Gloria was on screen, I saw my half-brother Tim's face in hers. My eyes peeled themselves on her like she was a magnet. Was she really that mesmerizing or was I waiting for her to tell me something? You know, break out of character, look straight into the camera at me, time travel to the twenty-first century, and say, "That stuff about your father and half-brother Tony? . . . "

Tony, my father's first son, had an affair with Gloria, my father's second wife, when Tony was barely a teenager. Nick wanted everyone to believe that Tony was the one who seduced Gloria and made sure that that was the story that got around Hollywood and was cemented into Hollywood lore. This is what Tony told me really happened:

When Tony was twelve years old, he moved out of his mother's tenement apartment in New York City and into Nick and Gloria's Cape Cod-style beach house on Colony Road in Malibu, California. Tony was a troubled kid who had been in and out of military schools and homes for juvenile delinquents since he was five years old. As soon as he'd arrived in Malibu that summer of 1950, Gloria set the wheels in motion that led to Nick accusing Tony seducing his wife.

Nick, who was busy on the RKO lot, in pre-production on *Flying Leathernecks*, had sent Gloria to pick Tony up at the Los Angeles International Airport. Tony had never met his stepmother. Even though she was a movie star and her photograph graced the Hollywood trades, Tony was unaware of what she looked like.

Tony waited anxiously for his father to appear in the baggage claim at LAX. "All of a sudden I was wrapped up in the cashmere sweater that this beautiful woman was wearing. 'I'm Gloria. I've been wanting Nick to bring you out here so badly.

97

I saw a picture of you right after we married. I had to have you out here.'"

Tony was ten years old in that photograph.

Within weeks Gloria was saying things to Tony like, "You're awfully cute. I wish you were ten years older," and then invited him into the bathroom to watch her take a shower. She told him to turn his back as her nightgown was falling to the floor. But he watched as she stepped naked under the water. When she was done, she wrapped a towel around herself and asked Tony to dry her back as she lowered the towel to her waist. Instead of running away, Tony did what she asked. Another time she asked him to join her in the bedroom. She patted the space on the mattress next to her and he sat down, soaking up the scent of her powdery perfume.

In his unpublished book about his and Gloria's affair, Tony wrote: "She reached over and mussed my hair. She lay across me, put a finger on my nose. She kissed the end of my nose then bit it and bounded out of bed. Her white nightgown barely covered her."

She told him she wasn't interested in taking his mother's place. She said, "We'll have our own relationship."

She admitted to Tony that she liked children better than adults, because they were more honest. She invited him into her bedroom to listen to Édith Piaf records.

"She was like a teenager playing going out. She had taken the bright white bulb out of the lamp by the bed and replaced it with a soft red one. The drapes had been pulled closed. She was sitting cross legged on the bed with a drink in her hand."

She French kissed him and said, "I've been waiting to do that ever since I saw the picture of you playing stickball on the street."

She slipped her hand down his pants.

"I don't know how to approach this," Tony told me. "But Gloria and I ended up having a lot of foreplay. A lot of sexual activity."

Tony wrote, "Gloria came into my room. She sat on the edge of the bed. It was like a dream. I tried to put my arms around her. She told me to lie still. She pushed back my hands and rolled me over on my back. I could barely make out her face in the dark, but I felt her breath, then her mouth. I raised my head toward the kiss and lifted my hands to hold her. She told me to keep my hands to myself. Her fingers ran over my shoulders, then my chest and stomach. They stopped at the elastic of my under shorts. She was still kissing me. Then her hand slipped into my shorts and wrapped around my penis."

At the end of the summer Nick sent Tony to Harvard Military Academy in Westlake Village. He didn't see Gloria until Christmas. On New Year's Eve Gloria was in a rage because Nick wasn't home for dinner. She had prepared a duck and was purposefully burning it when Tony walked through the door and into the smoke-filled kitchen. He ran to the stove, turned off the oven, and opened the window. Gloria slapped him across the side of his head and yelled at him to get the hell out of the house.

Tony thought that if he could find Nick and bring him home in time to celebrate the New Year than maybe Gloria wouldn't be angry anymore. He walked from Colony Road to the Pacific Coast Highway and then to the Inn, where he knew Nick sometimes rendezvoused with Marilyn Monroe.

Nick wasn't there.

Tony was afraid to go back to the house without Nick, so he decided to kill time by sitting in a Malibu coffee shop drinking coffee until the sun came up. In the morning he went back home. As he was approaching the house he noticed Nick's clothing, slashed with a razor blade, thrown in front of their beachfront property.

Tony found Gloria lying in her bed with the covers pulled up to her chin. She was furious because Nick had called her in the middle of the night refusing to tell her where he was. Tony went to console her, and she started screaming irrational accusations.

"You've broken into the house. Go away. You're darling father might walk in. How would he like to find his son in bed with his wife?"

Tony panicked, "'You haven't told him anything? Have you, Gloria?'"

He pulled the blankets off of her and it was revealed that she was holding a gun.

Gloria called the police.

"This is Gloria Grahame at 14 Malibu Colony. My stepson tried to rape me. Get here fast."

Tony tore out of the house and ran to the rocky cove where he knew there was a cave he could hide in. The State Troopers came after him, along with two local Malibu Sheriffs, one who knew Tony. Tony was afraid, rightfully so, that he would be accused of rape, and sent away to a juvenile detention center, or worse yet, prison.

The State Trooper eased Tony's mind and was able to eventually coax him out of the cave. "'Didn't you know? I called your house a half an hour ago. I told Mrs. Ray we were coming to take you to your father. She hung up on us.'"

Unbeknownst to Tony, Nick and Gloria had separated and Nick had moved out of the Malibu home and into the Garden of Allah hotel in West Hollywood.

When the State Troopers went to the house to retrieve Tony, Gloria confessed that she had lied about Tony's attempting to rape her. The Malibu Sheriffs then drove Tony to Nick at the Garden of Allah hotel.

That night Nick took Tony out to dinner at an Italian restaurant where Nick was a regular. The maître d' asked if he would like his usual drink, Old Rarity. Nick said yes and ordered the waiter to keep Tony's drinks coming. First came the screwdrivers, then the Chianti, and finally, the brandy. Nick accused Tony of coming to live with him and Gloria as a diabolical scheme to destroy his marriage, a payback for having left his mother, Jean. Nick accused Tony of competing with him for the love of Gloria. And then he slammed the words, "You're fucking Gloria," against his son.

Tony went numb.

Nick handed him a small trinket wrapped in tissue. Tony unwrapped it. It was a button from the jacket of his military uniform. "It tickled my ass when I climbed into bed one night."

Tony had never worn his military uniform in Gloria's bed.

There was a long silence.

Then Nick said, "I want you to make recordings about this, Tony. They will save me thousands of dollars in divorce court."

Tony spent the next day sequestered in his hotel room, with a guard standing outside the door, and confessed on tape about having had sex with Gloria.

The next day he was sent away to a military school in Missouri.

Nick played the tapes at Hollywood parties.

Betty

"**I** heard about Nick's son Tony through Nick, who was going through a lot of angst about him. He told me he had walked in on Gloria making love to his son. So, I knew about a Tony, but I didn't know the Tony I knew was Nick's son," Betty said.

Tony Ray was enrolled in the Movement for Actors class that Betty taught at the Rainbow Studios in Hollywood. She had realized that actors' bodies didn't flow naturally in character along with the words they spoke. "I felt [actors] needed to experience moving within the character they were playing," Betty recalled. "Being a ballerina where everything is exposed without words enabled me to create all kinds of movement to communicate. That's the kind of thing I taught as well as limbering and strengthening the body."

After class one day, Tony and Betty hopped into his convertible and picked his mother, Jean, up at Los Angeles International Airport. She had flown in from New York City to spend time with her son and her brother, Morris, who was an executive secretary at the Directors Guild of American.

On their way home from the airport they stopped at an outdoor café on the Sunset Strip. They were seated at the table waiting for their food to arrive when Jean started combing her fingers through Betty's windswept bleached blonde hair and making comments that gave Betty the impression Jean thought she was Tony's girlfriend. "It was awkward,"

Betty remembered. "And then Jean said, 'Tony's so like his father,' and began describing Nick. I realized she *was* talking about Nick. I couldn't get out of there fast enough. I didn't want either of them to know that I even knew Nick Ray."

In 1956, Betty was twenty-two and living with Joy in a one-bedroom apartment across the street from Plummer Park in West Hollywood. Her brother, David, was getting his PhD in Romance Languages at the University of California, Berkeley. At twenty-five he became the youngest professor ever hired at Princeton University. "He just didn't want to be interrupted to take care of our mother," Betty said.

After their father Karl's death, the responsibility of taking care of Joy fell on my mother. It wasn't that Joy couldn't work. She had worked as a substitute teacher when Betty and David were children but stopped once my mom started dancing in movies in 1948. Joy just wanted to stay home and drink and have someone take care of her.

When Betty was barely a year old Joy had fallen down a flight of basement stairs, fracturing her skull, and breaking both of her arms and legs. She was hospitalized for over a year. During that time David was sent to live with Joy's mother, my great grandmother Weidelman, and Betty was sent to live with a neighborhood family.

When Joy came home from the hospital she would make dinner and clean the house, but she was unapproachable, and remained in her own world. She was critical of her husband's drinking even though she was imbibing as well.

"I never knew she drank at all until she was older," Betty said. "When you grow up with alcoholism you don't notice it as such."

My grandmother was probably telling Betty that she was drinking water, like she had told my sister and I, but the water in my grandmother's glass was probably the same kind of water that was in the blue glass she drank from when I was a kid. The kind of water us kids weren't allowed to drink.

It was no secret in Hollywood that Nick was an alcoholic and a drug addict. Gavin Lambert said, "Nick's medicine cabinet was absolutely stocked with every kind of pill you could imagine. He had a vitamin cocktail—mainly vitamin B—and speed to treat depression and give him energy."

I admit my mother's naiveté was a sort of defense mechanism used to survive in the world of alcoholics and predators she had grown up in. This could have been one of the reasons she wasn't aware of Nick's dependency on alcohol and drugs. She also traveled in a different part of the Hollywood world than Nick did, so she wouldn't have heard gossip about him on the sets and stages she was dancing on. People who may have known would not have come running to her with the latest news because she kept her affair with him a secret. In fact, the only person she confided in about being in love with Nick Ray was her dance teacher Carmelita Maracci, who told Betty that she was making a grave mistake getting involved with him. "He'll ruin your career."

Of course, it was also hard to know how erratic he was because he would go a couple of years without calling her.

During one of his disappearances she became engaged to Dominic Frontiere, the drummer for the Luigi Trio, a dance troupe of which Betty and her best friend Roberta were members. They met the jazz dancer Luigi while taking classes at the Rainbow Studios. Eugene Louis Faccuito was an MGM discovery nicknamed Luigi by Gene Kelly while dancing *Singing in the Rain*.

During the late 1940s and early 1950s, Nick was a frequent guest at the parties Gene Kelly and his wife, Betsy Blair, threw at their home on North Alta Drive in Beverly Hills. On Saturday nights or Sunday afternoons you could just drop in and join a cast of characters that included Judy Garland, Lena Horne, Frank Sinatra, Betty Garrett, Johnny Mercer, Van Johnson, Norman Lloyd, and Stanley Donen, the director of *Singing in the Rain*, around the piano or in a game of charades.

"I did see Nick there one night. I heard something about how he'd lost a lot of money gambling," Norman Lloyd said.

"He'd come to my house," Gene Kelly said, "and just be one of the gang. We all came from New York and we were theater people, but we became very much in love with pictures. So, everybody in that group was thinking about movies and ideas. Nick would tend to disappear from time to time, but when he'd come back every once in a while he'd always drop in and say hello. As if he'd just gone down to the corner."

Nick spent the time he was with Betty disappearing. After their first sexual encounter, in 1951, he went missing for the greater part of three years. In that time, she dated and was proposed to by Bing Crosby. When it was becoming clear to her that Nick wasn't going to reappear, she accepted Dominic Frontiere's proposal.

Ten days before Dominic and Betty's wedding Nick called.

"Dominic was Italian, wonderful, charismatic. I was in love with him but I wouldn't let him near me," Betty said. She always told me that in her heart of hearts she knew she belonged with Nick.

Betty hadn't seen Nick in a few years. It was late at night. He wanted her to come to the Chateau Marmont, the hotel on Sunset Boulevard where he was renting one of the bungalows. She didn't think twice about jumping into a cab and spending the night with him.

In the morning Nick called her a cab to take her back to the Hollywood apartment she shared with Joy on North Fuller Drive. When she got out of the taxi, she noticed Dominic angrily waiting for her. He grabbed her by the arms and asked, "Where have you been all night?"

"With Nick." She couldn't lie.

"We're going to Vegas right now and we're going to get married," he said.

"No. I'm in love with Nick."

He shoved her with such force she nearly fell off the curb, got into his car, and drove away.

"I certainly deserved his anger. Here I was losing the guy that I was going to marry for a guy I didn't know whether I was ever going to see again."

Betty did not hear from Nick for another year. This time she was planning to marry the actor Vince Edwards, a dark-haired, dark-eyed dreamboat who had shot to fame after appearing with Sterling Hayden in Stanley Kubrick's *The Killing.* They had met while both were working at Paramount. He'd go on to earn megamillions playing *Ben Casey* in the hit television series of the same name. They would have made a perfect Hollywood couple. The blonde goddess—she really was—and the handsome television star.

"Vince and I did a lot of Hollywood hopping. We'd go to dinner, do different things. He knew Jimmy Dean. Nick was making *Rebel* at the time I was tight with Vince," Betty said.

Edwards had been friends with James Dean and hung out at the same places, like the Honey Hole, owned by a Texas millionaire's son named Johnny Franco who was friends with James Dean's sidekicks, Jack Simmons and Maila Nurmi, the Man Ray model, ghoulish television host, and confidante of James Dean.

"Maila Nurmi was Finnish like me. We did a *Playhouse 90* together, 'Jet Propelled Couch.' It was a ninety-minute live program. We played goddesses living in outer space. Anyway, Maila and I became friends. That's how I found out she was seeing Jimmy. Not romantically. They were close friends," Betty said.

Once when Tony was in Los Angeles, auditioning, and needed a place to sleep, Betty suggested he call Franco and ask if there was any room at The Honey Hole for him to stay.

"We'd all go smoke grass at Franco's place. I'm not sure whether Franco was a pimp or a drug dealer," Dennis Hopper later told me.

Did Nick call Tony hoping he would know where Betty was? Had he called Rainbow Studios looking for her and been told she went on tour? It didn't matter who gave him the information. What mattered was that he knew where to find her. It was like he was the wolf on top of the mountain watching the white bunny joyfully hopping through the valley below.

"Nick was gone a long time," Betty recalled. "Jimmy was killed. And then Nick came back."

Nick tracked Betty down again in 1956 when she was in Texas on a personal appearance tour for MGM. More than a year had passed since they'd seen each other. Why was she suddenly on his mind? Had he heard of her engagement to Vince Edwards? Did he want to stop the marriage?

Nick called Betty at the hotel in Texas where she was staying.

"Where are you?" he asked.

"Nick?"

"Yes, darling."

"You know I'm in Texas?"

"When will you be back?"

Years ago, when Betty first told me about Nick tracking her down, I thought it was so romantic. He must've loved her so much to hunt for her like that.

"Three days later I was sitting in a beauty shop getting my hair done and there's a picture of Nick and Marilyn Monroe on the cover of *Confidential*," Betty said. "I just died. I thought, Oh God, if he's seeing Marilyn, that's it. So, I get home. He calls me. I meet him at the Chateau. Gavin Lambert, his lover, answered the door with a limp handshake. I looked on the couch and there was Marilyn Monroe sitting cross legged in one of Nick's sweaters and nothing else. 'Nick's upstairs,' Gavin told me. So, I went upstairs and spent the night with Nick."

* * *

During the 1970s, in Hollywood: walking into a room with cocaine mirrors on coffee tables, sun-bleached and tan women sitting on the couch staring blankly at the air, and the faint smell of baby oil drifting out from the dark bedroom down the hall. I knew doing the coke meant I would be walking the darkened hallway. It was the price I had to pay, and I was okay with it because cocaine was the local anesthesia I needed to shut off my brain. I liked downers, too, Quaaludes, Tuinals, Percodan, and I would often take one of either of those before I left home so that by the time I got to the powdered mirrors and dark hallways I'd be relaxed. You didn't want the older men to see you nervous. And I wasn't. I knew all men lived in their cocks because that's what Betty would tell me. She would stand in my bedroom doorway, drunk from wine and an evening of sex, and tell me so.

It was dull and cold indoors, but sunny and clear outside, the salty ocean breeze wafting over me as I walked up the stairs and into the drug den. I was sixteen and knew there was something wrong with my being there, but before I gave myself a chance to come to my senses, I detached.

When I studied acting with Nina Foch from 1984 to 1986, she encouraged me to study the Alexander technique, a technique whose philosophy is to lengthen and widen the body. In my experience it released the emotional trauma I'd stored in various parts of my body. I physically existed in two parts. There was my upper half—from the hip bones to the top of my skull, and my lower half—from the upper thigh to the tip of my toes. My vagina was the netherworld. It didn't connect to my upper or lower body. It was a region in and of itself.

It's what us victims of sexual abuse do. We split our bodies into two and our vaginas lead us into the dark. If I wore the right slinky body-hugging dresses, a pair of high heels, and my hair long and flowing, I got the attention of men who had a lot of money and wanted to give me a lot of cocaine. There were mirrors covered with powder drawn into neat lines ready for me to snort. I'd hold my hair back off of my face and lean into toward the glass, line the straw up perfectly to the coke and take it all up my nose in one blast. I would do all of the lines the men drew out for me. The coke made me sparkle and turned me into Aphrodite. And all I had to do was lie there in their beds and let them fuck me. Cocaine tricked me into believing I was the one getting something over on them. I didn't feel any-thing about it until I woke up the next day, cold stone sober. The only way to deal with my shame was to go to the drug den again. Throughout my teens and early twenties, I thought being targeted by men meant I had power.

Rebel Without a Cause

"James Dean ate Nicholas Ray," Charles Bitsch, the *Cahiers du Cinema* writer, said.

It's true. The movie, *Rebel Without a Cause*, never goes away because James Dean is in it. You say, "Nicholas Ray was my father," and people get a puzzled look on their face. You say, "He directed *Rebel Without a Cause*, you know, James Dean," and they get starry-eyed. Ever since I was seventeen years old, the age I was when Nick died, people have asked me if I knew James Dean. I'd always do the math in my head. He died in 1955 I was born in 1961. There was a six year difference between his death and my birth. I tried figuring out a way that I could've known him. People seemed to want that from me.

Rebel Without a Cause is a ghost tapping my shoulder so I won't forget who my father was. So many times I've wished the movie would go away. So many afternoons I have not wanted to think about Nicholas Ray but then just when you least expect it there's James Dean in that red jacket leaning against the wall on that poster or you turn a page in the newspaper and there's an article, "Rebel Without Shoes" or "Rebel Without a Clue" or "Rebel Without Applause." When I first started hanging out at punk rock shows in 1979 word got out I was Nick's daughter and people started calling me the Rebel with a Cause. I never could figure out what cause they were talking about. All I wanted to do was get wasted.

I saw *Rebel Without a Cause* for the first time in 1995, when I was thirty-four years old. I believe, wholeheartedly, that I could not have watched it without having been in college.

In 1993, at the age of thirty-two, I was finally ready to go to college. With twelve years of sobriety, three years of therapy, and nearly a decade of acting classes behind me, I had the confidence to sit in a classroom of my peers. I decided I wasn't going to let lack of money stop me from getting a college education. I borrowed every dime, taking out student loans I won't be able to pay off until I'm one-hundred-eighty years old. I took classes at the New School for Social Research as a non-matriculating student for a year before applying and getting into their undergraduate program. My Uncle David, the Princeton professor, called the New School the progressive university. A fellow classmate of mine and I used to refer to our college as the weirdo school, perfect for two ex-punk rock misfits like us. We knew how to fend for ourselves on the street, but for me, school libraries were a mystery.

As a matriculating New School student, I had access to the massive New York University library on East Fourth Street across from Washington Square Park. I hadn't been in a library since I was in junior high school. I couldn't remember how to use the card catalogue system. I knew how to get myself out of hairy situations, like escaping from two men who picked me up while hitchhiking, but checking a book out of the library? Forget it. I was humiliated telling the librarian I needed to be shown how.

Little by little I developed a confidence in myself I had not known. I even started taking film history and theory classes (I'd avoided taking film theory classes that had anything to do with my father's movies) and made a short 16mm non-sync film that was included in The New York Underground Film Festival and The Bumbershoot Arts Festival. Without having reached these personal milestones I could not have shown up for the screening of *Rebel Without a Cause* when I was thirty-four.

I was sitting in a classroom at the New School when my professor began lecturing about *Rebel Without a Cause*. The professor claimed that in the movie Nicholas Ray was saying that the family is a ball and chain. I sat in my chair thinking my father hated me.

Not long after the lecture, *Rebel Without a Cause* screened at the Museum of Modern Art. I wanted to prove the professor wrong. I called asking for tickets. It was the first time I'd called a venue that was going to show my father's films and identified myself as his daughter. The night of the screening was a rainy Friday night. Downstairs in the theater lobby a long line was forming. I expected there to be two older film nerds and me. The theater was packed. People were sitting in the aisle by the time the movie started. There was clapping when my father's name appeared on the screen.

There's a scene in the movie where you can see how disappointed Jim Stark (James Dean) is in his father. Jim has just come home after agreeing to participate in a chicken run with the neighborhood tough guy, Buzz Gunderson. Jim is in the kitchen, drinking milk from a quart bottle when he hears a loud crash coming from another room. He follows the sound and is walking upstairs when he sees a figure on hands and knees wearing a yellow ruffled apron. Jim says, "Hi, Mom," and his father (Jim Backus) answers back, "Hi, Jimbo." Backus is picking up the pieces of scrambled egg and bacon that have fallen off a dinner tray and littered the floor. Jim tells him to just leave it there. You get the sense that all hell will break loose if the mother discovers a mess has been left on the carpet. Backus refuses to leave the spilled food where it is even though Jim Stark is pleading with him not to clean it up.

Finally, Jim Stark pulls his father up by the apron's shoulder strap; he wants to know why his father won't stand up to his mother but can't get the words out of his mouth. You get the feeling that Jim Stark wouldn't have to participate in a drag race to prove himself to the neighborhood's tough crowd if his father wasn't emasculated.

I want to disagree with what my professor said about *Rebel Without a Cause*. My father isn't saying the family is a ball and chain. He wants family. He wants communication. He wants to discuss the struggle parents have talking to their children. He wants to sit down at the dining room table—in his case the dining room table was the film screen, and the movie theater, the chairs.

I want to believe that about my father. Of course, Nicholas Ray *ran* from family on three different occasions. First it was Jean and Tony. Second it was Gloria and their son, Tim. Third it was Betty, Julie, and me.

Near Death Party Girl Experience Or How to Kill a Party Girl Spirit Or How to Zap a Star of Its Shine Or It Would Have Been Easier to Kill Yourself Than to Have Married Nicholas Ray

When I was a child, Betty told me she and Nick eloped. I imagined them, in 1958, driving off the MGM lot after production on *Party Girl,* Nick's film for MGM about Chicago mobsters, wrapped in a red convertible sports car speeding across country far away from the city and into the woods. What really happened is they flew to Boston's Logan Airport where they were to change to a private plane that would take them to Maine.

Nick's friend, the actor Bing Russell, had suggested Betty bring Nick to his parent's lodge in Kennebunkport, Maine so that he could dry out.

On the way through Logan Airport to meet their connecting flight Nick started turning gray and clammy. He stopped at every bar, every store, searching for a bottle of vodka, but it was Sunday, and it was against the law to sell alcohol.

"You got any booze, baby?" he asked Betty.

"I don't drink," she laughed, nervously.

Nick collapsed at the stairs of the private plane. The ambulance came. He was taken to Boston City Hospital where he was immediately admitted. It all happened so fast, Betty got lost from him. The nurses wouldn't tell her where he had been taken because she wasn't his wife.

"To them I was a nobody, a chickie baby. I didn't know what to do," Betty said. "Finally, I found him late that afternoon.

They'd put him in a surgical equipment room. There were no available rooms. He had the delirium tremors. He thought I was his second wife, Gloria, and was ranting all of this horrible stuff at me. I tried telling him who I was but then I just backed out. I was scared shitless."

She found a nurse, explained who she was, and was told she had to spend the night at a nearby hotel. There was no way in hell she was going to leave his side. She demanded to sleep on a cot outside of Nick's room. In the morning she was rudely awakened by attendants who told her to check herself in to a nearby hotel.

Betty thought Nick was dying and called Tony in New York City, even though Nick and Tony's relationship hadn't improved much at all since the Gloria fiasco. But when Betty reached Tony, he rushed to Boston to be by her side. At the time, Tony was sharing an apartment on 4th Avenue and East 12th Street with Dennis Hopper, and working as an understudy in Elia Kazan's Broadway production of William Inge's *The Dark at the Top of the Stairs*. Tony took the midnight train from Grand Central to Boston and met Betty at the hospital. By that time, she recalls, "Nick was incoherent. He was talking about Jesus."

Tony stayed the night with Betty in her hotel room. "We slept in the same bed, but never fucked." she said. "It wasn't awkward. We were both bonded by Nick. You don't want to make love with someone else when someone who means a lot to you is dying."

Still, the next morning when Tony returned to New York City, he told Betty on his way out the door, "You're choosing the wrong Ray."

Betty stayed with Nick. "The doctor told me that Nick needed to stay in Boston for psychiatric help, but Nick met with the analyst just three times before we set off for Maine," she said.

She was apprehensive about going to Maine with Nick, even sharing with Joy that she had "qualms about Maine," but whatever warning bells were going off in her head she chose to ignore them, and ended up having a memorable stay.

When I was growing up, whenever Betty mentioned being in Maine with my father, it was as if this dreamy haze washed over her.

"It was the gentlest time. The most intimate time. Just me and Nick. We were so in love. He bought me a ballet barre. He was the kindest man. Just me and him."

When I was sixteen, I saw, for the first time, a black and white 8-by-10 photograph that had been taken while my parents were in Maine. Betty kept her photographs from the 1950s and early 1960s in a cardboard box stored on the highest shelf of her bedroom closet. My sister and I were not to look in them, under any circumstances. But I would get drunk on my mother's cheap Gallo white wine and spend the afternoon looking through these forbidden boxes. I found the 8-by-10 black and white photo that was taken of my parents when they were staying at the Kennebunkport Lodge on one of my drunken scavenger hunts through my mother's past. In the photograph, Nick is sitting across the table from Betty. His gray wavy hair is neatly combed. His eyes are calm. His expression is serious, but not sullen. He's heavier in this photo than I ever remembered him being.

Betty, on the other hand, was recognizable, because, as always, she was beautiful and super thin. She used to tell me, "Eating disrupted my digestion and interfered with dancing."

In the photograph, Betty's bleached blonde hair hangs to her shoulders, undone and free. There's a softness about her that I don't recognize.

From what my mother told me about their first weeks in Kennebunkport it sounded like it was the most tranquil time of her life. Nick had a ballet barre installed in their room so that she could practice every morning to the Beethoven Sonatas. It became a routine; she would practice at the barre and he would watch her. Betty loved to be watched. She commanded your eye go to her. I'd watched people gravitating toward her all of my life. I was also beginning to understand that my mother was willing to pay a soul-crushing price for this attention.

She wrote to Joy, "Nick sees to it I work out every day, while he sits watching with pleasure while I sweat it out. He's a perfectionist with me."

Perfectionist was a nice word for critical. After several weeks, Nick started criticizing Betty to the point where she felt like she couldn't speak to him in her defense. She wrote him a letter.

"I see you glowering at me. You are irritated hour after hour at me. I am hurt to the fucking core with your patient efforts to teach me to cut meat, stop cussing, etc."

To Joy she wrote, "We are two peas in a pod."

She told me, "We were so close. We slept in a twin bed!"

Whenever Betty spoke to me of their time in Maine, she painted a picture of Nick being her champion and soulmate. Of giving her a kind of strength she had never known.

On October 13, 1958, Nick walked into the kitchen of the Kennebunkport Lodge, where Betty was peeling potatoes for that night's stew, and announced that they were going to go to the justice of the peace and getting married.

"Nick had his hunting clothes on, and he was trying to put white cufflinks on a white shirt. He said, 'Darling, I need some help. I can't get the cufflink on there.' I looked at him in this hunting garb with the white shirt and cufflinks and I said, 'Where are you wearing that to?' And he said, 'Well, we're going to get married. There's a judge who can fit us in between milking calves.'"

Next thing Betty knew they were standing in the office of a justice of the peace who had never performed a wedding before. Nick was wearing hunting clothes and the justice of the peace was dressed in overalls. Bing Russell and his wife, Lou, loaned their wedding rings to Nick and Betty for the ceremony. Nick hugged Betty and said, "You're crazy, you know."

And she said, "I know."

They planned on staying in Maine, and away from Hollywood, until the end of the year. However, just as they were settling back into life on the lake Nick got a call from Ronnie Lubin, his agent at MCA, with an offer from Disney to direct a film called *Hurricane*. Nick and Betty returned to Los Angeles where they rented a house above the Sunset Strip on Miller Drive next door to the actor, John Ireland, who had been one of the friends who'd pointed out to Betty that Nick's drinking was out of control.

After the *Hurricane* project fell through Ronnie Lubin talked to Nick about a Paramount co-production with the Italian producer Maleno Malenotti called *The Savage Innocents*. Based on the bestselling novel *Top of the World* by Hans Ruesch, the film stars Anthony Quinn as Inuk, a polar Eskimo confronted with the morality of the Western world. It is one of my favorites of my father's films.

In Inuk's culture, offering another man his wife is the highest form of hospitality. When a visiting missionary refuses Inuk's offer of his wife, Asiak, played by the Japanese-French actress Yoko Tani, Inuk slams the missionary's head into the ice, instantly killing him.

Inuk and Asiak flee but are found by a state trooper, played by Peter O'Toole, who has been sent to bring Inuk to justice. Instead the two men befriend one another and try to understand the ways of the other.

Describing the film, Nick said, "In *The Savage Innocents* the landscape helped to put the spirit of man in relief. That man could survive in this environment, and in the process of his survival have the wish and the need to communicate the results of his observation to another man, however unsuccessful it turned out in the end—this was the drama. The tragedy of the story is that no matter how well intended the two men, each has to return to his way of life . . . . I think that the trooper's environment is just as tough to go back to as the environment the Eskimo has to go back to," Nick said.

* * *

I believe *The Savage Innocents* is a poem of a film and one of my father's treasures. I saw it for the first time at a Museum of Modern Art retrospective of Nick's films. At first, I thought, *Oh no it's going to be boring*—like *Bitter Victory*, his movie based on the French novel, *Amere Victoire* by Rene Hardy, starring Richard Burton, which Gavin Lambert described as a story of betrayal during World War II. "After an attack on Rommel's North African headquarters, the mission commander wins a decoration," Lambert said. "But he's a false hero, a coward and liar who left a younger officer, the true hero, to die in the desert."

The slow pace of *Bitter Victory* makes me cringe like the screech of nails on a chalkboard. Jean-Luc Godard declared "Nicholas Ray is cinema," after seeing it. I so disagree with Godard on this. What I mean is, I would declare "Nick is cinema" after seeing *In a Lonely Place* and my personal favorite of his films, *The Lusty Men*. But *Bitter Victory* had me silently screaming for a way out of the theater. *The Savage Innocents* swept me off my feet.

* * *

When Betty started sharing stories about what it was like to be married to Nick one story intrigued me the most. During shooting exteriors on location in the Arctic, the small plane en route to the Frobisher Bay Air Force Base where Nick, Betty, and the crew were staying, crashed. She made their life sound like a real-life action adventure movie. Much of the footage was destroyed but they survived unscathed. I imagined her and my father escaping the wreckage seconds before the airplane burst into flames. Now that was romantic.

Betty said, "I stayed in a Quonset hut near the Frobisher Air Force Base with two of the women who worked as secretaries on the base because no women were allowed to live there. At least that's what I was told and believed. Shortly after we arrived—before any of the location stuff —the two ladies took off to a party. It was a Saturday night. I went to bed. I woke in the middle of the night. All of the heating had gone off. It was colder than cold. I could feel my nose freezing. I kept putting on more and more clothes and jumping and dancing around. Eventually I couldn't move my hands. I would have frozen to death if they'd stayed out all night. They got home around two in the morning. First thing they did was rip off all my clothes and then they threw me into the snow naked and rolled me in it. That was my entrée into the Arctic. And that is where Julie was conceived. I started puking in the snow because of morning sickness. So, Nick said, 'I think we'd better go to London and have you checked.'"

The production was going to finish shooting at the British Pinewood Studios, anyway, so it wasn't a disruption in the film's shooting schedule to bring Betty to London so that she could get settled. Nick's friend, Joe Losey, suggested Nick and Betty stay with his friend, the producer, Hannah Weinstein. She had a castle in the English countryside where she let her American expatriate friends stay.

Betty wrote Joy that Weinstein had "made her fortune from peanuts, by charming and persuading many money peoples, five years ago, to invest in her ideas for television. Today she's a successful, wealthy woman, married to an attorney. They're both American."

Nick and Joe Losey had both been film directors under contract at RKO Studios when Howard Hughes took over from Floyd Odlum on May 10, 1948. When Hughes took charge, he made it his mission to weed out the communist sympathizers who were under contract. He tested directors' loyalty by offering them a chance to direct the movie, *I Married a Communist.* If they flat out refused Hughes determined they were communists and had their contracts terminated. Losey vehemently opposed directing the movie. He soon became a target of the McCarthy witch hunts and left America for London.

"Losey was an intellectual bastard," Betty remembered. "I loved his work and certainly honored him in terms of his being an artist. But his pompousness—I hated it in Nick, too. When he'd get into this pontificating, bullshitty, superior-than-thou bullshit. I hated it."

Losey spent his life as an expatriate, and made a name for himself as an acclaimed British film director.

Nick, however, agreed to direct the movie, and, with the help of his lawyer, who happened to also be John Houseman's attorney, squirmed his way out of the contract without alienating Hughes.

Like Joe Losey, Hannah Weinstein was an American who had made London her home. She was the same age as Nick, born in New York City, on June 23, 1911. She had been a professional journalist, writing for the *Herald Tribune* from 1927 to 1937, when she left to work for then-New York Mayor Fiorello La Guardia on his campaign to serve a second term.

Even though Weinstein left journalism and political campaigning to become a television and film producer, she never turned her back on political activism. Her house became a refuge for expatriates. It was there that Betty met Weinstein's close friend, Lillian Hellman, the writer of the Broadway hit, *The Children's Hour,* who had refused to name names before the House of Un-American Activities Committee.

There were rules to follow while living at Hannah Weinstein's. Everyone was required to gather for a daily formal breakfast, and to dress up. For Betty, "Finding something appropriate to wear was a bit of a puzzle. I didn't have any dresses, having just come from the Arctic. But I did get to the breakfast table. The first morning I was there I was seated next to Lillian Hellman. She was definitely holding court, and everybody was kind of spellbound by her. I didn't know who she was."

Betty, who was at least twenty years younger than the people seated at the breakfast table, had not been a part of the same Hollywood social circle. She wasn't even born until 1934, the year, for instance, Nick became a card-carrying member of the communist party. My mother compared eating breakfast with Nick's contemporaries to watching a television talk show, like *60 Minutes.*

"I was so lonely and so frightened about being pregnant, but Nick had to go back to the Arctic to shoot more location shots. Before leaving he found a realtor to help us find an apartment we could make our home base. The realtor didn't have time to take us, but, gave us the address, and said to ring the doorbell, because there was a tenant living there. So, we go, and to the door comes this dolly of a guy dressed in a bonnet and little frills. More frilly than I'd ever been as a girl. It was Dan Duryea. The actor. Anyway, he was doing some theater thing in London, and he didn't mind at all answering the door and showing us the flat," Betty said.

The minute they signed the lease, Nick was on his way back to the Arctic, and Betty was alone. The London apartment was in a landmark building right off Hyde Park. "The ceilings were like a thousand feet high. I felt like this little pea alone in this bed. There wasn't a television to keep me company. It was really spooky being there alone."

"Nick left me alone in London with one request. To go to as much theater in the West End as I could and to find him an actor who could play the part of the State trooper in *The Savage Innocents.* Paramount was going to stick him with a contract player, and he wanted a fresh face. So, I would go to the theater with the little terrier Nick had bought me before leaving and that I named MissYou. I would just tuck her under my arm. Nobody knew she was there. She was so close to me. We were like cat and mouse together.

"So, I saw wonderful theater, and one night I went to a play called *The Long and the Short and the Tall*," Betty said. The play was directed by Lindsay Anderson, who was a friend of Gavin Lambert's. (Before moving to California to be Nick's assistant, Lambert was a critic for the film journals, *Sequence*, for which he was one of the founders along with Lindsay Anderson, and for *Sight and Sound*).

When Betty saw Lindsay Anderson's play, she didn't think of the connection between Nick, Lambert, and Anderson. She said, "It was a really good play about the army. And onto the stage comes an actor who struck me as an English Errol Flynn. It was Peter O'Toole. And I thought, *Oh, man, I wonder if he could meet Nick and do the movie.*

"I went backstage and met Peter's wife, Sian, a Gaelic actress. She was also pregnant. So, I said, 'My husband is a film director,' and she said 'Oh, you're Nicholas Ray's wife. Oh, Peter would love to meet you. I'll convince Peter to do it,'" Betty recalled. "They gathered up these musical instruments and brought bottles of wine and Chinese food over to the Hyde Park flat. We spent the whole night drinking wine and talking and playing music. When Nick came back from the Arctic, I introduced him to Peter."

As soon as Nick returned to London from the Arctic, Maleno Malenotti, the Italian producer on *The Savage Innocents*, summoned Nick and Betty to join him in Rome. "We were met at the airport with fanfare," Betty said. "Photographers, publicity news, and the wives of the men connected with the film came to greet me and offered their help getting me acclimated."

Betty wrote to Joy, "The world should be this magnificent.

This is no city. It is an expression of life! Walking through the streets sends you into a magic dizzy. It must be the tourist center of the globe. It's as a great museum should be. . . . The citizens of the city are as curious of you as you are of them. So, that also creates a pleasant blushing sensation. Nick, being entirely engrossed in most consequential business here, has been away most of the day. So, I've soloed."

At first, she was so excited just to be in Rome but after a few weeks she felt alone again, isolated in a foreign country. In later letter to Joy, she wrote, "The strangeness of the people, the language, their way of life, though everyone has been polite and friendly, the undercurrent is uneasy. We are rich Americans. They are poor Italians. I despise not being Italian when in Italy."

Moreover, Nick started criticizing her again.

"The other night at dinner with a group of Italian art critics I got a toothpick and started picking my teeth," Betty wrote. "Nick laid into me and I started crying. Another night, Nick nudged me during a performance of a play because I laughed at the wrong moment, a moment the rest of the audience, including Nick, was taking very seriously. And then, on a different occasion, we were socializing with an Italian film actress, who I've forgotten the name of, and Nick was so excited being with her that he completely neglected me."

She was twenty-four years old. He was forty-eight. She was without her mother and her best friend. She was pregnant. She was no longer living a dancer's life, the only kind of life she had known since she'd been seven years old. She wanted to believe that, together, she and Nick would create artworks that could somehow make sense of the human experience.

She grew hopeful when, finally, they moved out of the hotel and rented a flat in old Rome. Nick became interested in a project called *A Day in the Life of an African Boy*. "I was so excited, because I had learned enough from Nick about what turned him on. He was not going to do mega-movies, he was not going back to the Hollywood movies, but to do more documentaries, to do more intimate things."

Or so Betty thought. Without her knowledge, Nick had signed a contract to direct *King of Kings*—an epic with the same grandeur of a *Cleopatra*—for the ill-fated Samuel Bronston Productions. Nick was paid $75,000 for twenty-four weeks at $3,125 per week plus two percent of the western hemisphere gross from the first dollar. In addition, he received living expenses of $500 a week, a car, and a chauffeur. His salary as well as expenses commenced on Monday November 23, 1959, six days after Betty's twenty-fifth birthday.

Betty found out about Nick's commitment to direct *King of Kings* on Christmas morning, 1959. She was due to give birth to their first daughter, my older sister, Julie, in a couple of weeks. That Christmas morning Nick walked her to the window of their apartment and pointed to the brand-new Jaguar parked outside. "It's yours," he said.

She said, "Nick, I don't even drive."

Babies, Speed, and Movies

On Sunday, January 10, 1960, Betty and Nick were entertaining John Houseman and a few of their film friends at their farmhouse on the Via Appia Antica in Rome when Betty's water broke.

"I was in the kitchen preparing beef burgundy stew, and the guests were talking, and my water burst. We were off to the hospital and at ten to seven—Julie was born. It was probably the most thrilling thing that had ever happened to me—having this beautiful baby girl—and I could have just left the planet with her. That's how fabulous it was. Nick was there for the fast delivery and then disappeared with John Houseman."

Betty had never felt any warmth from Houseman. She took a walk along the Via Appia Antica with him one afternoon and he acted like a jealous lover; he didn't get why my father had married her. Houseman made my mother feel like she would she would never be part of their world.

Dance had always been the glue that kept Betty together. But she hadn't danced professionally since *Party Girl*. She felt motherhood could replace what dancing had given her once Julie was born but Nick was adamantly opposed to her being a full-time mother. Nick insisted the quality of time you spent with the child was more vital than the quantity of time. Against Betty's wishes he hired Jenny, a nurse from the hospital where Julie was born, to be the nanny. She begged him to wait, to let the baby settle into life, to give it a few more months before bringing a stranger in to watch over her.

* * *

First, Nick took Betty away from her tribe of dancer-gypsies. Then he took her away from dance. Then he got her pregnant. Then he hired a nanny and took motherhood away from her. Then, a month after their daughter, Julie's, birth, Nick left Betty alone and went on a business trip to New York City, called his twenty-four-year-old niece, Gretchen, and asked her to meet in his suite at the Sherry Netherlands Hotel.

* * *

The last time Nick and Gretchen had seen each other was at her wedding in 1957. He had wanted to bring Jayne Mansfield as his date, but Gretchen had begged him not to. "Who was going to notice me, the bride, with Jayne Mansfield there?" On her wedding day, Nick "was standing next to me, and said, 'Do you like my tux?' I said, 'Yes,' and he said, 'I'm not wearing anything underneath.'"

Three years later, Nick called Gretchen and "asked if I wanted to come see him in New York. I was excited to see him." She took a four-hour bus ride from Newark, Delaware, where she lived with her husband and two children.

"Nick had dinner served in his suite. We talked about Bertolt Brecht. Music was my thing. I was just so happy to be there," Gretchen said.

The next morning a dark-haired woman with an olive complexion and a French accent paid Nick an unexpected visit. Nick ushered Gretchen out of the suite and told her to come back in an hour. He handed her a stack of twenty-dollar bills and directed her to nearby Sixth Avenue, where he thought she could find a couple of record stores that would carry albums by her favorite musicians.

When Gretchen returned the mystery woman was gone but she noticed boxes of syringes in plain view on the bedside table. Nick explained how they were for his vitamin B12 shots. Not only had Nick started drinking again he was shooting drugs again, too. By the time his second to last film, *King of Kings*, went into production in April 1960 he was carrying "a *farmacia* that he lugged around, it was a doctor's bag full of medications. Thorazine was one of them. There was a whole bunch of them. They were all for psychosis," according to Betty.

On the second night of Gretchen's visit, Nick "was very physically aggressive. I focused on his toes. My mother, who had rheumatoid arthritis, had toes just like him. I kept pushing him away. 'No, Nick. Please don't.' I pushed him hard. He left, furious. I locked the door. And in the morning, I packed my bags and took the bus back to Newark. I was disappointed in myself. I was thinking on the ride home, 'You dumb shit.' Women, you know, always take full blame."

* * *

Nick once said, "I feel rather poetic about women, whether it's savagely poetic or lyrically poetic—but not poetic in the Victorian sense, the pedestal sense. I feel poetic about getting them off the pedestal."

* * *

The next thing Nick did was call Tony.

"I got a call from Nick asking me to meet him at the airport," Tony said. "His visits over the years were always out of the blue. So, it didn't surprise me. That was Nick. We sat at a table at Kennedy [then Idlewild Airport] and he asked me if I wanted to come be his assistant on *King of Kings*. I said, 'No, I'm going to go to California and look for work.' I'd been in John Cassavettes film, *Shadows*, and in the soap, *Search for Tomorrow*. And then Nick said, 'If you're going to California why don't you look up Gloria.' And he gave me her phone number, which was really weird. I was shocked. I was totally taken aback."

When Tony landed at Los Angeles International Airport, he had the napkin Nick had jotted Gloria's phone number on in his pants pocket.

"It was a very foggy night and I was parked at the corner of Laurel Canyon and Ventura boulevards in front of a Thrifty Drug Store," Tony said. "I called her from a payphone."

"Who's this?" Gloria asked.

"Tony, Tony Ray."

"Tony Ray?"

"Yes."

There was a pause.

"Where are you?" Gloria asked.

He told her.

She said, "Don't move. Stay right there. I'll be there in twenty minutes."

"My heart was pounding. She showed up with a suitcase, a box of groceries, and we drove immediately to the guest house I was renting in Laurel Canyon and we fell into each other's arms and she didn't go home for a couple of weeks. Her mother watched Tim. Gloria and I were inseparable. For the next few months she was only visiting home. On May 8, 1960, Gloria and I drove to Tijuana and got married."

Betty recalls, "I thought Tony and Gloria's marriage was a holler. I just thought it was the funniest thing in the world. I mean—I just thought it was a holler. What can I say?"

Betty had had no contact with Tony since Nick had landed in the Boston City Hospital and she certainly had no idea that Nick had met Tony at Idlewild Airport and given him Gloria's contact information.

"Nick and I did the mean thing and got married and there was no connection with Tony at all. I don't know where he was or what he was doing. No, once Nick survived, that was the end of Tony, you know, he and Tony being in conversation at all."

Tim, the twelve-year old son of Nick and Gloria, was living in Van Nuys, California with his mother when he found out that his half-brother married his mother.

Tim's mother married Tim's half-brother and Tim's half-brother became Tim's stepfather.

"I remember when Tony first showed up," Tim said. "I was playing baseball on the street with a group of the neighborhood kids and there was this really weird looking adult walking down the middle of the street. He gave me a bunch of quarters and took me to a baseball game. I can only remember that much. I didn't want to be there anymore. Nobody talked to me about my feelings."

The first thing that entered Tim's mind were the words, "*get out.*" He didn't want to live with his mother, who was now his sister-in-law, or his half-brother, who was now his stepfather. "I ran away to my grandmother's house."

And with the help of his grandmother, Gloria's mother, Tim tracked down Nick in Spain. "I knew pretty much nothing about my dad," Tim said. "I didn't really have any ideas about him."

Betty recalled, "Tim called us and said he wanted to come out. He didn't want his brother to be his father. Nick was very busy. So, I was the one that told Nick that Tim wanted to come."

She added, "Nick said, 'Just for the summer, you know, he's not my son.' I thought it was ridiculous and tried to convince him of that. I felt absolutely he should come. He's a little boy. I was very maternal, and I was dying to have him meet Julie."

What Tim would walk into when he arrived in Madrid that summer of 1960 was perhaps as, if not more, chaotic than his mother marrying his half-brother.

Nick and Betty were renting a house in La Florida, Spain while filming *King of Kings* at the Chamartín studios in Madrid.

"All of these production wives started coming into Madrid, and I said, 'Oh, Nick, I'm not a wifey-wifey, I don't want to go team shopping, I just don't know how to get out of this.' He said, 'Well, throw 'em in a class, a noontime class, and give 'em some jazz dancing.' So, I said, 'Okay, I can take a break from twelve to two.' I opened up the class, and it became a huge success— not only with these wifeys in there, but all the actresses came, and other actors who were living there or working in other productions, and then the flamenco dancers, so my world really became, for the most part all day long, dancing."

* * *

"I believed so much in Nick's work," Betty said. She believed Nick had been grooming her to direct until her dying day. Nick enlisted Betty's help in choreographing Salome's dance. She had a difficult time working with the actress, Brigid Bazlen, who was cast in the role.

"Brigid Bazlen was a little girl who could not dance, who was not in touch with herself and who had claws for fingers, who was really like a spider woman. Hands in playing and dancing are very important. Nick had me imagining myself as Salome and kept asking questions about what feelings I'd have and how I would behave. We worked on who she was: a rebellious teenager with a focus. Then he got me on the stage, where we worked with the scenic designers and the composer. But what I worked out with Brigid at rehearsal wasn't playing out on the set. So, Nick started to work the camera settings. He said, 'We're going to construct a big bird cage, and she'll go to let all the birds out and there'll be torches, lots of torches.' He said, 'We've got to affect her, rather than just take this actress [who can't dance]. . . .' That was the start of my knowing how Nick directed; how he would use every element [at his disposal] and make a happening out of something that wasn't happening."

When I first saw the movie in the late 1980s and watched Salome's dance, I saw my mother's movements in Brigid Bazlen.

Working with Nick on *King of Kings* was like being in film school, according to Betty. "Talking and working. I used to go into the editing room and watch how they'd edit and how Nick would make his selections. A lot of the arithmetic of film-making I was into. I was doing more of that and my dance thing than anything else I can remember during *King of Kings*. We were both busy. But Nick was home every night and we made love and got up in the morning and went off again and that was our life. Busy, busy, busy."

Nick wasn't letting her sleep. It was like he was sucking the life out of her. She turned to Viveca Lindfors, an actress in her dance class, for advice.

"We became friends, and we went out for coffee, and we got into girl talk. I told her how exhausted I was. And that Nick wasn't letting me sleep. I was exhausted. She told me about these little pills that you could get at the pharmacies. They're just like aspirin. They came in tubes.

"I was taking two Preludin a day, at first, then two every four hours, then entire tubes full," Betty said.

Tim remembered these days in Spain, fondly. "Betty was out of her mind on speed, but she was great with me. She really spent a lot of time with me and was very loving. Got me flamenco boots and castanet lessons and took me to bullfights. I'm tagging along behind her through the amphitheater, and there are fifteen guys with their tongues out trying to look down her blouse. She wasn't wearing a bra and was dressed all in white. She just had no idea."

Occasionally, Tim visited Nick on the set. "They were shooting the crucifixion and the actor Jeffrey Hunter showed up on set with his armpits shaved. Nick was furious. They spent the whole day doing, you know—Jeffrey on the cross, trying to look good—and then they—so they're wrapping it all up—putting away the cameras and the lights and everybody is leaving and we were in a valley and just down the valley was this massive like—two-hundred foot white cross that they had put up on a mountain and the sky got really dark and a hole opened up in the clouds and this beam—bright sunlight—went onto that cross and I ran up to Nick and I said, 'Dad, Dad—here's the real deal. That's what you should be filming'. And he just kind of looked. He stopped and looked."

Tim reminded me of myself. He sounded just like I did, making this rather ordinary moment into a life-changing event. When I was sixteen Nick sent me a note that was supposed to have come with money—money I never saw, and on the note, he wrote, "Don't spend it all on gaucho pants." I thought the note was so great I put it in my scrapbook of saved memories. On the set of *King of Kings*, Nick stopped and looked. It was incredible. Just the way he stood there. And looked. He *looked*. It was amazing. He saw what I saw. He looked at what I was looking at. It bonded us for life.

But overall, Tim said, "There wasn't a whole bunch of contact."

Tim didn't want to go back to the States at the end of the summer. And Betty didn't want him to. He had become her buddy. If you think about it, Tim was closer in age to Betty than Nick was. They were thirteen years apart whereas Nick and Betty were twenty-three.

"I was really sad and fought Nick about sending him back, but there was no talking about it," Betty said. "It wasn't my decision to make. It was Nick's."

After *King of Kings*, Nick and Betty returned to Italy where Joe Losey introduced Nick and Betty to the sculptor, Beverly Pepper, and her husband, Bill, a foreign correspondent for *News-week* magazine. Every Sunday the Peppers had an open house at their villa outside of Rome, on the Piccolo del Mas a Mi, where their guests would drink wine, and play bocce, a game similar to bowling, but played outdoors, on a lawn.

Beverly Pepper called Rome at that time, Hollywood on the Tibor. In an effort to draw audiences back into the movie theaters, the major studios, like Paramount, were pumping out the sword-and-sandal epics starring big box office names such as Charlton Heston, Kirk Douglas, and Elizabeth Taylor. Instead of creating Roman Empire sets on Hollywood back lots, the film industry converged on Italy and made the Cinecittà Studios in Rome their home.

"It was a very interesting time because people were more generous with each other," Beverly Pepper recalled. They were not competitive. They were trying to survive together. It was a very interesting enclave of people. We knew all of these Hollywood people, but we also knew Fellini, Antonioni, and Marcello Mastriani."

"I was with *Newsweek* at the time and they paid for a lot of the entertaining. You had to entertain. Being a correspondent, you had to have various contacts," Bill Pepper said.

They were also entertaining the intellectuals who had fled McCarthyism, like Ring Lardner Jr., who when called in front of the House of Un-American Activities Committee refused to name names. "The choice we faced was between being 'heroes' and being complete shits," he said. He fled to England where he published his critically-acclaimed book *The Ecstasy of Owen Muir*, a novel that could not find a publisher in the United States until the 1960s when it was released as a classic by the New American Library. His first Oscar win was in 1943 for cowriting *Woman of the Year*. He won his second in 1971 for best screenplay for *M.A.S.H.*

"[The intellectuals] were all refugees. They were finding out that they couldn't be touched. They were all interdependent. Nick was not a part of that," Beverly Pepper said.

What had Ring Lardner Jr. thought when Nick showed up? My father was friends with Kazan, who had named names, and he had worked on *Wind Across the Everglades* with Budd Schulberg, who, when asked why he had named names, said "my guilt is what we did to the Czechs not to Ring Lardner Jr. I testified because I felt guilty for having contributed unwittingly to intellectual and artistic as well as racial oppression."

Nick's peers during the 1930s, when he was a member of the leftist Theatre of Action, thought he had no real political convictions but rather that he was more involved in the drama of the politics of the time. Pete Seeger mentioned how his father, Charles Seeger, and their group of friends, suspected that Nick had named names. There's no proof that he did or didn't. There's just proof of character and Nick's character, as Elia Kazan described in his autobiography, was that of a chameleon.

Amongst the crowd of intellectuals who gathered at the Pepper's Sunday afternoon soirees, Betty was the real outcast.

What the intellectuals didn't understand, or care to know, was that Betty spoke with her body, as beautifully and profoundly as they used words. They treated her as Nick's wife. As if she had no identity of her own. The only thing that helped her fight off her sense of isolation was the Preludin.

Betty knew she had to start socializing with people her own age and sought out a friendship with Yael Dayan, a young Israeli woman who had published a novel, *New Face in the Mirror*, loosely based on her life as a powerful colonel's daughter. Her father, Moshe Dayan was the fourth chief of staff of the Israeli defense forces.

Yael Dayan invited Nick and Betty to Israel to spend the 1960 holiday season with her family. "So, we did. We stayed at her home," Betty said.

Meanwhile, Julie was left with Jenny in Rome.

"Moshe Dayan was a fascinating person. He was an archeological digger and had a whole wing of their home filled with these ancient artifacts. It was like a museum. And his wife, Ruth, was in charge of seeing that the orphaned children pouring into Israel from Yemen, South Africa, were processed into the different *Kibbutzim*."

Nick and Betty were in Israel when Julie turned one.

"Moshe Dayan introduced us to Ehud Avriel, the Israeli ambassador to South Africa, who gave us his place in the *kibbutz* in a valley near Galilee. Nick and I walked out into the desert, and this whole shipload of people had come in from South Africa. There was music, and we were riding on this ship, riding into the hills, and we danced, and we partied, and then we took off in the desert and made love, and Nicca was conceived."

* * *

Betty used to tell me a story of how after my birth she fell asleep and when she woke, Joy was sitting in the room with her. They asked the nurse to bring me in. The nurse arrived carrying a newborn with a dark mop of hair. Betty was confused. She thought it strange she gave birth to such an Italian looking baby, but she loved the baby from the start whoever's it was. Joy was the one who told the nurse to take this baby away and find me.

"Nicca was almost bald. This little blonde fuzz of hair. All blue eyes. Her whole face was eyes. I thought I had a little blue-eyed owl," Betty said.

* * *

Nick went to London during the first week of December 1961 for the premiere of *El Cid* with the sole purpose of getting Charlton Heston to play the part of Major Matt Lewis in Sam Bronson's epic *55 Days at Peking*, the tale of the Boxer Rebellion, which would be the film that ended Nick's career as a Hollywood director. With just a treatment to show, Nick intrigued the actor enough to make him consider working for Bronston again. Heston had starred in *El Cid* for the producer but had backed out of starring in his production of *The Fall of the Roman Empire*. Nick's doggedness proved to Charlton Heston he was serious. Even though Heston wanted to work with Nick he wasn't so sure about the film. "Must every film be the best one ever made?" he asked himself.

After Nick convinced Heston to sign on to the picture it was decided that we would move to Spain to be closer to the Bronston Studios where filming would take place. Betty found a house in La Moreleja, an upper-middle-class development twenty miles outside of Madrid, for us to move into.

"The house was gorgeous," Betty said. "You walked down to a sunken living room that opened onto this beautiful garden and the mountains and pool. The living room had a fireplace and a study all in one room. To the right of the hall-way was the dining room. There were three kitchens. There were casitas where the help lived. We had two housekeepers, a driver, gardener, cook, and a baby nurse. And there was a guesthouse. Upstairs was a huge master bedroom, a huge hall, Nick's bathroom, my bathroom."

Julie and I were kept in a separate section of the house, downstairs, closer to the help than to our parents.

* * *

Nick was fully aware that agreeing to make *55 Days at Peking* would be the fatal compromise. And yet he went ahead. It was the ultimate gamble. If it turned out he could pull off directing Charlton Heston in an epic telling of the Boxer Rebellion, he would win big; if he lost, he would lose everything.

From the first day of shooting the crew questioned his ability to lead them through the production. "It was my feeling from the very beginning that Nick was totally lost and frightened to death about the problems of making a large spectacle film," Bernard Gordon, the screenwriter, said.

Nick tried finding his way into the film through experimentation with multiple image. He wanted to have two different scenes playing in different parts of the frame at the same time. He wanted to break apart the frame the way Joe Losey broke apart the set on *Injunction Granted*, and the way Frank Lloyd Wright broke apart the box-like structure of the house. Or at least this is what I told myself years ago when I first started looking into the end of Nick's Hollywood career. Now I believe the use of multiple image in a conventional epic was clearly a sign Nick was lost and looking to his beginnings for the answer on how to proceed. I also think that his use of the multiple image was a sign that his mind was fragmenting. He had always shown himself in his films through character and camera movement.

"He was working the foreground and the background at the same time and using the screen in a different way, sort of ambitious and unrealistic and unrealized ideas," Bernard Gordon said.

The Spanish painter and production designer Manuel Mampaso recalled, "Ray told me that the eyes of the Empress would appear on one side of this huge screen, then you would begin to see what she was thinking about: the Boxers advancing. And at the other end of the screen you would see the English ambassador who was thinking the same thing. Then the screen would be filled by the two heads, while simultaneously you would see flashes, a little in the manner of Mondrian, of the fighting."

In his memoir of journal entries, Charlton Heston called the sets that Bronston had built at his studio in Las Matas the "most impressive he'd ever seen in a film. There on the Spanish plain they had reconstructed most of the essential features of Imperial Peking, including the Tartar Wall, the Gates of the Forbidden City, the foreign legations, and all manner of markets, canals, bridges, and houses, from palaces to hovels. . . . Unhappily, we never turned a camera on two-thirds of this incredible city."

Nick, being the mentally unstable visual genius that he was, needed to share characteristics with his star (James Dean, Robert Ryan, Robert Mitchum, Humphrey Bogart) that bonded them throughout the process of making a film. In his best movies it is as if the actor is a personification of Nick's character. They both need to trust one another in order to execute the emotional context of the story. What did he have in common with Charlton Heston? And where was the visceral emotion Nick was so good at putting a face to in the telling of *55 Days at Peking*?

Look at the movie with its thousands of extras, opulent sets, and the wooden Charlton Heston.

Heston, who held the director George Stevens in highest esteem and was more excited about the prospect of playing John the Baptist in Stevens' film about Christ, *The Greatest Story Ever Told*, than he was about working with Nick.

George Stevens and Nick Ray were polar opposites as were Charlton Heston and James Dean. When James Dean went to work on *Giant* after *Rebel*, he'd call Nick up in the middle of the night practically in tears over the difference in directing styles between Stevens and Nick. Dean felt that he had flourished with Nick in a way Stevens control wouldn't allow.

To Charlton Heston, George Stevens "was surely one of the best directors who ever lived." Heston felt he did his best work with directors like Stevens. At first, he was looking forward to working with Nick but as the days wore on Heston felt at a loss with Nick. "I can't put my finger on the lack of contact I feel there. He's intelligent, articulate, committed, but I feel a barrier . . . a performance, somehow," he wrote.

Stewart Stern, the screenwriter of *Rebel Without a Cause*, said it was hard to know who Nick really was because he always seemed to be acting. "Nick Ray *was* theater," he said.

Rather than go forward with making films like *A Day in the Life of an African Boy* he went ahead with making a film he knew would end his Hollywood career.

When Nick finally collapsed on the set on September 11, 1962, many were surprised it hadn't happened sooner. Working on a production where the only person he came close to relating to was the actress with the bad reputation who was an outcast and an alcoholic just like him, but whose behavior added more tension to an already tense production, sent him into cardiac arrest. When Charlton Heston informed Ava Gardner about Nick's collapse, she turned white with guilt. Nick was rushed to the hospital. Phil Yordan swore Nick faked the attack because he didn't know how to finish the picture. "He had no heart attack. He just quit."

He was kept in the hospital for two weeks. He discovered upon his release that he had been taken off the picture and banned from the set. He started drinking heavily.

On the day of the London premiere of *55 Days at Peking* Nick met Richard Burton, who had starred in Nick's 1957 film, *Bitter Victory*, and Elizabeth Taylor at the Dorchester for a light lunch while Betty was supposedly at the hair salon getting dolled up. When Nick returned to his and Betty's room at the Savoy Hotel, he found her lying on the bed in a near comatose state with an empty tube of Preludin in her hand.

Through Joe Losey, Nick got the name of Dr. Barrington Cooper, who had been treating Joe Losey for alcoholism since 1956. According to Joe Losey's son, Gavrik, as well as Beverly and Bill Pepper, Joe Losey was a terrible hypochondriac. He was able to go to Barrington Cooper at all hours of the day or night. "Barrington Cooper seemed to be able to get at what ailed people in a way that was almost Shaman-like. He was willing to turn up and be places and see people at any time of day or night. He was very much within the social doctor confine. Barry Cooper served the function of being an available source of drugs and psychological comfort," Gavrik Losey said.

Barrington Cooper was a short, well-built stocky man with warm brown eyes and a very English doctor bedside manner. After Nick found Betty strung out on the Preludin in their Savoy Hotel room, he had Cooper commit her to the London State Clinic. Betty recalled, "I was given a shot and I was out. I woke up forty-eight hours later, and these two musclemen were on either side of my bed. They lifted me out of the bed and hauled me to a bathtub. I felt like I was in *The Snake Pit.*"

At the same time that Dr. Barrington Cooper admitted Betty into the psych ward he admitted Nick into the London Hospital detox. He had been drinking around the clock ever since recovering from his heart attack.

"Nick showed up to visit me wearing his hospital pajamas and robe, visiting me, his crazy wife," Betty said. "I was so enraged. He was so obsequious with me. This was the icing on top of the cake. That he would come to visit his mentally ill wife. It was show time, folks. I got one of these musclemen to sit down with me. I said, 'I gotta get out of here.' He said, 'Well, you can just check yourself out.' Yes!" she recalled.

"So, I checked myself out of this clinic. I was so surprised they'd let me go. I went to the Savoy, and of course they knew me, because we used to stay in the Savoy. I didn't have money on me, but they got word to Nick, and when he was released from the hospital he met me there," she added.

"I had this down-and-out confrontation with him about that little stork, Barry Cooper. What a slimeball he was. Ohhhhh, what he had done to me. Of course, at that point I wasn't quite willing to admit that Nick had orchestrated this whole scene with me, so I was blaming Barry Cooper," Betty remebered.

Gavrik Losey recalled Barry Cooper as "fairly unorthodox. If you viewed him as a villain, he certainly could be a villain. If you viewed him as a necessary part of existence then he was a necessary part of existence."

Betty disagreed. "Barry Cooper. That Harley Street doctor. He was the one who got Nick on methadrine. Barry turned it all around when he put Nick on that drug. Everything else was manageable, but that," she said.

As soon as Betty and Nick returned to Madrid, Dr. Barrington Cooper arranged for a nurse to come to the house to give Nick shots of methamphetamine. At the time the drug was legal and used to treat alcoholism and depression.

"Nick told me they were vitamin B12 shots. That he needed them for his nervous system," Betty said.

On some level she knew he was lying but went along with the lie in order to avoid any confrontation. She was determined not to lose her mind, again. She was off the Preludin and focusing on being "a mommy to the girls. I fired Jenny and hired Ronnie, an English girl. I didn't even ask Nick."

Then, Nick told Betty that "a friend of his was directing a film and we were going to Portugal for two to three days. We get there and twenty minutes after checking in at the hotel, Nick left to get cigarettes. He didn't come back. I had no passport, no money. I called a friend who wired me the cash to get home. Then, I went to the embassy and got another passport," she said. "I called Nick and his secretary, Maria, answered. She said Nick was home and would pick me up at the airport. He acted like nothing had happened. Like he hadn't even been in Portugal. I picked up the Preludin again."

In the fall 1961, right after the *King of Kings* premiere in New York City and before preproduction on *55 Days at Peking* started, Nick had announced to *Sight and Sound* an original idea for a film about a woman who finds herself in a foreign country without identification or money—the loss of both symbolizing the loss of identity. It was to be called *Passport*. He brought the story to life in the months after his collapse on and ouster from the set of *55 Days at Peking*. He didn't bring it to the screen. I shivered. My father purposefully set my mother up to be vulnerable and frightened. And to him it was a movie, an experiment, a macabre living theater.

"I thought that I was purposefully being driven crazy. I think he did it purposefully because he wanted to move on. And he didn't know how to get rid of me," Betty said.

Within days of the Portugal incident, Nick announced to Betty that he had optioned *Next Stop Paradise*, the prizewinning novel by the young Polish writer Marek Hłasko. Not only that, he had arranged for Hłasko to move into one of the casitas at our house in La Moraleja.

"We had a story-development company, called Carousel. I worked a lot with Nick on the scripts and reviewing the material that we'd get in. He'd say, 'Well, tell me the story in three sentences.' I had read Marek's book and loved it. I thought it would make a fabulous film. Nick orchestrated me working with Marek on the screenplay adaptation," Betty said.

"Nick was gone on a business trip the day Marek arrived. I heard this racecar come down to the driveway. I rushed out onto the terrace. And this gorgeous, tall kid who was my age hopped out of the car. He was wearing jeans and no shirt. There was a wooden cross hanging on his bare chest. He was something else. My heart leapt. Marek was very charismatic. He spoke with an accent. He was just too much."

As Betty recalled, "I was playing with the kids in the living room, and Marek came in. He was all dressed up and he said, 'I want you to go to dinner with me in Madrid. I'm meeting with some French friends.' I was so excited. I left the children with Ronnie and staff. I went upstairs and got really gussied-up fast. A little Chanel suit. We flew into Madrid in that car of his. We parked somewhere near the restaurant. We went in and there's this big round table filled with his friends. They all greeted him, and he pulled out a chair for me to sit, and I go to sit, and he picked me up and carried me out of the restaurant and ran down the street with me draped over his shoulder. Well, my little heart was going nuts. Finally, he dropped me down and I lost my shoes and we were running. We ran to an apartment building in old Madrid. He rang a buzzer and was let in. We took an elevator up and we made mad love until the sun came up," she said.

"Now, all I have is my little suit, it was a little silk suit, no shoes, stockings all ripped-up. I felt pretty stupid walking out of there. Then we couldn't find his car. So, we walked the twenty miles back to La Moraleja. Of course, the staff was furious with me. They scolded me in Spanish. Marek and I sat in the living room. We just laughed.

"The kids were outside. And Marek and I went upstairs and made love in Nick's and my bed. We were in the middle of sex and up came all of the staff and the kids. The kids jumped into bed with Marek and me. The staff pulled the covers off and started calling me a whore and all kinds of stuff in Spanish. Marek split to Nick's bathroom and I went to mine.

"Later, Marek said, 'Let's take the babies. Let's go to Munich. I have friends there. Come with me.'

"He was essentially saying, 'Leave Nick and take the babies and let's go.' And I said, even though I was desperate and crazy and all that, I said, 'No, no, no, no.' I said, 'I love Nick.' That was the bottom line.

"Oh, I was *in love* with Marek. So, Marek takes off. And then, within a month, Ronnie, the nanny, got pregnant. Nick said, 'Well, take her to Zurich for an abortion.' I guessed he was telling me to take her there, because they would do it legally. Mary, the secretary, booked the flight and when I got to Zurich, I contacted Marek in Munich. I don't know how, but I knew he was in Munich. I found him, and while Ronnie was in the hospital, I flew to Munich to be with Marek. I was just madly in love with him.

"I arrived at his hotel and rang his number. Marek's friend, a retired general, rang me up to his room. He told me how in love Marek was with me, but that, he wouldn't be seeing me. 'He's in love with you. He's madly in love with you, blah-blah-blah, but he won't be seeing you.'

"I was standing in the middle of the hotel room with this general, processing what he had just told me, and the phone rang. He handed it to me. It was Mary, Nick's secretary. It was like Portugal all over again. Mary said, 'There's a flight for you, you don't need to go back to Zurich, come straight to Madrid, and Nick will meet you at the airport.'

"The phone rang once more. It was Marek asking me to meet him in the hotel bar. I went downstairs. We sat at this little table. By then, I knew that Marek and Nick were in on this together. They had been setting me up. I was just wiped out."

Thirty-three years later, an acquaintance of Marek's confirmed it. Nick *had* put Marek up to it, but Marek had really fallen in love with her.

"Marek put his hand out, and I took mine and I went, POW! And left. That was the last time I ever saw him."

* * *

I first heard Marek Hłasko's name when I was twelve, in 1974, when we were living with Ward in Arleta. I overheard my mother talking on the phone. She was saying, "Marek killed himself? I was so in love with Marek. He killed himself?"

I stopped dead in my tracks and confronted her. "Who's Marek?"

* * *

In Munich, after leaving Marek, Betty retreated to the upstairs bathroom down the hall from the master bedroom. Bathrooms had been her safe place since she was a little girl—hiding inside them away from her father's leering. "I was in my bathroom like the *Glass Menagerie*, all fucked up on Preludin. I could spend hours just placing a figurine this way and that," Betty said.

"I knew I was nuts. I knew it. But that was it. Terrible to be conscious and crazy. It would be wonderful if you were unconscious and crazy but to be conscious and know you're crazy? That was one of the toughest things to reconcile. I would want to shake my head and find a new reality other than crazy but crazy was the only place to be."

"Nick brought over a doctor from California. He convinced me to meet with him. And at that point, the manner in which Nick presented this to me, I didn't feel threatened. I went to the Hilton and met Dr. Branshaft in the lobby. He was the first person that really looked at me and spoke softly to me. He said he could help me if I was willing to come to California.

"Dr. Branshaft said, 'You've got to get rid of all your Preludin. Before you come, you must not have any drugs in your system, or, I can't help you.'" Betty said.

"There was a man who met Nick and I at the airport who was this kind of a man-in-a-white-coat kind of guy Nick had hired to fly with me. I was really treated like a total mental case. It was like kind of the last straw with his aiding and abetting and setting up my whole suicide."

Nick had arranged for Gavin Lambert to pick Betty up at Los Angeles International Airport. He told Lambert he didn't know anyone else who could handle the situation as delicately.

"She was hysterical," Gavin said. "It was all right. I mean, I knew her. We were fond of each other. So, I said, 'Okay. Here we are. I know where I have to take you. I have a car waiting.' She thrust out a piece of Spanish pottery. 'It's Terra-Vera. It's real Terra-Vera.' Well, I said, 'Thank you very much. That's wonderful.'"

Betty said, "Gavin Lambert drove me to the hotel room and got me settled. Dr. Branshaft called and told me he'd meet me in the lobby at 10 a.m. the next morning. I just crashed. In the morning, the phone kept ringing, and I could barely answer it. It was Dr. Branshaft. I didn't want to get out of bed. I didn't want therapy. I just wanted to die. I kept responding, just let me die.

"Dr. Branshaft walked me through just getting up and out of that room. I took the elevator to the lobby, and he was there. He put his arm out and I hooked my arm in his and we did this very somber walk to his office.

"I'll never forget that very first session. I was seated. I wasn't on the couch. He said, 'I imagine you're angry.'

"He got me into such a rage. I was enraged!" Betty said. "But I had stuffed it. I found out that suicide often happens when rage implodes. It was such a lightning rod in my system that within a couple days I was able to get up and shower. I mean, just to know that I was angry was so major to me. He let me know within that first week that I was living with a diagnosed schizophrenic. He knew that Nick was a diagnosed paranoid schizophrenic through Nick's psychiatrist, Dr. Vanderhyde. They were colleagues. I didn't even know what schizophrenia was."

"Branshaft said, 'I don't like to talk in big words, and I don't want you to read any psychological books. I don't want you to get any more confused than you are. So, don't worry about his diagnosis. That's not your problem. What you need to remember is that you are not equipped to live with your husband. You don't have the skills.' I saw Dr. Branshaft every day for two weeks. I also started communicating with Nick and Branshaft helped me navigate through our conversations. Branshaft told me that it would never be as bad again. I've never forgotten that, and I've been through a lot of booze in my life since then, but it's never touched being as bad. I've never been as suicidal, or as wiped-out, or as addicted as that time."

A Dog Does Not a Father Make

Three months after leaving Madrid, Betty sent for Joy, Julie, and me.

"I remember saying goodbye to Nick and thinking he'd be there in a minute," Julie said.

I kept asking my grandmother, in Spanish (I didn't speak English at the time), "*¿Donde esta mi padre? ¿Está él en las nubes?*"

Where is my father? Is he in the clouds?

Julie recalled, "When I was on the airplane, I told myself I was going to travel for the rest of my life. I loved it. So, that's kind of come true. Nicca was scared. She was just scared, and I kept telling her not to be scared, because this was fabulous."

Betty was waiting for us at the end of the jetway when our plane landed at Los Angeles International Airport. She was so happy to see us, but I didn't know who she was. I started holding my breath. She picked me up and held me in her arms, but I still wouldn't breathe.

"I was repeating, *Nicca Nicca Nicca*," Betty said.

Julie instructed Betty to turn me upside down until I started breathing again.

I always believed Betty gave Julie the responsibility of being my mother because she didn't have time for me, and that Julie resented me for it. Now, I see Julie was both of our mothers. That little girl with the big brown eyes and chubby cheeks had been given way too much responsibility.

We picked our suitcases up from baggage claim and piled into the Buick Skylark that Betty had bought but didn't know how to drive. Joy sat in the passenger seat and Dorsey drove. Dorsey was a close friend and an actress Betty had met through the actor, Rafael Campos, in the 1950s. Julie and I sat in the backseat of the Buick with our mother between us. "It was the first time I'd ever had Julie and Nicca as my own children," Betty said.

Betty's heart pounded the entire time we were driving Pacific Coast Highway to our new Cape Cod-style house in Sunset Mesa, the hillside neighborhood off of Pacific Coast Highway with views of Will Rogers State Beach. Betty called it suburbia on the beach.

Julie thought otherwise. "This wasn't our house. I didn't know when we were going to go back to our house. I didn't understand that we were living there. I was really concerned that daddy wasn't coming."

But, for Betty, "Nicca and Julie saved my life. I was just so proud of them and so thrilled to have them with me," she said. "If I hadn't had them in my life, I don't know if I would have ever gotten out of that bed. I really had to get well fast. I was desperate that Nick would put them in a boarding school somewhere. I didn't know what he was going to do."

As the weeks wore on Betty was communicating with Nick less and less. Soon, her only contact with anything Nick-related was through his business manager, Rex Cole, who sent rent checks out of a fund Nick had set aside for us. The money was supposed to last one year. After several months the checks stopped coming.

It was clear that Nick was no longer going to be someone Betty could depend on for financial support. She was forced to move out of the house in Sunset Mesa and into a house in Laurel Canyon that Julie remembered as being a dirty hovel with turquoise and yellow walls. The rent was cheap, though, and Betty was still unemployed and looking for work.

"Roberta, my girlfriend, was dancing in Lake Tahoe and she talked to the choreographer and set me up to come and dance in Vegas," she said. Begrudgingly, Betty left my sister and I in the care of Joy.

"My mother would have periods where she was ravaged with pain and the cysts were growing on her spinal column. It was very painful for her," Betty said. "So, she would take to bed. My concern was that my mother wouldn't be able to take care of the girls."

What choice did my mother have? She needed to put food on the table and keep a roof over our heads. So, she went to Vegas and danced with Roberta in a show that was in the style of a Tiller, similar to the one The Rockettes put on at Radio City Music Hall every holiday season. "There were high hats and canes and I hated it," Betty said.

At the end of the month the choreographer offered her a contract, but she didn't want to raise her kids in Las Vegas. "Even though I would have had a guaranteed middle-class income I just thought, *uh-uh*. I wanted to have a normal life," Betty recalled. "A nine-to-five job, evenings and home and weekends with the kids. That's clear as a bell what I wanted."

But when Betty returned to Los Angeles from Vegas she got into a serious crash. She was hit by a car while driving the green Buick Skylark home to Laurel Canyon from her psychiatrist appointment in Beverly Hills. She was turning left onto Santa Monica Boulevard at Doheny and the Buick spun and hit a tree, throwing her out of the front seat and onto the pavement. When she came to a nurse who had been on her way to work and saw the accident was standing over her.

"Don't move," the nurse said, "the ambulance is on the way."

"I looked at my legs and arms and I looked fine, so I said, 'I'm going to get up,' and she said, 'No, don't move.' That's when I noticed the blood gushing out of my head."

She came home with her head covered in bandages.

"I was really scared she was going to die," Julie said. "She had this big thing on her neck."

Betty said, "I had tremendous headaches. I would have to rest and be quiet. If the kids ran across the room it was excruciatingly painful."

She locked us in our bedroom.

* * *

I don't remember Laurel Canyon or Sunset Mesa, Madrid, or Rome. I have no visual memories of my mother wanting or not wanting me. I used to think I lived in Rome for two years and would try convincing myself that this was true even though the math didn't add up. I used to think I spoke Spanish more fluently than I did. I mean, really, how many words does a two-and-a-half-year-old know?

My first memories are of sitting in the backseat of the Buick waiting at a red light on Charleville Boulevard, a street that runs through Beverly Hills. My memory is of a woman walking up to the driver's side window and asking my mother if she is Betty Uitti from the movies. The next memory is of a long narrow hallway in the house on Elm Drive in Beverly Hills. We moved from Laurel Canyon to Beverly Hills while Betty was still recuperating from the car accident. She'd found a Spanish-revival house with an even cheaper rent than what she was paying in Laurel Canyon, because all of the houses on the block were going to be torn down so the city could drill for oil. I've never understood how anyone could drill for oil in the middle of Beverly Hills and always tried picturing our house being replaced with the kind of oil pumps lined up along El Segundo beach.

When Betty recovered from the car accident Dr. Branshaft loaned her the money to enroll in the Westwood School of Business and she acquired the skills necessary to land a job as a commercial censor at ABC-TV.

"I came in on low-pay scale, but we had wonderful medical benefits and I was able not to worry about where the heck Nick was. We certainly weren't rich, but we weren't up shit's creek anymore," Betty said.

We moved to the Los Feliz neighborhood of Los Angeles and into a small house on Melbourne Avenue that Betty called a shack. It was a block away from where my mother worked at the ABC-TV lot on Talmadge Avenue. It was homey.

There was a big front window with a view of the street. The living room, where Joy slept on a red flowered couch, opened up onto a dining room that was big enough for an oval wood table that sat four. The kitchen had a built-in yellow breakfast nook with green seat cushions and was where Joy would bake the cinnamon coffee cake, prune tarts, and date crumbles that became the Thanksgiving and Christmas Day staples. There were a group of bushes in the yard that formed a cave and it made a perfect hiding place for hide and go seek. On birthdays Betty hung piñatas from one of the trees in the backyard and I would always squint when bashing the papier-mâché donkey with a baseball bat so I could see the exact spot where it had ripped and where the candy was falling from and where on the grass it landed.

There was a crawlspace under the house like the one under Robert Mitchum's childhood home in my favorite of Nick's movies, *The Lusty Men*. It is the story of a has-been rodeo star, Jeff McCloud, played by Robert Mitchum, who revisits his childhood home because he's trying to find himself now that his career is over. He thinks he finds the answer when he meets the prospective buyers of his childhood home, a young couple, Louise (Susan Hayward) and Wes (Arthur Kennedy).

Wes has dreams of becoming a rodeo star and asks Jeff McCloud to mentor him. A love develops between McCloud and Louise as they watch Wes turning into the cowboy star McCloud once was. In an attempt to reclaim his notoriety McCloud enters a rodeo competition, which kills him. His death wakes Wes up to what he's so close to losing: a loving wife and the dream of someday owning a home of their own.

I have often reflected on McCloud's placement within the frame during the opening scene where he is going back to his childhood home for the first time; the vastness of the land-scape representing the world he inhabits, the life he's lived so far. It's as if Nick is asking with all that is behind us, can we go home again? The script was developed from a 1950s *LIFE* magazine article about the lonely, transient lifestyles of modern-day cowboys. In a way Nick Ray was very much like Robert Mitchum's character in the movie. Nick's home was a film set in the same way Mitchum's is the rodeo circuit, and like McCloud, he became a transient.

The Melbourne house was torn down years ago and an apartment building was put up in its place. What would Robert Mitchum's character in *The Lusty Men* have done if he'd gone back home to find his childhood home gone? What would Nick look for when he would go back home to La Crosse? I've heard his mother, Lena, would sit by the front window waiting for him to walk up the pathway to the front door on the days he'd visit home after he'd made it in Hollywood.

I have a tendency to think my childhood was happiest when we were living on Melbourne Avenue. In comparison to the years we lived with my stepfather, Ward, they were, but in retro-spect I can see that those years were a breeding ground for my not feeling safe, too.

It was while we were living in the house on Melbourne Avenue that I first learned of my grandmother's alcoholism. Betty sent her to her brother, David, in New Jersey, and he put her in a sanitarium where she was given shock treatments.

I was too young to notice any change in Joy's behavior when she returned from getting her shock treatments. She spent most afternoons sitting in the red recliner watching television and drinking vodka from a tall blue glass. If my sister and I tried to take a sip, she would chase us through the house swatting our behinds with a wooden spoon. Other times, when we would refuse to take a bath or were making too much noise, she would grab us by our hair and drag us into the small bedroom we shared. She would force us onto our knees by pushing down on the top of our heads and then proceed to first bang our heads against each other and then to bang them against the wall. I joke that that's why my brain's a little scrambled.

I never stopped to think that the way she reprimanded us was abusive. I was never scared to be with her. In fact, she had always been the person I went to for comfort. I justified that she had to bang my head against my sister's and then against the wall because she was crippled.

I never told Betty about the way Joy punished us because Betty was always yelling at her for drinking all the vodka. If my mother were to find out about the beatings, I knew, or at least I thought I knew, she would show my grandmother the door. What if something bad happened to either Julie or me while our mother was at work? We weren't supposed to call her at the office.

We were so afraid of getting our mother fired that when we started a fire in the garage while smoking cigarettes, we didn't want her to know. I was seven and Julie was eight-and-a-half and we thought we could put the fire out ourselves. But when the curtains started going up into flames I ran into the house, screaming *fire*, which startled my grandmother out of a drunken nod. Joy called Betty, who came running home from work in a panic. Once she realized that the damage had only been cosmetic and no one had been hurt, she flew into a rage. How could my sister and I have been so stupid? What were we thinking? Smoking! Our stupidity could have cost her her job and our house, not to mention our lives!

A couple of years before the fire incident, Joy took Julie and me to Cuernavaca, Mexico where her son, David, was teaching. He was the closest person to a father figure I knew in those first years that Nick wasn't around. He was the kind of man who would squeeze your belly button and make a noise and have you laughing hysterically. We stayed with him and his family, his wife, Maria, and their children, Emi and Coco. The house itself was one story but there was a two-level yard. There were sliding glass doors that led out of the house onto a concrete landing with a swimming pool and a stone barbecue pit. The yard on the lower level was plush green with thick blades of grass always damp between your toes and a jungle of trees barricading it from neighboring houses.

While we were spending days playing badminton with our cousins in Cuernavaca, Betty was in Los Angeles and was heading home one day on her lunch break from ABC. She was crossing Talmadge Avenue to Melbourne when she noticed a black limousine parked in front of our house. Her stomach fell. She knew it was Nick. When she opened the front door, she saw him sitting on the couch with two of the Rolling Stones. "All I was seeing was Nick. My mind was all a-buzz," Betty said.

She went with Nick and the Rolling Stones to dinner at a restaurant on La Cienega and then to a club on Melrose where the Stones gave an impromptu performance. She called her coworkers saying she wouldn't be in for the next three days. They promised to cover for her.

"I hadn't killed the hope of getting back together with Nick. I was all ears and eyes, checking it all out. But, going back to the Bel Air hotel with him was not the same as it had always been. That was the beginning of the change. He was fairly impotent compared to his former self. He was not in good shape. It wasn't that I was turned off. It was that that wonderful physical emotional attachment we'd once had wasn't there.

"I made the decision I had to get back on track, get back to work. So, he came to the Melbourne house for a couple of days and we lingered together. I went out and got different things he liked to eat. And we're sitting at the dining room table and he said, 'The girls should have a dog.' And we went to a kennel and got Sugar, this little Sheltie, and brought her home," Betty said.

Nick was gone when we returned from Mexico.

"Betty told us, 'This is a dog from your daddy. He wanted you to have it to keep you company,'" Julie recalled. "I asked her why he had to go. I was just furious. I consoled myself, at least he got us a dog."

I loved Sugar, our new puppy, but I wanted my dad. I asked my mother why my father hadn't stayed long enough to see us. She said he was too busy partying with the Rolling Stones. I didn't understand.

That Christmas, 1966, Nick called. My mother gave me the phone. The receiver was longer than my face. He said, "I can't come home."

He was crying.

I told him, "Don't cry, daddy. It will be alright."

Julie had counted the days to Christmas, she was so excited about seeing Nick. When he called to inform us he wasn't going to make it, her heart sank. She said, "Don't ask me why I loved this man. Don't ask me why. I have no clue. All I knew was that he was way, way, way up there and that someday he would love me. And it never happened."

When Nick was in Los Angeles with the Rolling Stones that summer of 1966, he told Betty he was going to Germany. He promised that once he was there, he would check himself into a detox clinic.

Instead he stayed with his ex-girlfriend, Hanna Axmann, in Munich. She introduced him to Volker Schlöndorff, the German director whose first film *Young Törless* she'd had a small part in. Schlondorff was onto filming his second movie, *A Degree of Murder* starring the Rolling Stones muse Anita Pallenberg. Nick brokered the sale to Universal for $173,000 and earned a $60,000 fee. Nick's relationship with Lew Wasserman must've played a part in the sale although I sincerely doubt MCA was still representing Nick. Mega-agency MCA and Wasserman had taken control of Universal Studios in 1962.

In the early 1990s a friend told me she'd run into Lew Wasserman, one of the most powerful agents Hollywood ever knew, at a party. He was responsible for movie stars becoming independent contractors, which ultimately broke apart the studio system.

When my parents separated in 1964, Lew Wasserman and his socialite wife, Edie, offered to help Betty get back on her feet financially. She refused their offer. However, throughout my childhood Betty never neglected to mention how the Wassermans had wanted to save us from poverty. She said it like she had done a noble thing by refusing their generosity. That was how I was introduced to the Wasserman name. Lew and Edie Wasserman were people I had never met but who could have saved me from never having enough.

My friend mentioned me when she spoke to Lew Wasserman. He remembered me and asked how I was. He was the *King of Hollywood.*

Royalty. What does that mean? Kings and Queens and Guillotines. Once an agent said to me, "Who do you think you are? You're not Drew Barrymore." I had just read a script Nick had written in the late 1960s that was a speed induced rant going on tangents when it should've been finding its conclusion. "Yes," I told the agent, "I know." My lips crinkled. I refused to let her hear me crying over the payphone in the locker room at the Motion Picture Library. When people say to me, "You're Hollywood royalty," I don't know what they mean. I feel most things but never royal. I wore a blue Swiss Miss style uniform and white nurses' shoes while serving Rooty Tooty Fresh and Fruities at the International House of Pancakes.

Hollywood royalty is Irene Selznick, daughter of Louis B. Mayer, wife of David O. Selznick, son of Louis Selznick, one of Hollywood's founding fathers. George Washington. Cherry trees. The Cherry Lane Theatre in New York's West Village sits on Commerce Street. Tony lived near there when he was a boy growing up in the 1940s. In the 1970s, Tony was producing movies for the director Paul Mazursky. I saw *Blume in Love* in a theater in Westwood with my older sister. We hadn't seen Tony in several years. We clapped when his name appeared in the credits. When I was seven years old, my half-brother Tim was dating Jenny, the daughter of James Arness, who was starring in the long-running television show, *Gunsmoke.* Jenny left Tim for Greg Allman who left Jenny for Cher. I heard about Jenny's suicide on the five o'clock news and blamed Greg Allman for killing her. What did I know? I was seven. Years later, when I was twenty and sitting with Tim at his dining room table, he told me we were Hollywood royalty without the castle. I had just come off a six-year run addicted to alcohol and drugs where I ended up walking the then decrepit streets of Hollywood panhandling.

Royalty. If my father had just been an average man and not the man who directed James Dean in *Rebel Without a Cause,* he would have likely ended up a drunken bum on Skid Row. In the years following his separation from my mother, in 1964, he wandered through Europe, where I was born, conning people into giving him money to make films I don't think he ever intended on making. He, along with his older sister, Helen, used to steal pints from their father's stash and drive the fourteen blocks to the Mississippi River where they would spend the afternoons getting drunk. It's rumored that Nick was using cocaine as early as the 1930s. It's a fact that during the 1950s he carried a doctor's bag overflowing with pharmaceuticals.

By late 1966, Nick's doctor was sending him boxes of speed in glass ampules to treat his alcoholism and depression. Nick was renting a small two-story house on Sylt, an island off the German coast, not too far from Paris. He loved the island's landscape, the dunes, the light, and how the scenery changed every few miles. He called it a cameraman's dream. And of course, in all of his methamphetamine-induced grandiosity he claimed he wanted to build a film studio there. He couldn't even pay his rent. My father once hid naked in the bushes from the landlord who had come to collect.

There were needles strewn all over the house and books about the effects drugs have on the brain. When the director, Barbet Schroeder, visited, Nick showed him photos and would say, "Look. This is the brain of someone who's shooting speed and it has shrunk." He was really lucid about it. At the same time, he would say, "For me it's different because I have this doctor . . . "

Stephane Tchlajeff, a young producer who had been sucked into Nick's craziness, shot up 2cc's of methamphetamine, like Nick routinely did, and didn't come down for two days. He was staying with Nick on Sylt to try and help Nick get financing to turn the French novel *L'Evade* into a film.

It was with this film in mind that Nick showed up at the 1969 Cannes Film Festival. In his article, *A Fine Director Unemployed*, the film critic Vincent Canby describes seeing Nick at Cannes. He wrote, "At a film festival, a movie director who hasn't made a movie in a long time is like a tourist in an exotic but slightly hostile land. He may be familiar with the terrain, but he cannot be a part of it, even though he may be something of an attraction himself."

When I was sixteen, in 1978, I found a yellowed copy of this newspaper clipping in my mother's box of photographs. That was the first time I read it. It made my father sound otherworldly and romantic and I wanted to be like him. The second time I read the article I was doing research about Nick's life at the Motion Picture Library in Los Angeles. The library was on La Cienega Boulevard and across the street from a park where my mother used to take my sister and I to play.

I walked out of the Motion Picture Library and saw the park across the street and remembered myself five years old going down the slide and feeling joyful. I was getting accustomed to not having a father. I was okay with it. The family unit I knew consisted of my mother, grandmother, sister, and me. I didn't need anyone else. Not until my mother remarried, in 1970, and my stepbrother started sexually abusing me.

I had read the rambling script *L'Evade*, the screenplay Nick had gone to Cannes with in 1969. Reading it left me feeling like I had been punched. I had tried making sense of the story of ex-convicts who escape prison and end up at a motel by the sea called the Motel Taurus. It is on a small island with one highway, a few thousand fishermen, and a prison. I understood that someone was murdered at the motel but could not keep track of the relationship between the characters or understand the story's plot. Nick made notes to himself in the margins of the script, but I could not decipher what he meant by them. It was like he was talking to himself through the characters and the dialogue became a rant between himself and the screenplay. It was alarming to see his mental disintegration on those pages.

I also read a letter responding to *L'Evade*. It was written in

1969 by Paul Kohner, an agent, and said, "I do not know about the novel, of course, from which this is taken but to my knowledge Edition Eleuve Noir is one of the more lurid and less highly regarded Paris Publishers. This screenplay is unredeemable bad. Reading it, one comes to the conclusion that Nick must have lost his marbles to write such an incoherent, disjointed screenplay peopled by such unexplained and senseless characters and especially for him to submit it in this form to anyone. Charles Bronson could easily suspect us from having lost our marbles if we were to submit this to him for his consideration to play a role in it."

It was at this time I began acknowledging that Nick wasn't this otherworldly romantic figure and started to face the fact that my father was just like some of the speed freaks I'd known when I was doing drugs and living in a one-room apartment with a syringe spray-painted on the bathroom door and the words Meth Monsters written next to it. His brains were scrambled.

I walked out of that library and I felt like I was carrying my father's insanity on my shoulders. It left me feeling stark.

Nick was living in Chicago in a one room barely furnished apartment. He had left Europe and moved back to the States in 1969 after Ellen Ray, a political activist-turned-documentarian, presented him with the opportunity to direct her screenplay, *The Defendant*, which she described as "a film about a young boy on trial, ostensibly for possession of marijuana, but in fact for having possessed freedom of the mind."

Ellen Ray had also been to the 1969 Cannes Film Festival for the screening of *Gold*, which she called "a hippie movie political western" and had co-produced. She was telling Henri Langlois, the founder of the Cinematheque Francois, about her next project, *The Defendant*, and he suggested she get in touch with Nick.

Langlois told Ellen, "Well you know there's this American filmmaker who has your last name who's a natural to direct. We think he left the U.S. because of the McCarthy hearings."

Nick had not left to escape McCarthyism. He left because no one in Hollywood wanted to take the risk of hiring him to direct a movie. His drug addiction and erratic behavior had made him uninsurable.

Ellen Ray found Nick living on Sylt "looking like he was on his last legs."

She said Nick's condition didn't shock her; she "came from the drug culture. When I told him that I was involved with organizing the anti-war marches in Washington D.C. he got quite excited and said, 'This is the right time for me to come back and do something.'"

Nick arrived in Washington, D.C. on November 14, 1969 without even a suitcase to his name. It was the eve of the big anti-Vietnam War march where three-quarters of a million people stampeded the Capitol in protest.

Ellen Ray continued, "I think it just blew him away being in Washington. The energy. It was a beautiful weekend, stunning, gorgeous. People were on the street screaming. We had all of these different film crews. Eight, probably. Nick ran from crew to crew. We were shooting in 16mm. The footage shot was going to be used for our film, *The Defendant*, to show the massive insurrection against the United States Government, the laws, and Nixon."

During the protests Nick met Jim Hormel, the dean of the University of Chicago and an heir to the Hormel foods fortune. Hormel was a financial backer on *The Defendant* and suggested Nick come to Chicago to film the Chicago Conspiracy Trials. Seven people—Rennie Davis, Dave Dellinger, Tom Hayden, Abbie Hoffman, Jerry Rubin, John Froines, and Lee Weiner— were charged with inciting a riot at the 1968 Chicago Democratic Convention. The week of the convention the Chicago Police Force was ordered by Mayor Richard Daly to break up the crowds of anti-war demonstrators in Lincoln Park. They attacked protestors with tear gas and billy clubs, chasing hundreds of people into the streets where the once organized protest spun out of control. The Chicago Seven were blamed. When Ellen Ray and Nick left Washington, DC for Chicago to film the Chicago Conspiracy Trials, Ellen Ray still believed that Nick was intent on using the footage for *The Defendant*.

However, Ellen Ray said, "It became quite clear that Nick believed it was his documentary even though my co-producer and I hired him. We paid him. We got the film crews. I remember in Chicago coming into the courtroom. I remember the defendants flipping out because *there's Nicholas Ray!*"

Unbeknownst to Ellen Ray, Nick was pitching his own film, *Conspiracy*, using the footage that was meant for *The Defendant*. He was meeting secretly with Michael Butler, a producer of the Broadway smash, *Hair*, and got him to put up the seed money for *Conspiracy*.

It only took one month for Butler's assistant, Stuart Byron, to see how Nick's grandiose ideas about making a documentary that "captured the spontaneity of the last eight years," were too far-reaching for Nick to accomplish.

"He had no idea that the way he wanted to shoot the film was in a conventional Hollywood fashion [and that it] would cost three to four million dollars. He was thinking more like seven to seven-hundred-and-fifty-thousand. When the cameraman corrected Nick, Nick claimed he knew how to shoot in ways he didn't know about. What became clear to us was that really the only way he knew how to film was in the Hollywood way."

Tim was apprenticing with the cinematographer, László Kovács, who had just finished shooting *Easy Rider*, when he went to Chicago to see Nick and found him "living in a big empty space. I thought his living there like that was temporary. I thought he was on location."

In the March 1970 article, "Nick Ray Promises a Movie on Chicago Seven," the film critic Roger Ebert wrote, "He was carrying a small movie camera. People who didn't know him noticed him just the same and they wondered who he was. He is Nicholas Ray and he is in Chicago to make a movie."

It was another one of those *Aha!* moments where I realized Nick wasn't playing with a full deck. Nor was he in Europe making movies when Betty was married to Ward, like I had told myself throughout my childhood.

Ebert wrote, "He is in Chicago to direct the Chicago Seven in a movie about the conspiracy trial. He will make the movie, he says, and it will be the best movie he's ever made, even though some of our town's noblest citizens have done their damnedest to mess him up."

Ebert and Nick first met at a saloon where Nick devoured ribs and told Ebert his idea for the Chicago Conspiracy film. "His idea is to have the defendants play themselves. All of the action will take place on a courtroom set now under construction at a Chicago studio. The dialogue will be drawn largely from the trial transcript itself," Ebert wrote.

Nick was a lot of talk.

After the saloon Ebert went to Nick's home. "He was living in an apartment furnished with the things you absolutely can't do without, like a mattress (on the floor), a projector, a screen, an icebox with beer in it, and a transcript of the trial."

Left: Grandma Kienzle, Nick's mother.
Below: Nick's sister Helen.
Bottom: Nick's sister Alice and Porter.
Photos © Archives of Nicca Ray

Top: Grandma Joy with her daughter, Betty. Bottom left: Betty's brother David Uitti. Bottom Right: Betty's father. Karl Uitti. *Photos © Archives of Nicca Ray*

Nick and Betty on Maine honeymoon, 1958: fishing and playing checkers.
Photos © Archives of Nicca Ray

Betty and Nick in Rome c. 1959.
Photos © Archives of Nicca Ray

Top: Nick and Betty at the airport in Rome for *The Savage Innocents* production meeting.
Bottom: Nick on the set of *King of Kings*, 1960. *Photos © Archives of Nicca Ray*

Left: The Luigi Trio featuring Betty (right) with close friend Roberta Lawn and Luigi [Eugene Louis Faccuito]. Above: Betty (right) modeling, c. 1951. Below: Betty (foreground) on the set of *Androcles and the Lion*, where she met Nick, 1951 (author's note: While under contract at RKO, Nick was brought in by Howard Hughes to doctor scenes). *Photos © Archives of Nicca Ray*

Clockwise from top left: Betty (far right) singing with Desi Arnez playing on set of unidentified film; Betty with baby Julie on the set of *King of Kings* (Betty choreographed the Salome dance); Pay stub Betty Uitti from December 8, 1956; Wanda, Jimmy Durante, and Betty, on his television variety show.
Photos © Archives of Nicca Ray

Top left: Betty in Tijuana, 1960s. Top right: Signed photo from Betty's first dance teacher, Miss Evelyn. Bottom: Betty at the beach, balancing on a rock. *Photo by Bing Crosby. All photos © Archives of Nicca Ray*

Top: Betty at the beach with Vince Edwards, 1955. Bottom: Betty with Bing
Crosby. *Photos © Archives of Nicca Ray*

Top: Betty with John Houseman, 1960. Bottom: Joy Uitti with Charlton Heston at the opening of *55 Days at Peking. Photos © Archives of Nicca Ray*

Top: Betty with Nicca and Julie, front yard of Melbourne Ave., house, c. 1966.
Bottom: Nick, Julie, and Betty c. 1960 (author's note: there are no surviving photos of my mother and father with me). *Photos © Archives of Nicca Ray*

Top: Young Nicca in a photo Nick carried in his wallet. Bottom left: Nicca in Madrid, 1963.
Bottom right: Nicca at five years old at Franklin Avenue Elementary School.
Photos © Archives of Nicca Ray

Top: Julie and Nicca,
after trip to Mexico, with
Sugar, a sheltie left by Nick.
Bottom: Julie and Nicca with
umbrellas and doll, Los Feliz, 1965.
Photos © Archives of Nicca Ray

Top: Jean Evans
(Tony's mother; first wife
of Nicholas Ray).
Bottom: Tony Ray,
Nicca's half-brother, 1941.
Photos © Archives of Nicca Ray

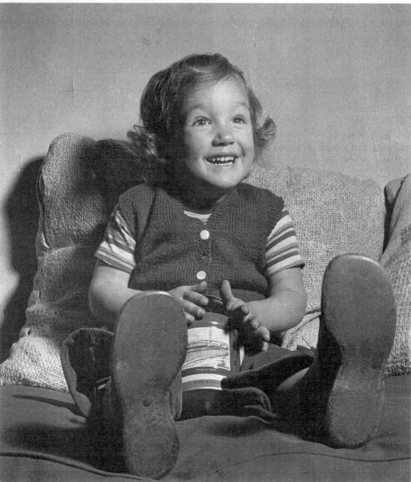

Top: Standing on the steps in front of the house on Wanda Drive. Photo taken in early 2000s. Bottom: Learning of the death of Nicholas Ray during a sleepover, Rachel (Tim's first wife), Tony Jr. on bed, Nicca Ray, with Betty (from back) on phone. Julie sits on chair, June 1979. *Photos © Archives of Nicca Ray*

animal arrives and announces
I'm here.

SO!

LOBOTOMY

1-2-3-4
I'm here I'm here
FEAR
BLA
BLA
BLA

Boots, Bandannas
and Chains.
HARDCORE!!

FROM - KILLFACE's

Wise up stupid!/Anarchy: Total individual freedom./Why all the clone agents
?/Cattle-a-grazing? Pigstey clicks? Baboons?!/Use your brain, not the jerks
next to you./Boring, Boring, Boring. That's what you are.!/Did you ever thi
nk 'bout it?/shoui 'bout it?/Stop hidding in mother's mansion/You
Scum!/You big NOTHING!/You multipal vitamin!/ah, go home!/
By the way, I don't wanna be like you!/copy of me./You can't
even do that well!/What next?/You follow so easily. LAZY sheep/
go home. go to sleep for 20 years./Stop lurking in the shadows/Come
out in the open/Show your dumb face/You listen to wordz!/Do you unders
tand 1/3 of them? Oh, I'm sure you do!/"Hey Joe, is it COOl?"/"Hey Bob,
It's the THING to do!/I got sick last night! Did you?!?/What does
Top Ramen and Thunderbird wine mean to you?/You call yourselves Punk
/Try going to the: Edge, Limit, ex
treme./You softie!/You are vile!!/I hate you!/we hate you!!/You are
your mothers' daughters/We are

Mother's Revenge

Clockwise from top left: Nicca, 1980, Hollywood; Animal (RIP) drawn by Anndoll (RIP);
Nicca, outside Beverly Hills disco, on Anndoll's moped; Flyer Anndoll, Nicca, and a
group of punk girls made and handed out at shows. *Photos © Archives of Nicca Ray*

Clockwise from top left: Anndoll in the Highland apartment, 1981. *Photo © Archives of Nicca Ray*; On the Venice Beach boardwalk, 1984; Nannette (RIP) and Nicca outside The Vex, 1981; Nicca at the Cathay De Grande with Top Jimmy, 1984. *Photos by © Gary Leonard*

Left: Nicca with Jesse,
1992, at La Brea Tar Pits.
Below: Jesse with Nicca
on the set of Nicca's film
She Was a Nice Girl.
Photos © Archives of Nicca Ray

Top and left: Nicca shooting *She Was a Nice Girl*, 1994–1995; Above: Still from *Cutting Moments*, a film by Douglas Buck. *Photos © Archives of Nicca Ray*

Top: With Norman Lloyd and his wife,
Peggy, at their home in Los Angeles.
Above: With Curtis Hanson at his office
on The Lot, Hollywood, 2007.
Right: Nicca with Brooke Shields in
Swatch advertisement, 1987.
Photos © Archives of Nicca Ray

Top: Nicca with Wim Wenders in NYC, 2011. Above: with Dennis Hopper at his home in Venice, CA, December 2008 *Photos © Archives of Nicca Ray*

Top: Nicholas Ray at SUNY with Dennis Hopper, c. 1971–72; Bottom: Nick at SUNY, Binghampton, 1971–72. *Photos by © Mark Goldstein*; Top (facing page): Two directors: Nicholas Ray and Samuel Fuller during filming of *The American Friend*, c. 1977. *Photo courtesy © Wim Wenders Foundation*

Above and left: Nicholas Ray in stills from *Lightning Over Water*, 1980, directed by Wim Wenders.
Photo courtesy © Wim Wenders Foundation

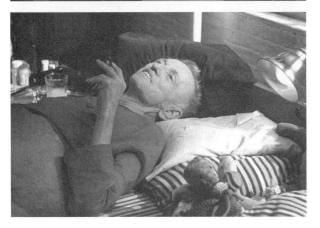

Family Ties

After we left Spain for California, Tim, Nick's son with Gloria Grahame, returned to Madrid and moved in with Nick in a two-bedroom apartment near Nicca's, the restaurant and club Nick had opened on the Avenida de Americas during the aftermath of *55 Days at Peking*.

While Betty was piecing her life back together and waiting for Nick to send a check so she could pay the rent, Nick was having an affair with the jazz musician, Hazel Scott. Scott had fled the states for Paris during the height of the McCarthy blacklist, and settled in Spain, where she reunited with Nick for the first time since appearing in his first film, *They Live by Night*. Nick had given her a standing date at Nicca's. According to Tim she moved into the two-bedroom apartment in Madrid where Nick and Tim lived.

"I'd go to Nicca's to hear her play," Tim recalled. "Some nights she'd be singing Billie Holiday songs. It would be around three or four in the morning, the place would be closing down, and she'd tell me, 'Go on baby, put your head on the piano,' and she'd play me old blues tunes and get me to sleep."

Scott was good friends with Ava Gardner who Nick remained good friends with after the *55 Days at Peking* debacle. In June 1964, when he was a juror at San Sebastian Film Festival, he used his influence to make sure Ava Gardner was awarded best actress for her starring role in John Huston's *The Night of the Iguana*. Tim met Gardner at Nicca's. One night when she and

Hazel Scott were drunk, they asked Tim to go skinny-dipping with them. He was seventeen at the time and too shy to go. "If only they'd asked me five years later," Tim said.

After Nicca's closed and Nick was through with Hazel Scott, or she was through with him, Nick called that doctor who had put my mother into the mental hospital and given her a sleep cure—the same doctor who had prescribed methamphetamine to Nick to treat his alcoholism and depression. Nick called him, Doctor Barrington Cooper, and the good doctor suggested Nick come with Tim to London and stay with him for a while.

"I packed my bags and we moved into Cooper's two-story mews," Tim said. "He was a short, stubby, fat, weasly-looking guy with a long-pointed nose. He was a member of the Royal Surgeons of England. I had the impression he had a lot of money because he drove a brand-new Jaguar."

Once Nick and Tim were settled in London, Tim enrolled in college, got a girlfriend, and started playing guitar in a band. Nick and Barrington Cooper formed a production company, Emerald Films, and developed two scripts, *The Doctor and the Devils*, based on a Dylan Thomas story about body snatchers, and *Only Lovers Left Alive,* based on a science fiction novel by David Wallis. "As an occupational therapy I suggested that we do some script development," Barrington Cooper said.

When Nick and Barrington Cooper made a deal with Avala Films, Nick moved to their base, in the former Yugoslavia. There, he shared a suite at the Hotel Esplanade in Zagreb with Hanna Axmann, his ex-lover and drinking buddy from his pre-*Johnny Guitar* days. After months of trying, unsuccessfully, to write the screenplay adaptation for *The Doctor and the Devils*, Nick traveled to Rome and sought the help of the famed writer and intellectual, Gore Vidal.

"The first sign when I realized that you could perhaps institutionalize him was when he came to my flat in khaki trousers with one leg torn to shreds," Gore Vidal said.

Nick had come from the zoo where he claimed to have held a lion and now was telling Gore Vidal that he was going to buy the lion for a pet. When asked how he was going to take care of it, Nick replied, "Oh it's not difficult. I'll find somebody to look after it."

Gore Vidal told me, in 2007, that Nick was a man who had ten different fantasies going at a time and no imagination. "He had no idea where reality began and ended," Vidal said.

While my father was going off the mental deep end, my mother was having a hard time relating to the other mothers who lived in our Sunset Mesa neighborhood.

"They were well-educated housewives who were married to doctors and lawyers," Betty said. "They had never worked. I felt like I couldn't tell them who I was or what was going on. I couldn't talk but I had to listen and play girl-talk with them. I couldn't really relate to any of them."

The only person Betty thought could possibly understand the depths of rejection she was experiencing was Nick's son, Tony. Dorsey reached out to him on Betty's behalf.

"I had never put his history with his father together in my heart," Betty said. "It was horrible that Nick had so rejected him. Now I understood. I really wanted to see him and let him know that I understood where he was coming from."

Tony drove to Sunset Mesa from Van Nuys where he lived with Gloria and their son, Tony Jr., born in April 1963.

He had remembered Betty as being this vibrant, fun person, but when he arrived at our house in Sunset Mesa he found her so depressed she could barely move.

"There was nobody anywhere that could possibly know where I was coming from, but Tony would," Betty said. I told him everything."

They sat on the floor in the living room talking about what had happened to her in Madrid. Then they went for a moonlit walk on the beach, fell into each other's arms, and made love on the beach.

"Tony was attractive, but that wasn't my motive. It was sort of an outreach. I didn't think it was nasty, or, wrong. It was very loving. It wasn't manipulated by either of us. It just happened."

According to Tony, "I never thought of leaving Gloria for Betty and Gloria never suspected that there was anything between us. Our affair wasn't a drawn-out thing. Betty and I slept together because we both needed each other. For comfort."

"Gloria had had a psychotic break," Tony said. "It had happened when we were on our way home to Los Angeles after doing the play, *The Country Girl*, with John Ireland, in Ann Arbor, Michigan. We were on the plane and all of a sudden Gloria started having these wild hallucinations that Nazi aircraft were flying up against our airplane. Shortly after we got home, I found her in one of the bathrooms with her wrists slit. That's when she went to the hospital. She had thirty-two shock treatments."

After that night on the beach Tony didn't see Betty again for a few years. A couple of months after their moonlit walk Betty realized she was pregnant with Tony's child. That child would have been my brother and my nephew, much like how, to Tim, Tony was his brother and stepfather. This is what it meant to be a Ray.

Betty found out about a clinic in Mexico that performed abortions for $1,000 from her friend, the actress turned political activist, Leslie Parrish. She asked Dr. Branshaft to loan her the money. She was furious when he refused. In her opinion, he was making a fortune off of her, and owed her. "I told him, 'There you are in your Sunset Tower.' And Dr. Branshaft said, 'All right, give me twenty minutes and I'll meet you down at Schwab's.'"

I always knew Tony and Betty had had sex and that she had gotten pregnant with his child. It should have been something out of Greek mythology, not everyday life.

I met Tony and Gloria for the first time in 1969. They invited us over for a barbecue at the house in Van Nuys, which in the 1960s was a predominantly white, family-centric, middle-class neighborhood like the kind where the fictional Brady Bunch family lived.

Tony had spent the 1960s working consistently as an assistant director on the television shows *The Rifleman, Gunsmoke, Hitchcock Presents,* and on the movies *The Misfits, The Apartment, The Prize, The Unsinkable Molly Brown, The Hustler,* and *Spartacus.* In 1969, he worked for the director Paul Mazursky for the first time as an assistant director on *Bob and Carol Ted and Alice.* This led to his being Mazursky's producer on such movies as *Harry and Tonto, Next Stop Greenwich Village,* and *An Unmarried Woman.*

Meanwhile, "Gloria was doing a little TV, three or four shows a year, and a little theater," Tony said, later admitting that their marriage had hurt her career.

Tony had just returned from Spain where he had spent seven months working on the film, *Valdez is Coming,* starring Burt Lancaster. On his way to California he stopped in Chicago, where Nick was living in a one-room apartment with a mattress thrown on the floor and thinking that he was going to make a groundbreaking docudrama about the Chicago Conspiracy Trials. Seven people—Rennie Davis, Dave Dellinger, Tom Hayden, Abbie Hoffman, Jerry Rubin, John Froines, and Lee Weiner—were charged with inciting a riot at the 1968 Chicago Democratic Convention.

"Nick sat me down and described the sets he wanted to build," Tony said. "He wanted me to raise a million and a half dollars. I was an assistant director. I wasn't in the position to raise money. The visit was over when he saw that I couldn't salvage his movie. I told him he was being unrealistic and left."

If Betty had any idea that Nick was in Chicago she sure didn't let on to Julie or me. I spent my youth believing he was in Europe making movies whereas my sister believed that the reason we never saw him was because he was in New York "and they didn't have any phones there."

That day we went to Tony's, Betty was parking her Buick Skylark in front of Tony and Gloria's house and Gloria was walking from the garage to the front door. Betty honked the horn and Gloria walked over to greet us on our way out of the car. Gloria was dressed all in black. Her blonde wavy hair fell loosely against the collar of her simple long-sleeved blouse.

She was a vision. She wasn't anything real. That's what I told the writer David Thomson when I met him in the early 2000s and he asked me if I'd known her. I said, "Someone as beautiful as she was who was married to my father and my brother? There's just something unreal."

We followed Gloria into the house and after bringing us to the backyard where Tony was grilling steaks she disappeared into her bedroom. It was weird they had this beautiful house with a swimming pool but there was a disconnect. Tony was standing over the barbecue in his own world while Jimmy, his and Gloria's four-year-old son, was running around like he had eaten a pound of sugar, and Tony Jr., who was six, was jumping up and down on the diving board. Polly, Gloria's teenage daughter from her marriage to the comedy writer, Cy Howard, lured Julie into the alley behind their house and introduced her to hashish.

"I thought Polly was our half-sister," Julie said. "She was a teenager and she took me back into an alleyway and introduced me to hash. I'd never had hash before. I was nine. Polly was the coolest girl. She was always in trouble. She was like Peggy Lipton on *The Mod Squad*."

We saw Tony six years later, on Thanksgiving Day in 1975. During that time Nick had come back into my sister's and my life for the first time in ten years. He'd lounged around the apartment in his leopard print bikini briefs, smoking Gitanes and letting the ashes fall to the floor. When he wasn't leaving cigarette butts in my mother's potted plants, he was dropping his silver coke spoon on the shag carpeting. Those six years had been traumatic for my nephews, Tony Jr. and Jimmy, too. Tony and Gloria had gotten a divorce and the courts had awarded Tony custody of their sons.

"Gloria was locked up in her room again," Tony recalled. "She refused to come out. She never fed the kids. She wasn't dressing them. She wasn't taking them to school. The school talked to me because the kids were showing up dirty and unkempt and unfed. The court sent an investigator to the house and determined that the kids were not being taken care of. It's kind of cliché but having had no family as a child somehow got me fixated on wanting a family of my own. I've done it all my life. I had my kids. And I was hooked on them."

Tony and Betty were alike in this way. They were hooked on us kids, but both had too many unresolved issues to be the best of parents.

After eating Thanksgiving dinner on that afternoon in 1975 with Tony and his sons, Betty banished us kids to the bedroom Julie and I shared. Tony and Betty wanted privacy. Betty hadn't kept her pregnancy by Tony a secret from my sister or me. My mother never shied away from talking about her sexual experiences. She kept a copy of the book *Joy of Sex* on our coffee table for years.

Naturally, all four of us children, Julie, Tony, Jimmy, and me, thought our parents were going to have sex.

I identified Tony as the man who had gotten my mother pregnant. He could have been the father of my younger sister or brother. Which would not have changed the fact that he was also my brother. Well, half-brother. As if just being a half-brother was supposed to make his and my mother's sexual relationship any less confusing.

Tony Jr. and Jimmy also seemed to know that Betty and Tony had had sex before. Or maybe that's what happens when your father marries his stepmother. You just assume that all of the adult members in your family have sex with each other.

And on that Thanksgiving Day in 1975, Tony Jr., Jimmy, Julie, and I were sitting on the two twin beds in my sister's and my bedroom getting stoned. As soon as we'd closed the door, Julie lit up a joint, and we started playing the "How Many Different Ways We'd Be Related If . . . " game for the first time. Here's a recap of the Ray family tree:

Tony's mother was Nick's first wife, Jean Evans.

Nick's second wife was Gloria Grahame, the actress.

Betty was Nick's third wife.

Nick and Jean's son, Tony, was born on November 24, 1937.

Nick and Gloria's son, Tim, was born on November 12, 1948.

Nick and Betty's daughters, Julie and me, were born on January 10, 1960 and October 1, 1961.

Tony, Nick's first son, married Gloria, Nick's second wife, on May 13, 1960.

They had two sons. Tony Jr., born on April 30, 1963 and Jimmy, born September 21, 1965.

Julie said, "It was Tony, Mommy, me, Nicca, Tony Jr., and Jimmy. Us. And Gloria? I just didn't understand where she fit into the picture."

Julie wanted Tony and Betty to get married. She didn't think there was anything wrong with our half-brother and mother saying *I do*.

"I had it all figured out. I thought I was really smart," Julie said.

The four of us were thrilled by the prospect of our parents' future marriage and our living together. We were family already. Why not be brothers and sisters and live under the same roof? Preferably theirs. They had moved out of the Van Nuys house and into a house with a black bottom pool on Laurel Grove Drive in Studio City.

We were living in a two-bedroom apartment with cottage cheese stucco ceilings and no pool in sight.

I was fourteen and Julie was almost sixteen, but she'd been acting like she was thirty ever since she was three. Tony Jr. was eleven and Jimmy was nine. We were young to be their aunts. We should have been their sisters. It would've made more sense.

"If our mom married your dad, you'd be our nephews and our brothers," Julie said to Tony Jr. and Jimmy.

She opened our bedroom window and lit a cigarette to cover up the smell of the pot.

"Nicca and I would be your aunts *and* your sisters." She looked Tony Jr. and Jimmy in the eye.

"That's fucked up," I said.

The four of us started laughing—pig snorts and all.

The next time I saw Tony Jr. and Jimmy was a couple of months later when Tony invited us over for an afternoon visit. Their swimming pool was designed to look like a pond. "The pool was done with stonework and tiles. I designed it. We brought a boulder from the desert to use as a diving board and had to lift it over the house with a crane," Tony said.

Not only was their pool like none other I'd ever seen, Tony Jr. and Jimmy had their own personal pinball machine. I was so envious because my mother had trouble affording to buy my sister and I winter coats.

How was I to know at the age of fourteen that my half-brother, who was twenty-four years older than me, was strung out on cocaine?

"I had a period at the Studio City house, where I locked myself in the house for six months, just before we made *Next Stop, Greenwich Village*," Tony recalled. "And I wouldn't come out. And the kids were with me. I would go out at night and buy groceries and cook dinner, but I wouldn't see anybody. People would leave notes on my gate if they wanted to contact me. I was really in trouble with drugs and depression. There was a lot of cocaine going around in the industry and Paul Mazursky knew that I was doing coke. Mazursky's psychiatrist helped me. His name was Milich, and he came to my house because I was too paranoid to leave mine and go to his office. Finally, after days, Milich said, 'Tony, you have to go back to work. You've got to reclaim your sanity.' The next day I got in my car and went back to work. Paul Mazursky and I were inseparable for years. He became like a father."

I saw Tony Jr. and Jimmy again on October 1, 1976, for my fifteenth birthday. I hadn't planned on spending it with my nephews. In fact, Betty was taking my friend and me to Knott's Berry Farm, the amusement park in Buena Vista. It had fun rides but always paled in comparison to Disneyland. Still, I was looking forward to spending the night riding rollercoasters. I hadn't expected Tony Jr. and Jimmy to come along for the ride or for my mother to pick up a Hells Angel. She brought him home with us like he was a prize she'd won at the arcade.

He made himself comfortable in our apartment for several days. It was awkward coming home from school and having him in our apartment while Betty was at work. At this point in my life, if I had been frightened of him, I would not have acknowledged it. However, I was relieved when after a week of his lounging around on our couch Julie took Betty aside and demanded she tell the Hells Angel to leave.

I looked at Tony Jr. and Jimmy's life and thought they had it so much better than we did. You know, because their father, my half-brother, was a successful producer and they got to go with him on film shoots. When Tony could he would take his sons with him on location but that stopped once Jimmy's behavior turned violent.

"I was in Montana working as an associate producer on *Rancho Deluxe*." Tony said. "Frank Perry, who had directed *Diary of a Mad Housewife* and *Play It As It Lays* was the director. Tony and Jimmy came with me. It was arranged for me to leave the kids at the state senator's ranch. It was kind of neat. They rode horseback to a one-room schoolhouse. They enjoyed that. There was a lot of trout fishing. The owner of this ranch gave me a couple of Chesterfield rifles. They were very expensive guns. When we got back to Studio City, I kept them in the house. Jimmy got a hold of one and started firing the guns through the window. The police came. I had trouble with Jimmy. I had real trouble with him. So, I got rid of the guns. Another time, Jimmy was running across rooftops of the houses in our neighborhood with a toy gun in his hand. The police were chasing him. They could have shot him."

When Tony was working on *Next Stop, Greenwich Village* he had brought Tony Jr. and Jimmy to New York City with him. They were staying at One Fifth Avenue in a two-bedroom suite on the twelfth floor with a balcony. "I came home one afternoon, and Jimmy was standing on the ledge of the balcony with a knife in his hand threatening to jump off. After that, Mazursky told me I couldn't bring the kids on location with me anymore."

I was sixteen years old the first time I realized that maybe Tony Jr. and Jimmy didn't have it so much better than me. Tony Jr. appeared at our door on Christmas Day. It was out of the blue, like he had been wandering the streets of West Los Angeles, where my mother and I were living at the time, looking for a family to spend the holiday with. I didn't ask him where Jimmy was or where his father was. A friend of mine had come over and the three of us went to the Beverly Hills Cafe on La Cienega and met a man who asked us if we wanted to come over to his house and snort some cocaine. You know, make it a "white Christmas." By then I had been snorting coke for a year and never turned down an opportunity for more. So, we went to this guy's estate in Beverly Hills and got coked. Later that night Tony Jr. and I were in my bedroom talking and he shared with me how lonely it was having a father who was always gone on film shoots. He said he had had a girlfriend for a while who lived in Beverly Hills and her parents were always gone, too. He said they would sit in her palatial estate wondering why their parents didn't care about them. In his opinion I was lucky to have a mother who made it a priority to be home.

When Tony sold his house in Studio City, he built a house on Broad Beach Road in Malibu. It was where Jimmy lived, mostly on his own, because Tony was working most of the time in New York and Tony Jr. was going to boarding school in Ojai, California.

Gloria was living in an exclusive trailer park on Pacific Coast Highway across from Will Rogers State Beach, and even though it was not far from where Jimmy was living, she didn't go see him once, according to Tony.

In October 1978, Tony was in New York and "got a call that Malibu was on fire. It was one of those fires caused by the Santa Ana winds and it ended up destroying three hundred and sixty homes. It went from Ventura, all the way across the mountains, and to the ocean. When I got to my house it was on fire. And Jimmy was on the roof with a garden hose and no water was coming out of it. Fire trucks were lined up along PCH doing nothing because they'd run out of water. They had nothing to fight the fires with and my house burned down. I got Jimmy off the roof. And that night it was really an inferno. There were horses and animals on the roads. It was like a war scene. My house burned down. There was a family who Jimmy had been spending time with, the Kojevski's and I asked them if he and his family could take Jimmy in, and they said yes."

I was in high school at University High in West Los Angeles when my mother told me that Jimmy was wanted by the FBI. At this time, Tony was an executive in charge of East Coast Production at Twentieth Century Fox and living in Scarsdale, New York with his second wife and her three children. It was during this time that Tony brought Jimmy home to live with him and enrolled him in Scarsdale High School. But, soon after his arrival, Jimmy was caught stealing and buying drugs.

Then, according to Tony, "The FBI came to my house looking for Jimmy. It turned out he had been involved with a gang in Malibu led by a group of adults that had the local kids robbing houses and bringing the stolen goods to them in exchange for cocaine and other drugs. Apparently, they murdered a teenager on the beach. I got a criminal lawyer to defend Jimmy. The FBI said they weren't interested in prosecuting Jimmy. They wanted him to testify against the adults who ended up going to prison for a long time."

Tony said, "I got Jimmy a job working in the grip department of a movie I was working on and that got bad, too. I came in one morning to work and I didn't see Jimmy and they told me they had him upstairs on an empty stage sweeping the floor and I asked why, what happened? And they said, Jimmy's stoned. I put Jimmy in a rehab. He refused to take medication. He had a lot of violent outbursts and then Jimmy just disappeared."

Gloria moved to New York City and into the Manhattan Plaza, a subsidized housing for theater professionals. She had had breast cancer in 1974 and was in remission, but the cancer came back in her stomach.

Tony said, "Gloria was always having to have her stomach pumped. She developed this odor about her. You could smell the illness. I visited her a lot at Manhattan Plaza. She was about to go to London to do *Macbeth*. She went to a garment bag in her closet and pulled out this little purse and handed me a Cartier cufflink. 'This is for you,' she said. 'I want you to give the other one to Tim in case I don't see you again.'"

Gloria died on October 5, 1981. I was living in New York City at the time with my father's last wife Susan. I rented a room in the loft they had shared in the years leading up to his death on June 16, 1979. She had taken me in, in 1981, after I landed on her doorstep at 3 a.m., drunk and holding a bra in my hand.

I had only seen my father three times from 1974 until his death. Once when I was twelve. Once when I was fifteen. Once when I was sixteen. I had seen Tony in 1969 and in 1975, when I was seven and fourteen. I was nineteen when I saw him again in 1981.

Julie, who was also living in New York City in 1981, had been in contact with Tony and four months before Gloria passed away, Tony, Julie, and I met in Tony's apartment on the Upper East Side. He took out a sandwich baggy full of cocaine and a small coke spoon, and the three of us got high. I wasn't supposed to be doing drugs or drinking because I was sick with hepatitis. But I had my priorities straight. I wasn't going to let a bad liver put a damper on this impromptu family reunion.

After Julie went home Tony and I decided to go eat dinner in Chinatown. We were driving downtown on Second Avenue in his Mercedes when he turned to me and asked if I liked sex. I didn't know how to answer it, except to say, "I don't."

I saw that we were approaching the Kiev Restaurant, a Ukrainian diner on 7th Street, and asked him to stop so that I could go to the bathroom. I felt like I had when I was seventeen and had jumped out of a porn producer's car on Little Santa

Monica Boulevard in West Los Angeles. Like I had to run for my life. That night in 1981, I'd waited in the Kiev bathroom stall for what I thought was enough time to get rid of him. When I left the diner, he was gone.

The next time I saw Tony was in 1986. I was living in Los Angeles again and met Tony at Characters, a Chinese restaurant on Melrose Avenue that was owned by an ex-boyfriend of Julie's. Joining us were Betty, Tim, and Tim's friend, Gwen Welles, an actress known for her work in Robert Altman's 1975 classic, *Nashville*. I thought it would be like a family reunion. I was disappointed when I discovered at the beginning of our lunch date that Tim and Tony were more interested in listening to Gwen than they were in talking to me.

In 1989, I saw Tony Jr. in New York City. He was in town visiting friends. He came to see me in a play a group of us from acting class had put on in a rehearsal studio space in the West 40s. I was studying with Suzanne Shepherd at the recommendation of the actor, Harris Yulin, who was married to Gwen Welles, and was also friends with Tim. Afterward the performance, we went to one of the actor's apartment in the Manhattan Plaza. I had not known that Gloria had also had an apartment there. Nor had I known that Tony Jr. had lived there with her and been living with her when she got sick.

"I'd gotten this call that Gloria collapsed on the stage in Liverpool," Tony said. "So, Cy Howard and I arranged for Polly and Tim to get in an airplane and go to Liverpool and bring her back. Cy sent a limousine to the airport to pick her up. I sent an ambulance. The ambulance met the plane and took her to St. Vincent's Hospital in Greenwich Village. The plan was I would be called when she got to the hospital. Instead, the call I got was that she was dead. So, I never got a chance to see her before she died."

He added, "Tony Jr. was finishing high school at Rhodes Prep School on West 54th Street. He suddenly developed hives. I brought him to the house in Scarsdale and he was only there a couple of weeks when he came into my bedroom one night and said, 'Dad, I'm going to hurt myself or hurt somebody else.' He was having a breakdown. I took him to the Westchester County Hospital. It took me about five or six weeks to go through the legal work of getting him out of there. I transferred him to Hartford Psychiatric Hospital, and he was there for about a year and a half."

When I saw Tony Jr., in 1989, he talked about being a teenager in the 1970s and working as a production assistant on the films his father was producing for Paul Mazursky. At the time I was jealous of how easily it had been for him to just go work on a movie set. I certainly didn't know how fragile Tony Jr.'s state of mind was. Tony Jr. was trying to grab onto something that would stabilize his life, but if he thought it would be me, he was wrong. At that point, I only had enough strength to get myself on a stable track. I couldn't eat or sleep and for a short time I was cutting myself. I started seeing a therapist and slowly, very slowly, I began putting my life together. But, at the time I saw Tony Jr. I was not in a state of mind to be of emotional support.

In 1990, Tony and his third wife, Eve, a stabilizing force in his life, set sail for the Bahamas on the twenty-eight-foot Freedom cat ketch sailboat he had bought while working on the movie, *Turk 182*.

"I took the boat to the islands. I knew nothing about sailing and engaged a good Irish racing sailor to crew with me," Tony said. "Eve and I stayed on the water for seven months, never drinking or doing drugs. Without knowing what I was doing at the time, I was setting about to save my life."

When they returned to land, they settled in Cape Neddick, Maine and Tony admitted himself into the McLean Hospital in Boston where, finally, he was treated for the bipolar disorder he had been suffering from all of his life.

Tony was finally settling down when Jimmy showed up at their door.

"Jimmy was always high on meth and alcohol and he'd have violent outbursts," Tony said. "I helped find him work doing construction, but he was fired for coming to work high. One afternoon, I found him in his room packing his little toolbox with thimbles, thread, and pocketknives. He was in this long overcoat that looked like a bum's overcoat from the 1930s.

"I said, 'What's going on?'

"And he said, 'I can't stay here, dad. I'm a drifter.'

"And then Jimmy disappeared. We learned he was on his way to Alaska . . . He had this fantasy that he was going to work on the pipelines and make a fortune.

"I did not hear from Jimmy ever again other than stories related to me by my elder son, Tony, that Jimmy was hearing voices that were telling him what to do and having violent outbursts.

"In July of 2000, I got a call from a policeman in Washington State. 'Do you have a son named James Ray?'

"'Yeah.'

"'He's dead.'

"They found him in the woods, in his Volkswagen camper, dead. The autopsy blood work showed no signs of drugs in his system, attesting to his mental illness," Tony said.

In July of 2000, I was staying with Betty and her fourth husband, Sandy, in Sherman Oaks California. I was thirty-nine, had just graduated from the New School University with honors, and was only beginning to go to the film archives at USC and UCLA, in search of answers to the questions I had had about my father since my first memory.

"We had a service in the South Bay in Los Angeles. We had this big photograph of Jimmy. All of Tony Jr.'s friends came. He was really devastated because he had been looking after Jimmy.

Mazursky was supposed to come but didn't. Tim didn't show up. The Kojevskis were there. It was a weird service. It was all right. I made arrangements to have him cremated and have the ashes sent to Tony Jr. and he and Polly and Gloria's sister, Joy, put them on Gloria's grave in the San Fernando Valley," Tony said.

I didn't go to Jimmy's funeral. I hadn't seen him since 1986. I had met him, Tony Jr., and Tim at Canter's Deli on Fairfax Avenue in West Hollywood. I had gotten close to Tim in the early 1980s. I thought he was going to show me how to live a healthy and sane life. He'd brought us together so that we could make a pact to be there for each other as a family.

How could any of us have followed through with that?

Six years after Jimmy's death, I contacted Tony. I got his email address off a group email that Susan had sent each of Nick's children in regard to Nick's estate, of which she is the executor. I was a little afraid to contact Tony. I had only met him on four different occasions: in 1969, 1975, 1981, and 1986.

I had no idea what to expect when I emailed my half-brother. I wrote, "Hi Tony, I hope this email finds you well and happy. I'm writing because I've been working on a book about our father. It's largely my personal story being the youngest of his four children. I'm very interested in talking to my family members about their relationship with him. Your stories are so important since I'm also trying to gain perspective on our family's history. I really look forward to hearing from you, Nicca Ray."

I didn't know what to expect. To tell you the truth, I was kind of afraid of him. I didn't know if he was still doing cocaine or if he'd just tell me to fuck off. I certainly didn't expect him to respond to my email within hours of having sent it.

Tony wrote, "I have stayed away from press and books—having written my own, unsuccessfully—largely because of my relationship with Gloria, which I kept private over so many years. But, yes, I would be happy to talk to you. I am afraid you are going to find I know very little about my father, but, what the hell. Love, Tony."

It took several weeks of back and forth emails, as well as conversations between Tony and Betty in which my mother reassured him that his story would be safe with me and that he didn't need to go to the grave with it. Soon, Tony committed to an interview.

Tony arrived in New York City on December 4, 2006. I met him at his hotel on 23rd Street, not the Chelsea Hotel, which he would have preferred, but a decent no-frills hotel all the same.

As soon as he opened the door, I knew he was not someone to be afraid of. He greeted me with a smile and a strong hug. He had put on a considerable amount of weight since I'd seen him last. He had been drug-free for over a decade. He was also being treated for bipolar disorder.

He had been living a normal life with his wife and daughter in a small seaside New England town for most of the last twenty years. It appeared that he was trying to keep things in check after a life spent moving from one chaotic episode to the next. He had never experienced calm.

He told me a story about the time he was living in Malibu with Gloria and our father, in 1951. He was describing a night when he was trying to fall asleep, but he was filled with a great sense of unease. Our father had bought him a motorized bicycle and early the next morning he took it on Pacific Coast Highway with every intention of running away. I imagined Malibu then must have been a wild and rural landscape, with the rustling canyons on one side and the roiling Pacific Ocean on the other. The landscape itself must have felt somewhat foreboding to a twelve-year-old New York City kid frenetically pedaling north, moving further away from a city and any people who could possibly save him from the lion's den his mother had sent him into. I knew his terror.

Identity Lapse

George, my mother's first boyfriend after Nick, would have been the perfect stepfather. She started dating him several months after Nick's visit and dog-dropping. He was a video engineer at ABC-TV, who she met while filling in as a script girl on the game show, *Let's Make a Deal*. Every Friday night the contestants lined up on Prospect Avenue in their outrageous costumes. It was a weekly Halloween party. Each week, Julie and I would run the block and half to see what kinds of crazy outfits people had on. We were beyond thrilled when Betty announced to us at dinner that she would be working as a fill-in for a few weeks. Neither Julie nor I ever expected her to bring home a boyfriend from the show.

"George was an engineer and he would run a lot shows I had to look at. So, he would be working with me. He was Armenian. He had a shock of white hair and a great smile and a gentle laugh—and just a sweetie pie and I liked him as a person. He had gone through a divorce and he was always asking me for dinner," Betty said.

I loved George the moment I met him. He took us out to Milano's Italian Restaurant, and we ate pizza with everything on it, salads, Shirley Temples, and got to pick out pastries, not just one, off of the pastry tray the server brought to our table.

"He spent more money on that one dinner than I spent on groceries for two weeks," Betty said.

I knew he was going to be the best thing to ever happen to our family. Especially when he bought us a refrigerator after not having one for over a year.

"I was cleaning house on a Saturday morning, and the girls were playing and a Sears man came to the front door and asked if I was so and so, and I said, 'Yes,' and he said he had a refrigerator for me. I said, 'I didn't buy a refrigerator, you must be mistaken.' He showed me the sales slip and it was signed, George Garunion. I was furious. I knew he was working that Saturday morning and I called him, 'Will you please talk to this guy and ask him to take this refrigerator back?' I felt like I was being bought, but the kids were overjoyed, you know—a new refrigerator," Betty recalled.

The Sears delivery men left without taking the refrigerator.

"After work, George came with loads of groceries. Well it was very sweet. And the kids adored him, and it just seemed, you know, an O.K. thing to do."

"When George came into the picture and bought us a refrigerator, I kept thinking where's my dad going to fit in?" Julie said.

I never knew my sister had fantasies of Nick coming home until I was in my forties. I thought she was just as content as I had been with the idea of George becoming our father. I was always happy when he came over. He took us to the International House of Pancakes and let us have strawberry pancakes for dinner before going to see movies at the Campus Theater across the street. On the weekends he brought home Der Weinershnitzel chili dogs for lunch and we sat at the breakfast nook in the kitchen and ate together like a happy family. Friday nights were the best, though, because he took us to Milano's Italian restaurant on Hillhurst and we got to eat too much pizza and drink Shirley Temples. He made me feel like we had a lot. I didn't understand why Betty wouldn't marry him.

"George genuinely loved the girls and me and the girls knew that," Betty said.

I never wanted him to leave. I always thought Julie felt the same way. I didn't know that her opinion of him changed after she "walked in on George and Betty having sex and I thought he was killing her. I screamed, 'What are you doing to my mother?' He was this big thing on top of her. After that I never wanted to see him again."

Well, she sure got her wish.

Dorothy, a friend of Betty's from the Mount Hollywood Congregational Church, had a brother, Ward, who came from Northern California to serve as the guest choir conductor. Betty thought he was "beautiful and a fabulous singer."

After the church service the congregants would gather in the courtyard for coffee and cookies. On Sundays I felt safe. I liked going to church. I liked seeing the same people every week. I liked eating the cookies in the courtyard and watching my mother mingle with the other congregants. She was an active member of the church and had become a lay minister. "I got very active with volunteering. I worked with the Quaker Friends and worked with women who were coming out of prison, organized clothing drives, set up and went with them to job interviews. I was doing that for my mental health."

On most Sundays Dorothy and her teenaged daughters, Wendy and Joyce, would join us for breakfast afterward. On the Sunday that Ward led the choir in song, Dorothy and her daughters didn't join us after the service. Usually we went to a diner where Hollywood and Sunset Boulevards intersect. It was small with tall glass front windows, a few tables that sat four, a counter, and no booths. The kids sat separate from the grownups and made strange liquid concoctions out of soda, creamer, sugar, salt and pepper and got amped up on waffles with strawberries, maple syrup, and whipped cream, while Dorothy and my mother talked about what looked like serious business.

"I respected Dorothy, but she was not a close friend like Leslie Parrish or Roberta. I had been working through Leslie with speakers, talent, and organizers for peace. We were a group of people who were educated in little seminar groups to go out and speak against the war to different places. I was very much against the war. I was active in women's rights for peace and I brought those ideals with me to the church," Betty said.

Betty's friendship with Dorothy wasn't based on political activism or on a shared past in movies. Like Betty, Dorothy was divorced and raising two daughters on her own. Dorothy's brother, Ward, was also divorced.

A week after Ward captivated Betty with his singing, Dorothy called and said, "'My brother really wants to meet you. Why don't you come over?' I went yippee!" Betty said. "I was attracted to him."

In all fairness to Ward, he was better looking than George. Ward had brown hair and blue eyes, a strong jawline, and sturdy features. He was six foot, of German descent, and physically lean. He was a casual dresser and mainly wore jeans with t-shirts and windbreaker jackets. I don't remember ever seeing him in a suit, except for when he married my mother. George was just a few fingers taller than Betty and could have stood to lose a few pounds. He wore glasses and had thick, silver hair he brushed off of his face. He wore button-down shirts, dark slacks, blazers and a tan overcoat. He may have dressed more conservatively than Ward, but it was Ward who never dared wear a pair of wrinkled pants. Ward was not someone a kid would want to play with. George was. When Betty and George were dating I didn't long for my father. I was getting used to, and liked, the family unit: Betty, Joy, Julie, me, and George. I was happy. It wasn't until Ward came along that I started imagining my father was going to come home and rescue me.

The way Ward suddenly replaced George felt like a jolt to my equilibrium.

Julie and I met him for the first time on Christmas 1969. It was clear that we didn't have any choice in the matter of Betty's love life. "She sat Nicca and I down and said, 'Your father and I are getting a divorce,'" Julie said.

Her divorce from Nick was finalized on January 1, 1970.

"I was mortified," Julie said.

I was really mad at her for choosing Ward over George. I know now that George was not the kind of a person she would ever marry. "It wasn't that I disliked him. He was a Republican. He was just not my type of close intimate person," Betty said.

No. George wasn't the kind of a man my mother would ever marry. He was too kind. "Ward showed taints of strangeness, but nothing, nothing like Nick," Betty said.

Instead of marrying a man who would nurture my sister and I to be our best selves, she married a man who had been married four times before; a man who had left his three children living in a trailer park in Savannah, Georgia with their alcoholic mother, his fourth wife. George would never abandon children, like Ward and Nick had. Not that I ever thought my father's absence meant that he had abandoned me. I didn't even begin to consciously consider that he had done that until I was in my forties. After my parent's separation I just thought he was gone and would come back some day when he was finished making movies. Although, on some level I must have known he wasn't. My best friend Val's father Richard was a film editor working on popular films like *Downhill Racer* and *The Candidate*. As a hobby he raced motorcycles with a club called The Viewfinders. Posters of the movies he'd worked on lined the walls of the garage where he kept his motorcycles. On some level I must have been aware that Nick wasn't making current movies. I mean, where were the posters of his current movies?

"In school I'd write essays about how busy Nick was and how he lived in New York and how there was no telephone service there," Julie said.

Julie thought he went from Europe to New York. I never envisioned him in the States. If he was in America, he would surely be with us.

Betty said she wanted to give my sister and I a normal childhood and that was one of the reasons she married Ward. If that had truly been the case, she should have married George. Instead, she opened the door for more insanity.

"I was completely finished with Nick," Betty said. "I knew there was going to be no future. And I really didn't feel comfortable with having a series of lovers. And I was much more attracted to Ward, than I had been to anybody since Nick."

I can say this now, as an adult, as a daughter who knew her mother very well, and had to piece together her mother's life in order to face parts of her own. Betty married men who were good in bed. That was a deciding factor in her marrying Nick and in marrying Ward. She was also attracted to men who evoked danger.

As Julie remembered, "I hated Ward from the very first night I met him. He didn't know a damn thing about my mother or us. He didn't want to know us. There wasn't an honest thread in that man."

"He was a lesser version of a Nick Ray," Betty said.

And still, after everything Nick had done to her, she married a man who was like him.

"She'd given up on my father and thought Ward was good looking and they had great sex," Julie said. "That's why she married him."

Ward was tall and stern. He was not huggable like George had been. George was safe. You didn't get the creeps when you sat on his lap or when he wanted to give you a hug. Ward was foreboding. Not that I knew what that meant when I was eight. I just knew I didn't want to go near him. At first it wasn't anything that he did that made me feel that way. It was just his aura. He was just wrong.

"I remember weeks before we married, Ward took the blankets off the bed in some sort of rage and ripped them onto the floor and that shocked me. It was like, "Huh? Where did that come from? It scared me. I was startled to see this kind of rage out of the blue."

What's scary is that she married him anyway.

"Neither one of us wanted to have an affair and I had no interest in anyone else. We decided that we couldn't continue this relationship without getting married and getting a house."

Betty found the house while walking through the Franklin hills. It was around the corner from the Shakespeare Bridge, built in 1926 in a Gothic style with steeples and mid-nineteenth century lampposts. Julie used to walk along the stone railing like it was a balance beam. If she missed a step, she could've fallen off into the hillside below. She never fell, though. Not even when she was stoned. She started smoking pot almost as soon as we moved into that house, once taking me around the side one afternoon and handing me a lit joint. "Smoke this, Nicca. It'll make all of this okay." I turned it down that day. A few years later I couldn't get enough.

To this day, one of the most distressing things about living with Ward and his children in the house on Wanda Drive was that it was the most beautiful house I've ever lived in. I should have happier memories. What went on inside, which I am getting to, didn't match its grand exterior. The house, built in the Spanish Revival style, stood majestically in the middle of a street with only five houses on it. There was a flight of stairs with thirty steps that wound their way up from the street to the thick wooden engraved front door. Halfway up the steps, on the left, was a sundeck with wrought iron fencing. On the right was a three-tier garden where wild poppies grew and where Ward planted sunflowers and a cement pathway that circled around the house to the backyard, which had plum, orange, and grapefruit trees, and where Ward eventually planted straw-berries and tomatoes.

We were able to rent the five-bedroom house cheap, because the hippies who had lived there before us had left it a pigsty. A lingering scent of stale beer and urine permeated through-out the hallways and rooms. The bathtubs in both bathrooms were caked with vomit that we had to scrape out with a weed-ing knife. We had to step carefully between the shards of glass covering the stone tile floor of the second story balcony. Down in the basement more broken glass littered the cement ground. Nothing had been cleaned or dusted, not the wrought iron railing of the spiral staircase or the pane of the bay window in the sunken living room. We scrubbed and we scraped and swept and dusted and returned the house to its grandeur. There was one contribution to the house that Betty loved and refused to change: the hippies had painted psychedelic murals on the walls and ceilings of both the master bedroom and the bedroom that would become mine.

I could see the clay-tiled rooftop from the playground of Franklin Avenue Elementary, where I went to school. I was just finishing the third grade. When I told my teacher, Mrs. Goodman, that I was going to be a bridesmaid at my mother's wedding she smiled big and said, "You must be so excited."

I was filled with dread.

Betty only dated Ward for six months before marrying him. She asked Hugh Anwyl, the minister from Mount Hollywood

Congregational Church to officiate, but he refused because "he saw danger," Betty said.

Betty never discussed Ward in depth. *Hugh Anwyl saw danger.* What kind of danger do you think he was talking about, Mom? *He saw danger.* And that wasn't a sign that maybe you should steer clear? "I thought he'd make a good father for you girls because he was a teacher and sang in the church choir." But what about the danger? "I thought he'd be a good father."

Ward's brother, Gavin, who was a bishop back east, flew out and married them in our new house. Ward, Gavin, and Dorothy were minister's children. After their marriage I never saw Gavin again and our weekend Yahtzee games with Dorothy's daughters ended too.

On the night of their wedding, Betty stood at the top of the spiral staircase, and waited for the musical cue signaling it was time for her to meet Ward at the bottom of the steps. She was a stunning bride dressed in a flowing white gown with a baby's breath crown. The way she was smiling no one would have suspected she was scared to death of marrying the man.

"That night I knew I was making a big mistake," she said.

Then why didn't she take my sister and I and get the hell out of there?

"He threatened to kill me if I left," she confided in me a few years before she died.

From the moment she became Mrs. Ward Schwab, Betty dissociated from the reality of what she had done and lived in a fantasy that we were going to be some kind of real-life Brady Bunch. Ward wanted Julie and I to change our last name to Schwab. Betty didn't voice any objections. I did. I adamantly refused. There was this assumption that he was going to replace my father. There was no way. I have always been possessive of my last name. I can't imagine ever having another. I have always felt strongly that I am a Ray and no other. I sure as hell wasn't going to let some Ward take that away from me.

Delving even further into her denial that she had made a terrible mistake marrying Ward she convinced him to move his two oldest children, Mark and Kristen, in with us. This infuriated me because Ward refused to let my grandmother live with us. She had always lived with us. It was like my mother traded my grandmother for Mark and Kristen. She went so far as to convince Ward's ex-wife, Iris, to move to Los Angeles with her and Ward's youngest, Heidi. Betty even helped Iris get a secretarial job at an engineer firm and found her an apartment next to the Hillhurst Liquor Store on the corner of Prospect and Hillhurst, a five-minute drive away from us.

"I wanted Mark and Kristen to be able to see their mother," Betty said. "I remember my friends thinking how bizarre I was helping the ex. But I didn't look at things that way. I just thought of the kids having access to their mother. I didn't like abandonment. I didn't like being married to the father and abandoning his three children. And then I discovered he really didn't like any of his kids."

Mark and Kristen had thick southern accents and called Betty "ma'am." Kristen, who was twelve, had brown hair down to her ass. She parted it in the middle and let it hang in her face. She wore bell-bottom blue jeans with a patch sewn on the crotch that said "Keep on Truckin'." She listened to Ten Years After and Nazareth. She spent most of her time reading romance novels. She rarely spoke. When she did, it was so softly, I had to strain to hear. She didn't have any friends. Once, Julie found out she made out with a boy she had a crush on and that did nothing to boost her popularity.

Julie recalled, "I was going steady with Larry, but I wouldn't sleep with him because I was only twelve. Kristen was a year older than me and one afternoon she went and had sex with him. She said, 'Guess where I was?' Ugh. I hated her."

Kristen was a master at making her presence unknown. She slinked around the house as if wearing satin slippers. Her breath was a whisper caught in the wind and blown out to sea. She could be sitting next to you on the couch watching television and you would forget she was there. Making herself invisible was her way of keeping out of harm's way.

Betty said, "Kristin was kind of a low-life with brown hair and very removed. She stayed in her room most of the time. She was not an unattractive girl, just you could see all she knew was misery. That's how she walked and talked and looked."

"She was the neighborhood slut," Julie said.

Mark wasn't a likeable kid. He didn't have friends. He had brown stringy hair and bad acne. It wasn't like he tried any of the ointments that would clear it up. I don't even think he washed his face.

"He was a big pimple," Julie said.

He would just let the whiteheads mount. His bedroom reeked of dirty socks and the walls were covered in *Playboy* centerfolds and posters of a barely clothed Raquel Welch in the 1966 movie *One Million Years BC*. At dinner he poured ketchup over everything he ate and slouched over his plate and shoveled his food into his mouth. It drove my mother crazy. One time she poured the contents from the wooden salad bowl over Mark's head. He sat motionless while the iceberg lettuce, tomatoes and shredded carrots slid down his face.

Betty said, "I had a hard time stomaching Mark. There was some vibe about him that I didn't like. You know when you really don't like a kid."

Soon after Mark and Kristen moved in, Ward started beating Mark up. I feel like it started happening right away. Ward would catch Mark drinking milk out of the container and hit Mark up the side of his head. Mark would be walking up the stairs too slowly and Ward would scream at him to move faster. Mark would get home from school a half hour later than usual and Ward would meet him at the front door and pound the shit out of him and leave him lying on the stone floor in the foyer.

The beatings precipitated Mark's sneaking into my bedroom at night. I never understood why he forced himself on me until I was an adult. How could I have? I was eight years old when he started coming after me. At first it happened only at night after our parents had closed their bedroom door. I could hear him walking down the hallway from his bedroom to mine. The door creaking open. He would stand over me, unbutton his pants, and shove his penis into my mouth. He threatened to hurt me if I screamed and then he would twist my arm to give me an example of the pain he'd cause if I turned him away. I hated him. I feared him. I felt sorry for him. Mostly, he terrified me.

Years later, when I was in therapy, I was talking about Mark coming to me after the beatings and thought maybe he was coming to me afterward for comfort. It didn't make the pain go away, but it gave a reason to why Mark did this. I needed for him to have a reason. I couldn't think he was just depraved with no conscience.

"Mark would try to stick his hands down my pants," Julie said. "I stopped him. I never thought he was doing that stuff to Nicca because she was the baby of the family."

Ward had stopped beating Mark and had started going after Julie. He didn't like it that she was popular with the boys in the neighborhood. He thought she was a whore. Sure, she was beautiful, and a lot of the neighborhood boys had crushes on her, but the main reason they came over to our house to talk to her was that she played on the boys little league team and they came to take her to baseball practice.

"Ward tried to kill me," Julie said. "He had me pinned up in the garage and he told me he was going to kill me. I believed him. My mom pulled up into the driveway and they sent me away for the summer. I stayed with a friend and her family. She knew he was abusive, and she did nothing. I harbor such bad feelings about that man I don't like to talk about him. I still blame her. I don't care why she did what she did. She threw away her chance to start over marrying him. She ruined our family."

You might think that Mark stopped coming after me once Ward stopped beating on him. He didn't. When we were home alone, he would chase me through the house and tackle me to the ground. Usually in the foyer at the foot of the spiral staircase like I was a bunny rabbit and he was a fox. Sometimes, at the start of the chase, I would get enough of a lead that I could hide in the coat closets next to the front door before he had a chance to pin me down. But then he'd open the closet door, and there I'd be, and, well, you can guess.

I wasn't even safe in my mother's car. On Saturdays in the summer she loved to go to Venice Beach. He would sit next to me in the backseat and put a towel over my lap while he fondled me. I wish I could have screamed so that Betty would have seen what was happening and stopped him but by the time this was happening it was as if I was wearing a muzzle.

When I was in my early twenties, I started having nightmares where a rapist climbed through the window of my house and the whole dream was about the chase and my trying to escape (I still have them from time to time). The dreams got me going to a therapist and for the first time I started dealing with what Mark had done to me. I was so angry at my mother that in those therapy sessions I would scream, "Where were you? Why didn't you see?"

When I was twenty-five, I confronted Betty face to face. We were sitting in the Rose Café near Venice Beach. "I didn't know," she said.

"How could you not have known? We were in the backseat of your car."

"I didn't see."

"But you were right there."

"Nicca, please."

"What?"

"Not so loud."

"Where were you?"

"Oh please. Don't cry. Not here. Not now. I didn't see. I didn't know."

"But why?"

She could never give me an answer. Not then. Not five years after that. Not in her last month alive. She did say she was sorry, and I believe she was truly sorry for what had been done to me, but she could never take responsibility for her part. She could never admit to me that she had failed me by not protecting me. When I was in my thirties and the subject came up, she would say she was sorry for being such a bad mother and I would comfort her and tell her she wasn't a bad mother. I'd say, "If you were a bad mother, I wouldn't be talking to you now."

I wanted her to say it was all of her fault. That my trauma was a result of the choices she made. I wanted her to be able to say that and take responsibility so some of the responsibility would be taken off of my shoulders. Eventually, I accepted that the responsibility was all mine. I had to find ways to heal my trauma. She couldn't do the healing for me.

When I was twenty-four, I started reading books, such as *Betrayal of Innocence: Incest and its Devastation*, to overcome my experience with incest. At the time I wasn't at all cognizant of the generational patterns in families where there is incest. In the book, the author, Dr. Susan Forward, contends that incest isn't the reason a family falls apart. The family was already in trouble before the incest happened. "Incest [was] the result of such a breakdown in the family."

On so many afternoons I would be in my bedroom and hear Ward shouting at Julie and Julie yelling at him to leave her the fuck alone and then I'd hear the front door slamming and I'd look out my bedroom window and see my sister running down the front staircase onto the street and down the hill to the Shakespeare Bridge. And then I'd wait for her to come home but sometimes she wouldn't come home for a week and there'd be no explanation from my mother about where she was or when she was coming back.

"I always made friends with other people's families," Julie said. "I became the surrogate daughter of other people's families. You know, families that really cared about family. I would find these families that had moms and dads and normal breakfast on Sundays."

Val's family was my surrogate family. One of my happiest childhood memories is going with them to the motorcycle races where her father would race with The Viewfinders. Early on Saturday mornings or late on Friday nights we'd pack up their RV and head out to the Mojave Desert or Indian Dunes hauling his Hodaka and Maico motorcycles, and the Yamaha mini-bikes Val and I would ride, in a trailer hooked to the back of the RV. I don't remember if I ever told Val point blank what Mark was doing to me, but she knew my house was a dangerous place to be. So, we devised a plan where we'd always be together on the weekends, either spending the nights at my house or hers. Mark never came after me if Val was with me. And on the weekends Ward kept his hands off of Mark and Julie, because my mother was home.

On the nights Julie disappeared, after Mark, Kristen and I had gone to our bedrooms, Ward and Betty would start fighting. My mother would scream, "You leave her alone. You bastard.

She's just a girl. You leave her alone!" Her voice writhed with such anger it sent chills through my body. Then, all sounds stopped. It would get quiet and I would start to close my eyes but be stirred back awake by the sounds of their lovemaking.

There is one day I remember as if it happened yesterday and not forty-eight years ago.

I heard Ward screaming at Julie to get in the fucking house. I ran to bay window in the sunken living room. She was standing on the street, in front of the garage, talking to the boys on her baseball team. That day the boys weren't swarming around her because they wanted to be her boyfriend. They were making plans for the next baseball practice. Ward marched into the kitchen, got a silver mixing bowl, a pair of scissors, and rushed back outside. He grabbed Julie and pulled her into the backyard by her waist-length hair.

"I remember thinking he just wants to have sex with me," Julie said.

I spied on them from the window above the kitchen sink. He pushed her down on the grass. She started to get up. He forced her back down. He put the silver mixing bowl on top of her head. He cut her hair along the line of the bowl. Chunks fell to the lawn.

She closed her eyes.

He kept snipping.

Her chin, mouth, cheeks, and nose scrunched up.

Snip snip snip.

I wanted to push him away from her. I wanted to take the scissors and stab him, but my legs were paralyzed. Ward walked away and left my sister sitting underneath the plum tree. He left the scissors by her side, the bowl on top of her head. When he was out of sight, she took the bowl off of her head and placed it on top of the scissors. She stood, brushed the hair off her jeans, and disappeared into the neighborhood.

And where was Betty in all of this?

"I couldn't articulate what was going on. I went into a haze."

At least she wasn't locking herself in the bathroom like she had done when she was married to Nick. That was an improvement.

Ward once wrapped a thick bicycle lock around the refrigerator when milk prices soared. "Mark would eat a dozen eggs and drink a quart of milk after school and his father put a chain around the ice box," Betty said.

The night Ward chained the refrigerator Betty took Julie and I by the hand and we stood in front of the fridge and she giggled this nervous little girl giggle. It was as though she wanted my sister and I to tell her how to deal with the situation. Later, perhaps after we'd gone to sleep, she confronted Ward, yelling at him, "Get that chain off there, that's ridiculous."

Ward was in charge of making dinner on the weeknights because Betty got home from work later than he did. Once a week Ward combined all of the leftovers in one pot and put it in the oven. It didn't matter if the combined ingredients included spaghetti, meatloaf, and tuna casserole. It went into the pot, baked at 350 degrees, and landed on the dining room table an hour later. He called them mish-mashes. On mish-mash night he'd set a bag of potato chips out on the dining room table but forbid us from crunching when we ate them. I figured out the way not to crunch was to wet the chip down with my saliva and press down on it with the roof of my mouth so it would flatten and slide down my throat like a magic carpet.

We weren't allowed to eat cereal or watch cartoons. We had to clean the crevices between the tiles on the foyer floor with a toothbrush. The wrought iron staircase railing had to be polished weekly. The laundry had to be folded. There couldn't be noise. I tiptoed through the house in an attempt to not make a sound—not easy to do when all the floors are hardwood or stone tiles. He hated laughter.

When Julie was home, she broke the dinner table tension with jokes. "Mommy, Mommy—my pigtails are too tight," she'd say and pull her pigtails back tight so that her eyes would squint. "Bus driver bus driver open the door," she'd say with her hands pressed against her cheeks smooshing her face. I'd bust up. Then catch Ward's glare. He never laid a hand on me.

"Ward loved Nicca. He never gave her any trouble. She was the little favorite of all the kids," Betty said.

I felt guilty. I looked up to Julie. I wanted her friends, her athletic talents, her beauty, her intellect. But she was always gone. It got to where I felt like she hated having me anywhere near her. I felt terribly guilty Ward didn't terrorize me, too.

The years Betty was married to Ward were a four-year nightmare—not just Mark's abusing me and Ward's terrorizing Julie but day in and day out existence in that house was so bad that sometimes when I look back on them I want to believe that the house was haunted, that that was why people behaved so badly. Many afternoons I cried on my way home from school because I didn't want to go home but didn't know where else to go. Walking uphill on Franklin Avenue from Talmadge to Holly Knoll throwing my hair into my face to hide the tears. I feared what I was going to walk into when I walked through the thick wooden front doors. Julie brought me around to the side of the house and offered me a joint because it was the only way she knew how to cope with what was happening. She couldn't rescue me from Mark just like she couldn't rescue herself from Ward, but she could anesthetize us. Like I said earlier, I abstained from smoking the pot the first time she offered but when I was thirteen and she offered it to me again I accepted. By then so much had happened that getting stoned was the only option for survival.

What did help me get through was writing. When I was ten, I brought all of my stories to my fifth-grade teacher and he would read them to the class. Of course, I excused myself right before the reading and hid in the bathroom for the length of time it took him to read. I dreamed of having my stories published in *Highlights* magazine. I was waiting for Betty to show me how to submit one of my stories even though she never had time to read them. When I was eleven, I threw all of them away in the garbage cans out in the backyard. I'd been following my mother up the spiral staircase asking her if I could read her something I'd just written. She shooshed me away. I gathered every single handwritten paper from my dresser drawers and threw every sheet into the trash. It was a turning point in my young life. I didn't write again until my late twenties. From that point on I stopped going to Betty for anything.

I was twelve and had just started the seventh grade at Thomas Starr King Junior High when we moved out of our five-bedroom, two story Spanish Revival house in the Los Feliz hills and into a cramped two-bedroom tract home on a viewless street an hour away, in the Arleta neighborhood of the San Fernando Valley. The reason we moved was that the owners of the Wanda house wanted to sell and even though they offered to sell it for fifty grand Ward and Betty declined. When I was in my twenties, I asked her why they didn't buy it and she said she knew the marriage wasn't going to last much longer and she didn't want to own anything with Ward. At the time, though, we weren't given a reason for moving.

I finished the seventh grade at Pacoima Junior High. It was isolated and felt a world apart from Los Feliz and Val and everything familiar. That's what Ward did. He took away everything familiar. I hated him and I was really beginning to hate my mother for staying with him. At least Mark had stopped coming after me. He had started smoking angel dust and that seemed to distract him from me. His drug use got so bad that after my mother left Ward, Ward sent Mark to Synanon, a cult-like rehabilitation and therapeutic community that was started in Santa Monica and expanded to Tomales Bay in Northern California. The organization was corrupt beyond measure, accused of using violence to keep members in line with their practices, which included severing ties with the outside. The last I heard of Mark was decades ago and that he was homeless in San Francisco. I feel bad for him, in a way, because I don't think he ever had a chance. But if I were to ever see him again, I would tell the motherfucker to get the fuck away from me fast.

We lived in Arleta for six months. In that time, I was sent to the dean's office at Pacoima Junior High three times; this was the beginning of my reputation as a bad child. The new house was smaller, but we were more isolated from each other than ever before. I had my own bedroom, which was the one closest to Betty and Ward's. Julie and Kristen shared the den. I couldn't tell you when they started getting along although I'm pretty sure it had something to do with getting stoned. I still hadn't smoke pot, but I had tried white crosses that a friend from school gave to me. I liked the way they made me feel pretty and light and interesting. I didn't take them again for another couple of years, though.

I stayed in my bedroom most of the time watching television shows like *The Streets of San Francisco* and fantasizing that some-one like Michael Douglas could be my dad. My dad. He seemed so far away like a blip in time. Gone.

I had two pet rats, Ms. Bigstuff, who I'd gotten after seeing the movie *Willard*, and Musky, who I got from a neighborhood girl. I let my rats out of their cages and talked to them as if they were my friends. I didn't talk much to anyone in the house. By the time Betty got home from work it was 6:30 and the last thing she wanted to hear was about my day. In fact, she didn't want to hear about anybody's day. I had been given the responsibility of cooking dinner on weeknights, which was a godsend because it meant we didn't have to suffer through any more of Ward's dreadful mish-mashes. Betty always prepped the food that I put in the oven. The only things I had to cook were the rice or noodles we served with the main dish. Oh, and I made salads.

At dinner nobody spoke, we just ate our meals and went to our bedrooms. Ward was always sullen and mostly silent. He wasn't threatening Julie or beating Mark or yelling at Betty. He was just morose. If Ward and Betty spoke to each other it was after we had all gone to sleep.

Ward started sleeping on a mattress in the living room. There was no explanation as to why. Not one single word was said about it. Julie, Kristen and I just looked at each other with the expression of *what the fuck now?* And Mark was gone in his dusted haze and hardly ever came out of his bedroom, which was the pantry room between the kitchen and garage. Betty came home from work, we ate dinner at the table, Ward included, and then we each went our separate ways to our bedrooms and Ward to his mattress. It was near the end of the school year. I have a sense that it was just days before the end only I can't be sure because I've blacked out the following memories.

I've been told by Betty that the day we left Ward she'd been driving to Safeway Supermarket when she realized she'd left the grocery list at home. She drove back to the house to get it. When she walked through the door, she saw Ward slamming a vacuum cleaner into Julie's back.

I was home. I'd seen the altercation happening. I blacked out. I've been told by Betty that it was the Saturday after the 1971 school year had ended. Julie and Ward got into a fight over Julie leaving to meet up with friends.

I have no recollection of my last days at Pacoima Junior High or how my mother, Julie, and I went from living in Arleta to living in a two-bedroom apartment on top of a hill between Hyperion Avenue and St. George, back in the neighborhood where I'd grown up. One minute I was living in the San Fernando Valley and the next I was sitting at a white dining room table in a two-bedroom apartment watching Betty making fresh tomato sauce for spaghetti. We never discussed what had happened. Both Betty and Julie were able to just move on with their lives. Julie was extroverted and popular. Betty was always able to put her best face forward. I dreaded waking up.

Those years shaped me, colored my view of the world. I only recently understood how I have befriended the enemy ever since Ward and Mark came into my life. I always prided myself for being able to get myself out of scary, even life-threatening situations when I was a teenager going to clubs in Hollywood. I could calm a beast. I also always know my escape route. Can't walk down a street without knowing which way to run. I walk through life feeling as if I am prey. It can be exhausting.

There's a loop, a thought loop accompanied by pictures, that I live in, and that I can't break out of sometimes. I fall backwards in time, back into the house on Wanda Drive, where Mark is shoving his penis in my mouth, and Ward is threatening to kill my sister, and Betty is screaming at Ward to leave Julie alone, screaming, "For Christ's sake she's just a child!" And then I hear my mother and Ward having sex, and I can't get out of the house, out of the loop, and I can't remember that this all happened over forty years ago, and my mind and my life become a decades-long loop, and I am paralyzed, stuck in bed, stuck in a rut, stuck like a mouse in a glue trap.

I spend the first hours of my day reminding myself that I am safe now. I look around at my surroundings and visualize the faces of all of my dearest friends and I look in the eyes of my partner for the last nearly thirty years and tell myself no one is going to hurt me, not now, not ever again.

I try to remember who I was before Ward and Mark came into my life. I was shy. I was precocious. I followed my sister around like she was a goddess. I had good friends. I liked presents and birthday parties and church and pizza and movies and watching *Felix the Cat* cartoons with my grandmother. I don't remember if I looked in the mirror and understood who I saw staring back at me. But I do remember being fourteen, seventeen, twenty-three, twenty-seven and looking in the mirror and not being able to define who I was to myself.

When I was in my late thirties, I thought I still didn't have a solid sense of self because I hadn't known my father. I thought that if I could just get to know him through the legacy he'd left behind, I would somehow be able to see myself more clearly.

I know now, trauma is what stole my identity. It wasn't my absentee father.

In 1970, Nick was spiraling further inside a drug-induced whirlwind that began at a Grateful Dead concert at the Filmore East in New York City. He was hanging out backstage with Dennis Hopper when they were approached by a Brian Jones lookalike named Arthur Whittal, a young New York University film student turned drug dealer whose stepfather was one of the founders of Suffolk Downs race track.

"I sort of recognized Dennis. He looked like somebody interesting. He had a big beard. They both looked bizarre. You know, big tall Nick with the eye patch and shorter Dennis covered in a beard. I had a big bag of cocaine in my pocket, about a half an ounce," Arthur said. After the show Dennis and Nick brought Arthur and his wife, Phyllis, a clothing designer, back to the Chelsea Hotel.

"I was cutting Bolivian and Peruvian flake. A little bit of that goes a long way. We were all just talking away like mad. It was life in the fast lane," Arthur said.

Dennis returned to his thirteen-bedroom house in Taos, New Mexico where he was editing *The Last Movie*, a film he had been wanting to direct since the early sixties from a screenplay he'd cowritten with *Rebel Without a Cause* scribe, Stewart Stern, but couldn't find the financing for until the success of *Easy Rider*.

Within days, Nick joined Dennis in Taos, and shortly thereafter, Arthur, Phyllis, and Nick's young girlfriend, Susan, flew in from New York City. They took a private plane from the airport in Albuquerque to Taos. The night they arrived was windy. There were a thousand stars and mountains everywhere you turned. Nick walked towards them, the ancient Peruvian poncho he was wearing blowing in the breeze, like Clint Eastwood in *A Fistful of Dollars*.

At Hopper's there were at least forty people in the house at one time as well as a punch bowl filled with white powder. Nick was writing on scraps of paper and taping them to the ceiling so they would hang down at eye level. He wanted Dennis to bump into them so that he would "come to present time consciousness," Tim said.

Tim had driven from Los Angeles in the white Porsche Tony had bought for him from Donald Sutherland after working together on the Paul Mazursky film *Alex in Wonderland*.

According to Phyllis, Nick's need for attention was insatiable. "One morning Arthur and I were in bed. Susan was downstairs sleeping. Nick crept up and tried to jump my bones. He made an offer to swap Susan for me. He was in the mood for playing," Phyllis said.

"One of the days we were first there Nick disappeared to take a bath. He came out of the bathroom wearing bikini underwear. He had dildoes, which we had found in an upstairs closet, strapped to him so that he had these protruding penises all over his body. They were coming out of his head like a unicorn, coming out of his breasts like elongated nipples, one coming out of his stomach. It was so funny," Phyllis said.

Then Nick ran up a $2,500 phone bill.

So, Dennis Hopper kicked him out and did my father this great service and called the experimental filmmaker Ken Jacobs, who, along with Larry Gottheim, started the film department at Harpur College at Binghamton. Dennis got him a paying lecture gig, which led to a two-year teaching contract. He didn't just kick him out on the streets.

At the lecture Nick made such an impression on Tom Farrell, a star-struck student who was thrilled that the director of *Rebel Without a Cause* was on campus even though he had no idea who he was. When Nick brought Farrell up to the stage, he singled the first-year student out of a crowd of three hundred people and made him feel more important than anyone ever had. Speaking in front of the class about a demonstration he had been to in DC, Farrell "became so passionate relaying the story. Nick said, 'This is an example of acting.' I didn't know what he meant but I was fascinated."

During the lecture Nick was adamant that the only way to teach film was by making a film and had the faculty bring out equipment to prove his point.

"Nick believed film was a collective art. He felt that it was not to be analyzed or taught in a lecture hall. That the only way one was going to learn how to make films was to actually do it," Richie Bock, one of the students, said.

Following the lecture Larry Gottheim, Tom Farrell, Nick, and a crowd of twenty students got a few jugs of wine, gathered in a room in the cinema department, and continued talking.

Farrell said to Larry Gottheim, "'Hire this guy!' Everyone knew he was prospecting for a new professor. So, when people heard me say, 'Hire Nick,' they all chimed in and said, 'Yeah. Get this guy,'" Farrell said.

At the beginning of Nick's first semester teaching he announced to his class they were going to make a feature film.

He used all of the school's film equipment to make this movie with his students and didn't care that he was leaving the other film teachers and their students without any equipment. Richie Bock, one of Nick's students, was spit on for being a part of the "Nick Ray cult."

Tom Farrell thought acting in the movie that was to become *We Can't Go Home Again* would make him a star.

Nick's students thought they were making a masterpiece film with a genius director.

"In one of the first scenes in the film we get to meet the Hollywood director. I roll backwards and that's what James Dean did. I was playing a modern version of James Dean," Richie Bock said.

In the scene, the students are asking Nick if it was true that he'd directed *Rebel Without a Cause*. He looked like he'd been turned inside out; like he was an outline of a coloring-book drawing and someone had colored him in with blue watercolor. His thickness, weight, and substance were gone.

Instead of having his students make their own short films he enlisted them in making his comeback film, *We Can't Go Home Again*, a "ninety-minute feature film where we discover that the decade has led us away from the confrontations with the establishment and institutions that were so much a part of the sixties. Each individual in *We Can't Go Home Again* has turned the confrontation inward, into a search for the self," Nick wrote.

The movie could've been such a revealing sociological study if he hadn't been so psychologically frazzled. He was taking the explosiveness of the 1960s and relating them to the human implosions that were surrounding him, something like what reality television does today when they throw a group of people together in a house and instigate dramas that audiences can't wait to watch unfold. Who are we? What are we? Why are we?

Scenes were created out of improvisations based on the lives of three of the students in particular, Leslie Levinson, Tom Farrell, and Richie Bock.

"We never shot improvisation and used it in the film. We shot a scene we memorized based on our lives," Levinson said.

Leslie told me she didn't know Nick had two daughters for a couple of years. She was glad she hadn't known.

There is a scene where Leslie's running around half naked talking about getting the clap on purpose because she likes feeling dirty. She sells her body to make money to pay to keep the film going. She gets sick from shooting bad speed and Nick helps her get through it.

In his article from September 24, 1972, "Nicholas Ray: Still a Rebel With a Cause," Vincent Canby writes about going to Harpur College in Binghamton, New York for a screening of Nick's film, *We Can't Go Home Again*. He wrote, "The screening room was leaking . . . . The screening room, which also functioned as a cutting room, classroom and storage room is in the basement of the Lecture Hall at Harpur College, one of the colleges that make up the State University of New York at Binghamton. Here, for the past year, the man who directed such Hollywood movies as *In a Lonely Place, The Lusty Men,* and *Johnny Guitar*—phenomena that are as much a part of the American of the 1950s as Eisenhower, the Korean War, loafers and James Dean—has been teaching film by making a film."

Nick always talked about breaking apart the rectangular frame when talking about *We Can't Go Home Again* and sought to do this by using 35mm, 16mm, 8mm, and video synthesizer. In fact, he was using the synthesizer when he turned himself inside out.

Nick set up shop at the Chateau Marmont, taking over Bungalow 2, the same bungalow he lived in when he was at the top of his game in the 1950s. But, instead of having James Dean over, he had Richie Bock and several other former students staying with him in an attempt to edit together a screenable version of *We Can't Go Home Again* to show at Cannes.

My father was in Los Angeles, not too far from where we were living in Arleta—a nowhere area of the San Fernando Valley sandwiched somewhere between Van Nuys and Pacoima.

Nick spent the year after Cannes wandering with all of those cans of *We Can't Go Home* footage. At one point he landed in New York City, in the basement of the Bleecker Street Theater, founded by the documentarian Lionel Rogosin (*On the Bowery*) in 1960, and where William Starr was publishing *The Film Society Review*. Vincent Canby, the film critic who had sat in on his class at Harpur and written an article about the making of *We Can't Go Home* urged his colleague, film scholar and collector, Gene Stavis, to meet him.

"There was this man who looked like he could've been a bum on the Bowery. He hadn't shaved or washed in days," Canby told Stavis. "It's heartbreaking to see him there struggling, trying to put this thing together. Can you give him a call and see if you can help him?"

There was an editing facility housed in the basement alongside the publishing quarters of the *Film Society Review*. A few NYU film students were attempting to help Nick edit *We Can't Go Home Again*. He was cutting and recutting, cutting picture without sound. He was tearing everything apart. I don't know what the NYU students were thinking or how long they stayed but Gene Stavis could only stand to be around Nick for a couple of weeks. Nick wasn't making much sense. At one point he pointed to the Steenbeck monitor and said, "I'll come out in a long shot on the stage and when they see me the audience will think, 'There's the director of *Rebel Without a Cause.*'"

Stavis asked him, "They will?"

I thought of Nick as a wanderer because I didn't see him for ten years, from the time I was two until I was twelve. I never knew where he was during the years he was missing. So, I just thought of him as this man who refused to be pinned down. I'd wanted to think of myself that way, too. As someone who would end up feeling trapped if they stayed attached to any one person, place, or thing for too long. The truth is that I want those attachments.

I was walking off the grounds of the American Film Institute, where I had listened to a lecture my father gave at CalArts, and it was really beginning to dawn on me that my father had not been in Europe making movies like I had led myself to believe. He had been lecturing in Valencia, a forty-five-minute drive from our house in Arleta with Ward.

I was standing on the corner of Franklin Avenue and Western looking up into the hills. Where Western Avenue curves into Los Feliz Boulevard is the entrance to Ferndell Park. When I was nine years old, in 1972, Mark and I went hiking in the hills of Griffith Park.

Betty had driven us in her second car, a red Volkswagon 411, and dropped us off in the parking lot of the Planetarium, where Nick had once shot scenes between James Dean and Sal Mineo for *Rebel Without a Cause*. Betty waved to Mark and me as we ventured through the parking lot and into the mountainous terrain. Mark and I had been walking a trail for a half an hour when he pulled me off of it and into an area hidden from passersby. There, he unbuttoned his jeans. His hand moved toward my head and I knew that he was going to push my face down on his penis and I broke free. I ran back up to the trail. I ran as fast as I could away from him. I threw my hair into my face so when I passed by other hikers, they would not be able to see my tears. I ran not knowing where I was or if I would ever make it out of the park, which spanned four thousand and ten acres in the eastern end of the Santa Monica Mountains. After what seemed like hours, I was suddenly running downhill and into what I knew was Ferndell Park. I ran to where Franklin Avenue hit Talmadge, the avenue where my grandmother was living and had lived since my mother married Ward. My grandmother, who, when I arrived, out of breath and with a tear-streaked face, let me lie next to her on her twin bed and rest my head on her round belly, while she sipped from her blue glass of vodka.

When I stepped off the grounds of the American Film Institute, I was standing on Western and Franklin Avenues and the memory of running away from Mark on those very streets was as vivid as if they were happening to me in present time.

When I was in my late teens and early twenties, I walked the stretch of Franklin from Western to Gower all the time. I walked it drunk, stoned, and sober. I walked it with bags hanging off my shoulders. I walked it knowing where I was going to sleep at night and not.

Nick had said during the lecture, "I prefer the outlaw to the sanctimonious and the righteous and the indignant people who modify our culture, our earth, our sex lives, and our desires to fly. I'll choose the alcohol anytime."

I'm sober a long time, but I can still feel whiskey going down my throat, how it burned. That burn made me feel powerful enough to conquer anything. I also know when drinking stopped making me feel that way and how my friends changed and how I felt like an outcast and how feeling that way made me feel superior to the masses—to the people who "modify." The way I drank? I lived for it. It was my life from the time I was thirteen until I was twenty. Alcohol dictated the choices I made. And it almost ruined me, like it helped ruin my father.

As I walked the stretch of Franklin Avenue passing the Scientology Celebrity Center and the Mayfair Market, I was carrying two bags, one filled with overnight clothes, and another stuffed with notebooks, tapes, and a mini-recorder I was going to use to interview the film editor, Frank Mazzola, who had played Crunch in *Rebel Without a Cause*.

I turned left on Argyle and took Argyle to Vine. I passed the Palace nightclub where I saw the Ramones play when I was twenty-two. After the show an old friend I hadn't seen in years ran up to me, gave me a big hug, and said, "Oh my god. You're alive."

I walked on Hollywood Boulevard pressing the heels of my shoes into the names that were engraved into the center of each star. Gloria Grahame's name is engraved on this same path, at 6522 Hollywood Boulevard.

I got to a bus stop and waited. I was meeting friends on Melrose. It made sense to me that I should be able to catch a bus here and transfer to another bus at Fairfax that would take me to Melrose. A bus stopped and the doors opened. I asked the driver, "Do you go to Fairfax?"

"No. But I'll drop you there. Hop in."

I stepped inside the empty bus. The driver didn't charge me. I sat in one of the front seats that are reserved for the elderly. He was an aging metalhead with stringy, shoulder-length brown hair.

"I've been driving fourteen hours," he said. "Is there a Rhino records store near here?"

"I haven't lived here in a long time," I said.

He pulled the bus over to the curb and let me out. I met my friends for dinner.

"I've had the strangest week," I said.

Dearest Betty,

I learned from Tim, with considerable dismay, that
your last marriage has, at least temporarily, gone
sour. I don't know why, nor do I have any intention of
asking why. As I tried to explain to you at our last and
most fulfilling encounter—the most dangerous part
of my decision not to see Nicca and Julie again lay in
the hope that any image of me would disappear, and
I was happy they were in Mexico with your brother
when we last met. The risk I was taking was that there
would be no feedback from them—that their father
had rejected them, didn't love them. My darling Betty,
the only photographs I carry with me, daily, are those
I have of Julie, Nicca and you, and the three of you are
and have always been my only loves.

I, in my unmailed letters, told them that I would either
write or send them one of my obituaries which would
declare, if any did, my undying love for them. Not having had the chance to write my own obituary, except
in this film when I say, "I was interrupted," I doubt if
any cinema history or gossip columnist would include
it. But, "I was interrupted" has as much to do, or more,
perhaps, with my resolution to see the three of you
again and setting the record of love straight than any
other personal statement I have been able to make
in any of my films. As an actor, swinging in a barn
with a noose accidentally slipped around his neck,
and which his weakened arms could not release—the
only "adjustment" I could take for that scene was that
I hadn't, as yet, faced up to the responsibility I feared
would come from my decision not to be a weekend
father who could not keep his promises. Deeply, I
think I was right. As deeply, I think I was wrong.

Nick

Homecoming

Nick met Bernardo Bertolucci when he was in New York promoting *Last Tango in Paris*. Bertolucci was always influenced by Nick's relationship with his work. And being in his presence that evening was magical. Nick effortlessly won the affections of the ladies who circled around him rolling the rather large joints he continuously smoked while drinking non-stop. He was funny, seductive, a connoisseur of pleasure. He floated throughout the apartment dancing and ever so freely sharing himself with others. His lack of inhibition made Bertolucci think of how "Nick was always fighting for his freedom, to be himself with every movie he did. Sometimes it worked better than others, but you could feel in his movies the constant tension of expressing himself poetically. He was someone who was closer to a poet than a director."

Talking to Bertolucci over the phone in the early 2000s and hearing his refusal to pass any moral judgement on Nick helps me see past the mess my father was so that I can get a glimpse of the beauty of his spirit. Watching Nick, Bertolucci thought of frivolity, and said to Nick, "We are doing our night of frivolution."

I laughed when Bertolucci said this. A revolution of frivolution. Don't we all need to let loose . . .

Tom Luddy, the producer and co-founder of the Telluride Film Festival, said, "I met Nick in 1973 at a party near Lincoln

Center during the New York Film Festival. He looked ravaged but in a kind of attractive way. He was charming. I remember him standing a little sideways. He was wearing his eye patch. Bernardo Bertulucci introduced us and suggested that it would be great if I got Nick out for a retrospective of his films at the Pacific Film Archives."

Luddy was a well-known programmer who had gotten his start programming for the university film societies while he was a student at Berkeley. He was running his own movie theater, the Telegraph Cinema, when Sheldon Renan, the founder of the Pacific Film Archive, called "begging me to come help him with the programming. I started there in 1972. When he left, I became the person in charge and stayed until I left to work at Zoetrope as a producer in 1980."

Luddy returned to Berkeley after the 1973 New York Film Festival and started organizing for a retrospective of Nick's films at the Pacific Film Archives. He also agreed to pay Nick for shipping reels of *We Can't Go Home Again*, thinking that the film would be included in the program. "But what arrived in my office was about twenty boxes that had many other things in them, like vacuum cleaners and pieces of clothing," Luddy said. "My administrative guy said, 'Why are we paying for this? This is a bottle of rubbing alcohol and an electric toothbrush. What does that have to do with showing films?' He arrived right after the boxes came. It became clear he didn't have any place to go."

Tom Luddy put Nick up in the spare room of the apartment he shared with his wife. "It wasn't unusual that I would have film directors who were in trouble staying with me. He would have jugs of Almaden Mountain White Wine. He was obviously alcoholic, but you know the students and other filmmakers were attracted to him so entourages would develop around him. He would hang with other filmmakers, like Roberto Rosselini, who was excited to meet him, and go to parties. Sometimes people were shocked by his condition.

"So, Nick started telling me about how he had his students coming to work on the film, and the film arrived, sound reels, 35mm, and I paid for all of the shipping," Luddy recalled. "It was a little exorbitant. It wasn't electronic like how it is now. It was real film and it was always in a messy state. I was very close friends with Francis Coppola from the time Zoetrope started in 1969 and he would always have film screenings at his house in the Pacific Heights. I introduced him to Nick. He had this amazing building where he was doing the postproduction for *The Conversation* and *The Godfather Part II* and I asked Francis if he could help Nick and Francis said, 'Well, after hours when everybody goes home, if he doesn't mind working all night, he can use our editing tables—As long as he doesn't make a mess and you leave in the morning,'"

Nick moved into Zoetrope, which was housed in a warehouse building on 5th and Folsom in San Francisco. The esteemed film editor, Walter Murch, was cutting *The Conversation* there during the day and it was imperative that Nick be gone when Murch arrived in the morning. Nick was also expected to leave the editing room neat, to not make long distance phone calls, and not to trip the alarm system.

One morning, Nick, unaware that the business day had begun, groggily made his way out from under the couch and in front of the screen where *The Godfather Part II* was being screened for Robert Evans, the head of Paramount.

"Nick freaked everybody out," Luddy said.

"I remember coming in one morning and finding Nick asleep under the pool table," Phil Kaufman, who was editing his film, *The White Dawn*, said. "He had long hair, an eye patch. People were more into costumes, then. He was dashing. He'd been up all night, carousing, editing."

Another time, Nick was passed out at the bottom of the staircase. Two journalists were there to interview Francis Ford Coppola and when they passed a *Rebel Without a Cause* poster, they asked Luddy whatever happened to Nicholas Ray. Luddy pointed to the man sprawled out on the floor next to a jug of Almaden wine, and said, "There he is."

"Nick wasn't working so much," Tom Luddy said. "It looked a little bit like this pathetic film was a crutch that he was doing to give the illusion he was still doing something."

Jerry Jones, an East Coast photographer who used to date Arthur Whittal's cousin, was living in Mill Valley—Whittal had joined Nick in San Francisco. Jones, an admirer of Nick's movies, invested $25,000 in *We Can't Go Home Again*. According to Sheri Nelson-McLean, Nick had deluded himself into believing that the Cannes screening was a brilliant success. Jones had connected Nick with his friend Sheri, who'd recently arrived from Texas and Nick handed her the *We Can't Go Home Again* script he wanted organized. She happily agreed to help him when she returned from an already planned trip to South America.

Tom Luddy saw through the farce. "I saw *We Can't Go Home Again* a number of times. I screened it, double system, a beat-up work print with scratches. It seemed self-indulgent. An exercise that might have been good in a classroom. It wasn't coming together as any kind of compelling film, in my view. It was not a great work of art by a tortured artist. It was a mess that kept a guy in bad shape going in a sad way. Most of my friends thought it was a mess. We didn't know how to say that to Nick, though."

Coppola, exasperated with Nick's drunken shenanigans, asked Luddy to find somewhere else for him to stay. Luddy called Peter Gessner, a filmmaker and founding member of Cine Manifest, a Bay area film collective whose mission was to make political films that were rooted in real stories like the film *Northern Lights*, which focused on the family farms of North Dakota.

The films they were interested in making were the kinds of documentaries Nick had fooled Betty into thinking he dreamed of making when he and Betty were first married.

Nick was too stoned-out to see what could've been a great opportunity to get involved with a new group of young filmmakers and a way to leave *We Can't Go Home Again* behind.

Steve Wax, a member of the collective, recalled, "Peter called me and said, 'Tom just called me, and Nick Ray is over at Zoetrope. He wants us to come meet him. He wants to know if we have some space for Nick.'"

Wax added, "It was late at night. We go over to Zoetrope. We go upstairs past the pool table into this room where Nick is sitting at a mixing table that has three screens and at least eight plates so you were able to run eight different tracks or films simultaneously. We're introduced to Nick but he's working. So, we watch. He was running all of these tracks of that film. We're looking at it trying to figure out what the hell it is. It was incomprehensible. He's yelling at this kid, his editor, to cut two frames here and two frames there. Then he said, 'Bring down the janitor's laugh.' There's a guy walking in the snow at night in upstate New York. Nick's saying, 'Bring down the janitor's laugh.' There's no laugh on the track."

Peter Gessner said, "I'm looking at the footage trying to see the whole picture. I'm trying to see what the film's about. Right away I knew we were on different wavelengths."

"Peter and I—our eyes open up," Wax said. "We're electrified. This is the craziest thing we've ever seen."

Nick arrived at the Cine Manifest building on Folsom and 11th with five of his students, a flea ridden dog, reels of film, and a dozen or so brown paper bags in which he kept his personal belongings. The Cine Manifest group nicknamed Nick and his tribe, Nick and the Greasers. He was the king and they were his court.

"His students struck us as a lot more naive and younger. We were eight years out of school. They were sycophants. We identified with him because he had been kicked out of Hollywood. A lot of us had had run-ins and decided not to go mainstream," Steve Wax said.

"There were people who said they didn't find it such a great romantic thing to be involved with Nick Ray. While to the young kids, he was like a god to them. I was like that, too. We were all enamored with the idea that we were hanging out with one of the great filmmakers, even in those days, even the kind of horrible shape he was in. It made people think this is all because he's such a great artist. He's paying such a price for what he's going through. He never sold out. He could've been sitting by a swimming pool in L.A. like all the other ones but he's trying to pursue a different track. It was part of his hustle to have young people find him heroic in that way," Tom Luddy said.

Nick and his students, who were never invited, took over the Cine Manifest workspace and offices. Nick would leave his waterpik and eye patches lying on the arm of the couch where he slept. He was prone to dropping his pants and sticking a needle into his buttocks at any given moment no matter who was standing in the room with him. He told the same lie he'd always told—that they were vitamin B12 shots. One of the first things Rob Nilsson, also a Cine Manifest member, noticed about Nick was his swollen elbow—he thought maybe it was from water build up.

Nick had been admitted to the hospital twice while he was in San Francisco. Once for what Tom Luddy said the doctors called alcoholic hemorrhaging. Luddy had called Tony informing him that his father had been hospitalized, that there was fear he wouldn't make it.

Tony told Luddy, "Sorry. Been there done that." Another time Nick was in the hospital John Houseman was in town doing book signings. Luddy contacted him about Nick. Houseman had the same reaction as Tony. "Been there done that."

On shaky mornings when Nick and his drug dealer, Arthur Whittal, were wandering the streets coming down from the coke and needing a drink they frequented the Freak Bar, though its unclear whether that was actually its name or what Arthur called it because most of its patrons were missing body parts.

"Nick was just another part of the atmosphere," Peter Gessner said.

"He looked like a death mask. He had these wild eyes, this long face, the eye patch, unruly white hair," Rob Nilsson said.

It only took one month for the collective to kick Nick out. From there he moved into a sewing factory in Sausalito. There he set up a Movieola, a standing editing machine, in the back area of the factory.

Sheri Nelson-McLean, who'd returned from South America, found Nick at the sewing factory. I don't know if the students were still tagging along but Arthur was with him and they were spending all of the money Jerry Jones had invested in *We Can't Go Home Again* on cocaine. When Nelson-McLean found out she took the checkbook away. She brought Nick to her house in Mill Valley. He told her he was filled with regret over not having had contact with my sister and me. He wanted to see us but was afraid he wouldn't know what to say if he did. She encouraged him to make contact. That was in August of 1974.

Betty didn't tell Julie or me that Nick was coming home. She didn't want us to be disappointed if he didn't show. I was about to turn thirteen. I hadn't seen him since I was two and a half. I hadn't talked to him since I was five. The morning of his homecoming I stumbled half-asleep past the bathroom and into the kitchen to fix myself a cup of Taster's Choice instant coffee.

Betty was washing the dishes and singing a song she had made up, "*Lovesick lady playing with dreams so deep/Let me take you from your sleep/into his arms/Lovesick lady, are you really there/Or are you just a child crying?*"

"What song's that?" I'd rubbed my eyes.

She didn't look up from the sink. "I'm taking you clothes shopping today."

We usually shopped at the Green Stamp store on Hollywood Boulevard or at the discount warehouses in the San Fernando Valley. Green Stamps were stamp booklets you could buy at the local Food King supermarket and every time you bought groceries you would get green stamps in addition to your change. Once you filled the booklet with stamps you could go to the Green Stamp store and buy clothes and household goods for less than what it would cost in a department store.

Built in 1927 it had a huge neon sign on the top of its Renaissance style building. One of the first department stores in Los Angeles, it became known as The Broadway Hollywood in 1931 and went on to gain the reputation of being a cutting-edge retailer, having introduced women's pants to shoppers even before its New York City store. We only got to go shopping there on special occasions. I hadn't heard of anything special. I wasn't complaining. I never turned down new clothes.

Julie chose a white cotton dress with three-quarter sleeves and blue embroidered flowers around the neckline. I picked a pair of baby blue hiphugger flares and a blue long-sleeved t-shirt with a beaded Indian's head covering the front. As soon as we were home, Betty closed her bedroom door and spent the rest of the afternoon and early evening on the phone. That night at ten o'clock she appeared in our bedroom doorway and said, "I'll be back in a couple of hours. Put on your new outfits and don't go to sleep."

"Where are you going?" we asked.

"Timbuktu."

She used to always tell us Timbuktu when she didn't want us to know where she was going. For the longest time I imagined her popping herself over to Africa like Samantha in *Bewitched*. I was surprised when in high school I was on my way to Palm Springs to spend Easter vacation partying in the sun with friends and we passed a green sign that said: Timbuktu Next Exit.

"You can imagine the state I was in going to the airport," Betty said. "And then seeing him? It was the same incredible bigger than life rush I had when I saw Nicca and Julie getting off the plane from Spain. Nick didn't look bad. His movement and stance hadn't changed. On the drive back to the apartment we didn't talk much. I didn't fill him in on this, that, or the other thing. On the ride home from the airport Nick and I didn't do a lot of blah blah. I parked the car in the garage, and we walked up the two flights to the apartment. He stopped me from opening the door. I could see him getting himself grounded," Betty said.

It didn't strike me as weird that my mother expected my sister and I to get dressed up in our new clothes and wait. By that time in my life plenty of weird things had happened in my life to not think it was strange. You know, like Ward sleeping on a mattress in the middle of the living room for no apparent reason.

Julie and I sat on my twin bed, dressed up, and waited. It was past midnight when the front door opened. An old man stood behind Betty. He ducked on his way in; the top of his head skimmed the frame. His white-gray hair hung to his shoulders. He wore black jeans, a black shirt, and black cowboy boots. A black pirate's patch covered his left eye.

It was my father.

I ran to him, jumped into his arms, wrapped my legs around his. He lowered his head. His hair fell on my cheek. I closed my eyes, nestled my face into the side of his neck, inhaled the tobacco scent of his skin, and whispered, "Daddy."

I really thought I was being saved.

"Darling," he said, holding me tightly for five minutes, before letting me down. Betty confirmed my memory of running into Nick's arms. "When we opened the door, the girls, looking gorgeous, leapt up and raced toward him."

"When he walked through the door, I was shocked and betrayed. Why hadn't my mom warned me he was coming? My first thought was what a mess. He smelled like cigarettes. I thought, what did she see in him? He was an old man with an eye patch. Broken," Julie said.

"There was a deep-down hope that we could find a way to be a family again. It wasn't the old being in love with him thing. It was like, maybe the search had ended. It didn't take but a few hours to realize uh-uh, no-way, Jose!" Betty said.

I only remember four things from his visit.

The first was how I woke from a nightmare where I was running through the house we lived in with Ward on Wanda drive. A baby was screaming. I had to find it or else she was going to die. I ran out of my bedroom, and down the upstairs hallway. On my way to the spiral staircase, I searched the bathroom, the towel cabinets outside my mother's bedroom, and the closet that led to the attic. Grabbing onto the wrought iron railing, I slid down the stone stairs, and landed on the foyer. The baby was screaming in Surround Sound. I opened the coat closet next to the wooden front door and saw the baby wrapped in a white blanket. I picked her up, and when I went to kiss her, I discovered she had no head.

I woke screaming. Betty and Nick ran to my bedside. They were wrapped in the same brown blanket. They took me with them into Betty's bedroom. She says Nick wasn't allowed in her bed, but I was brought in there to lay between them. Their boozy breath hit my neck. His knee touched my calf. I knew this was going to end up in a bad place. I did not know my father. And I did not trust my mother when she'd been drinking.

Once, when we were living in the five-bedroom Spanish style house on Wanda Drive, Betty had called me into her bedroom. She and Ward had just finished having sex, and she was sprawled out on top of the white sheet, naked. Ward was taking a shower down the hall. She caught sight of me as I walked past the doorway. I was headed downstairs for a glass of juice. "Nicca," she said, and patted the mattress next. "Come lie down next to me," she said. I noticed damp spots on the white bottom sheet. She looked me straight in the eyes and said, "Sex is beautiful," and then she put a finger up my vagina and told me how one day I would get to experience the beauty of intercourse.

In 1974, I was in bed with my mother and father and I couldn't get away from them fast enough.

"Nicca retreated pretty quickly. She shut Nick off. She shut me off, too. She shut all of us off," Betty said.

Nick's homecoming was just a continuation of the craziness I had already been living through.

He roamed the apartment in his leopard print bikini briefs, and nothing else. His stomach protruded over the waistline of his underpants. There was a yellowish tone to his skin. There was always a French Gitanes cigarette hanging off of his lip. He took up all of the space in our five-room apartment, even though he hadn't brought more than a couple of changes of clothes with him. When I would come home from school, he would be sitting at the dining room table, in his leopard print briefs, without his dentures, and making ornaments out of hanger wire and index paper like he was some sort of Picasso.

"I'd come home from work and he'd be hanging these Christo-like sculptures on the patio, and I thought, oh no, they can't go there. The neighbors will see them and wonder what kind of craziness is going on in here," Betty said.

In the mornings, he couldn't remember where he'd left his dentures the night before and Betty raced around looking for them in the silverware drawer, on the closet shelf, and in the soil of her potted plants. She took his silk and cashmere clothes to the dry cleaners and paid the bill. She yelled at him, "I'm not your maid. I'm not your keeper. You have to start taking some responsibility."

"He couldn't even sit on a chair without falling off. He was always fucked up. He was losing control of his bladder."

Next, he lost his address book. Nick was two hours late coming home, and agitated. Betty was mad, because she had prepared Chicken a l'Orange for dinner. When he finally came strolling through the front door he was with his drug dealer, Arthur Whittal.

"I hated Arthur," Julie said. "He scared me. He was sleazy. He had long, stringy blonde hair. He had bad breath and reeked of booze and cigarettes. You wouldn't want to be caught dead with this guy."

Nick was upset because he had lost his address book while taking the bus to the Social Security office.

Betty recalled, "It was like he lost his life behind that. Losing that book. I remember it from the time I ever met him. That was his maniacal Bible."

Nick called 411 and asked the operator for the bus company's phone number. He worked his way up the bus company's corporate ladder. "Hello, my name is Nicholas Ray, director of *Rebel Without a Cause*. I lost my address book on one of your buses."

He raised his voice. "I don't know which bus. I took four different buses today. One down Hollywood Boulevard, another across Fairfax, or, was it Western? Christ. How am I supposed to remember the bus number or the exact time? Listen, I'm Nicholas Ray . . . ."

He was name-dropping his own name, and nobody knew who he was. It was like the way he tried to impress Julie and me by telling us he used to hang out with Lead Belly and Woody Guthrie. We had no idea who they were. Hell, I didn't even know who James Dean was in 1974.

"He had become a shell of who he was. His whole person-hood had shifted. It was like seeing a man who had been emptied out. He had emptied himself out and was like a skeleton of what he used to be," Betty said.

With the help of her longtime friend, Leslie Parrish, the actress, writer, and political activist, Betty found him a studo in a post-production house in Hollywood.

"He pretty much lived in that studio which was a relief to me because his body wasn't in the house. At the studio working on *We Can't Go Home Again* he was like Geppetto. The more I looked at the footage the more confusing it was. I said, 'What is the story? What is the beginning? The end? Do you *have* a story?' He insisted he did."

I went with Betty to see him there, once. I sat with him at the Steenbeck. We watched the footage on the editing machine's small screen. The color was muddy like a foul mood.

A girl was naked. She was refusing to put on pants. She was trying to be sexy but to me she was scary. In another scene she confessed to Nick that she'd turned a trick in hopes of raising money for the film. She didn't get the money. She was talking to a journalist and my father was watching them from across the room. He was holding his forehead like he had a migraine.

Sometimes a shape—like one you'd see under a microscope in science class—cut into the top of the frame or was super-imposed over bodies. I thought it looked like a psychedelic amoeba shape. It made me squirm.

I left him alone with the gin and cigarettes at his side. He was not the heroic adventurer I wanted him to be. He was crouched over the turning wheels, his elbows on the edge of the machine, his chin in his hands.

Betty wanted to help him get sober and asked a couple she knew who were members of Alcoholics Anonymous if they could help twelve-step him. They offered their pied-a-tier in Huntington Beach as a safe place for him to dry out. No one anticipated how bad his delirium tremors would be. It took about twenty-four hours for him to turn "into a rabid dog." It was clear to Betty, and her friends, that Nick had to be under a doctor's care. Betty took him to Los Angeles County Hospital where she admitted him into their detox ward. When the nurse was wheeling him to the detox ward, Nick started winking at Betty, like a crazy person.

"I said to him, 'Don't you wink at me. This is not funny.'"

After he had been in the hospital for a few days, Betty brought Julie and I to see him. I recognized the front of the Los Angeles County Hospital building from the opening credits of the soap opera, *General Hospital.* Nurse Jessie Brewer! Doctor Steve Hardy! Save my father!

Julie and I stood outside of his hospital room peering in at Nick. He was sitting up in bed, wearing a white paper robe, and looking frail. We were afraid of him. Julie said, "I'm not going in. Are you?"

After Nick was released from detox Betty brought him home. Even though she saw how "his craziness was a continuation of the madness I'd experienced in Spain," she let him sleep on the mattress she kept in the living room. Even though she was "experiencing him to be chaotic and scary," she left my sister and I alone in the apartment with him. "Why did I leave the girls alone with him? The situation was just another piece of hell I had to get through. I was beyond worried."

I suppose our mother didn't want to be in hell by herself and that's why she was always bringing it home and sharing it with us. I just wanted a way out. That's all I wanted from my father, a way out. But, he was always looking for his own way out.

Julie came home from school and found Nick sitting on the edge of his seat waiting for her.

"Can you get me some coke?" he asked.

Betty had made it clear to Nick that his drug dealer, Arthur Whittal, wasn't allowed to step foot in the apartment anymore.

"I said, 'I can get you pot,'" Julie said.

"No. I want coke," Nick said.

Julie, who was fourteen, asked her sixteen-year-old boy-friend, Mike, if he knew where to score some.

"I was like, 'Mike, what are we going to do? We need to get my dad some coke.' I've never done coke. Do you know anybody that can get us some coke?" Julie said.

Mike made some phone calls and found out an address in Hollywood where he could score, and within a couple of hours, came back with a gram, that he had paid for with his own money.

"I asked Nick, 'Was the coke good? Did you enjoy it?'" Julie said.

"Ah, it was all right," Nick said.

"Like it wasn't good enough for him. He didn't even pay Mike back," Julie said.

That night, Julie told Betty that Nick had sent her out to score some cocaine.

"Nick sending Julie out to buy him cocaine? That was it. I called Arthur and told him to come and get Nick out of here.

Dear Betty,

It is imperative to me to try to make myself clear—or clearer to yourself than you think you are about me, therefore I must think it is to your benefit as well as mine that you understand some of these things with an insight somewhat bolder than that which has given you such magnificent recovery and exterior control.

I did not come to this unspeakable chunk of land and people to take anything from you. I need not go into Tim's call for me regarding you and I asked for a few days to deliberate ten years of keeping one's opinion, and acting on it rightly or wrongly could very well lead that person toward an easy touch. I did not take or come to take from you. Immodestly, I viewed my action in coming here in two ways (to be of help—for Tim had somewhat overdramatized, I think) and secondly to take selfish satisfaction from a rationale provided for me to abate the longer large hunger for the sight and sound and touch of you, Julie, and Nicca. I did not come to take from you. The purpose of the coming was to give what I could and expect nothing in return. Before entering the apartment I was hesitant and afraid. I still am. And I would ask none of you to do for me what I wouldn't try to do for you. No longer am I one to be lived with.

When we met so briefly in '66 you remarked that you couldn't remember the first three years of our marriage. Yet, you do some things at least, or have tried to. But I do not expect your insight can or should be bold enough for you ever to permit your suspicion of me to disappear or a forced evasion to be appraised as less than dishonesty.

Perhaps it would have been best for me to permit the "legend" to reach the highest cloud of absurdity and somehow disappeared within it. Should such a phenomena occur I will be seeing the three of you.

For practical reasons—many of them, it is best I live apart from you and our children—but above all others I can bring you no joy.

Ciao—

N

Boys and Drinks
and Dirty Old Men

I smoked joints with my best friends from junior high, Alysa and Val, in the alleys off Hollywood Boulevard. The three of us could've passed for sisters with our long, blonde hair and blue eyes. Alysa was the most responsible one—she was an honors student and a candy striper at the local hospital. Once when she was planning on running away with Val, she left her mother a note telling her not to worry. Of course, her mother knew she wouldn't skip out on her candy striper duties before running away so her mother went directly to the hospital after reading the note and rescued Alysa from spending the night in some garage Val had found through a friend. I wasn't privy to the runaway plan because Val and I had been like sisters since we were five and she knew I would tell her parents, because her family had been my surrogate family.

When Alysa, Val, and I got stoned in the alleys off of Hollywood Boulevard, we cured our munchies with ice cream sundaes from Swensen's. We ordered hamburgers and french fries from Howard Johnson's and watched the former actresses who were wearing too much red lipstick eat their Early Bird specials. We walked past the Gold Cup restaurant where the gay boys hung out. We avoided the scientologist who asked us if we were happy with our lives. We passed the stone lions on our way down the red carpet at the Egyptian Theatre. We crossed the street and touched all of the knick-knacks in the Chinese Theatre gift store. We looked through the poster racks in every head shop. Amongst the posters of Marilyn Monroe, Janis Joplin, and Jim Morrison was a poster of James Dean starring in the movie *Rebel Without a Cause*. I stared at the words: "Directed by Nicholas Ray."

In my stoned slumber I dreamed my father was the king sitting on a throne behind crystal blue beaded curtain. He was wearing red velvet and ruby bracelets. He was eating giant turkey drumsticks. He was King Henry VIII.

Drama was the only class I didn't go to stoned even though acting made me nervous. I knew that smoking a joint would calm me down, but I worried that being high would make me forget my lines.

I wanted my teacher to like me so that she would cast me in all of the productions. She had blue eyes and graying brown hair and almost every day she wore a gray and green plaid jumper dress. She was always smiling; always enthusiastic about the plays she was introducing us to. She cast me as Jack's mother in the school's year-end production of *Jack and the Beanstalk*. When I was onstage, I felt like I was the most important person in the room.

I wanted to be an actress. I was going to get Betty to help me. She'd started working in movies when she was fourteen. Why couldn't I?

She was about to serve dinner when I brought it up.

"You have to finish college first," she said.

"You didn't."

"Well, you will."

"I don't need college. I know I want to be an actress."

"I said no."

"Daddy would let me audition."

"What?"

"Nothing."

"What did you say?"

"Daddy would let me audition."

"Don't bring your father into this."

"Well, he would." I turned my back on her and ran out of the apartment and down the staircase, two steps at a time. I stayed away long enough to make her worry I'd run away. That way when I finally did walk through the front door, she would be too relieved to be mad.

After the final show of *Jack and the Beanstalk* Betty took me out to a celebration dinner at the Italian restaurant on Hollywood Boulevard where Julie worked. We sat in a red leather cushioned booth that surrounded a tiled table. Candles dimly lit the room. Live opera singers stood in front of a piano and sang as customers raised their wine glasses and sang along. All of the waitresses looked like beauty pageant contestants. Julie said that instead of filling out applications girls dropped off 8x10 glossies. I started working there a few weeks before graduating from junior high. That summer Val and Alysa moved. Vicki, one of the waitresses I worked with, took their place.

Vicki was the most beautiful girl I'd ever seen. She had thick wavy black hair and porcelain skin. When she walked her hair swept across her shoulders. She had long eyelashes and dark eyes and a soft soothing voice. She was three years older than I was.

Vicki looked out for me at the restaurant. Men came there and hit on the waitresses. It didn't bother them that I was fourteen. Some asked me if I was still a virgin. I didn't know how to respond. Vicki told me to say, "You'd like to know, wouldn't you?"

Vicki taught me how to not give them what they wanted without losing my tip. All I had to do was smile and shake my ass when I left their table. She protected me from Al, the owner, too. He was a short man with puffy palms, a round face, and dark hair. His pants, shoes, and pullover were beige. He wore a gold wristwatch and gold-rimmed glasses. He hired prostitutes and took them to the basement. Rumor was he did some of the waitresses down there, too.

He was hardly ever there on weekend days—the shifts I worked. Whenever he did show up, he pulled me aside and made comments about my appearance. "You shouldn't wear button down sweaters over low cut blouses. Unbutton one more button. Isn't that skirt too long? Part your hair further over to the left side. Some lipstick would be nice. Have you gone to the dermatologist? There's got to be something you can do for your skin."

I worried he was going to fire me because I wasn't as beautiful as the other girls. None of them had pimples. None of them had to be told how to dress or how to wear their hair. Every time he pulled me aside, I had to swallow my tears. And every time Vicki saw the agony in my face.

"Leave her alone, Al. I'll fix her," Vicki told him.

We squeezed into the small bathroom barely fitting between the sink and the toilet. She dusted face powder over my pimples, added a touch of brown eyeshadow, mascara, red or pink lipstick. She undid a button on my blouse and tucked it into my skirt.

"Just shake your hips when he's around and he won't notice your skirt's too long, and remember, he's an asshole," she said.

"But if I was pretty . . . "

"You are," she said.

Then she took a vial of cocaine out of her apron, twisted the black lid off, and dipped a tiny silver spoon into the powder. She held the spoon underneath her nostril and snorted. She dipped the spoon into the vile and then brought it to my nose. When a quarter of a gram was gone, I looked into the mirror and stared at my reflection. My pimples were disappearing. My eyes were glittery sapphires. I was free and fresh and clean, a bright, cool spring day.

Vicki almost died in a car accident. She told me about it when we were drinking codeine cough syrup at the Mulholland Fountain on Los Feliz Boulevard. The night of her near-death experience she was in a car with a group of girls going east on Sunset Boulevard at ninety miles per hour. They spun out just before Alvarado and crashed through the plate glass window of a furniture store. Vicki's seatbelt dug through her stomach and cut into her spleen. The doctors said she was going to die. When she regained consciousness the rumors around school spread:

The devil saved her life.

Some girls warned me to stay away from Vicki. They said she was the devil's daughter. Like that was supposed to scare me.

Vicki and I spent hours at the fountain getting high. One night when we were drinking codeine out of a medicine bottle, I asked her about her father.

"Never knew him," she said.

She lived with her stepfather. She said he never liked her. He'd married her mother when she was a baby. She had a half-sister who was the child her parents adored.

"Where's your dad?" she asked.

"Making movies."

We passed the cough syrup back and forth one more time.

"I'm a bastard," Vicki said. She took another sip of codeine and lit us each a Marlboro. We smoked them at the same speed. The cherries burned down the white paper; red sparks on brown filter. We let them fall to the ground at the same time.

The codeine was turning my head into one massive tingle. She was barely able to keep her eyes open. I was cradling my head in my arms and saying "bastard."

I said, "Vicki, say bastard slow like this: baaaaaaaaasssttaaard."

"Baaaaaaaasssttaaard."

"It doesn't sound so bad when you say it like that. It kinda makes it sound like a pillow feels," I said.

"Baaaaaaaassssttaaard," we chanted.

We laughed in slow motion. Everything moved slowly: the traffic lights changing from yellow to green, the cars on Los Feliz Boulevard, the twinkling of the stars, the cough syrup to my lips, Vicki's mouth on my cheek.

I was turning into a full-fledged, boy-crazy party girl even though I didn't have a boyfriend. I was still too shy to talk to boys. I had a crush on Bill, a high school graduate who was friends with Vicki's boyfriend. Bill was twenty-one but still going to the weekend parties. He had blonde hair and blue eyes, wore corduroys, and drove a red VW bug. All of the girls had crushes on him. Every third party or so I would gather up the nerve to smile at him. If I was drunk enough, I would manage to say hi. I was the last of my group of friends to have a boyfriend. It caused me great concern. I shared my worries that there was something wrong with me with Julie. She suggested I become this boy, George's girlfriend. Everyone knew he liked me. Except me. When she pointed him out to me at school I cringed. He wasn't much taller than me, wore thick glasses and was a bit on the chunky side. I didn't like him. Julie said it didn't matter if I liked him or not. If I was his girlfriend, then other boys would become interested in me. She was calculating like Nick was calculating.

The summer before I turned sixteen, I was busy hitch-hiking to Topanga Beach with Vicki. We turned our towels into sarongs and wore them over our bikini bottoms. Getting rides was easy. We stayed on Sunset Boulevard the whole way, from Hollywood through the Pacific Palisades. At the beach we spent the hours smoking pot, taking speed, snorting coke, drinking beer. Sitting on our towels with salt-water eyes we watched the surfers, the boats, the seagulls, the waves building and crashing and spraying our Coppertone skin.

We were always high when we hitchhiked home. Once we got into a white Lincoln and didn't notice that the driver was jerking off until he turned off Pacific Coast Highway and onto Sunset. As he was passing the Jack in the Box Vicki ordered him to stop the car. He did and we jumped out. But that didn't stop us from hitching the rest of the way home.

That summer, after a school year of Friday night parties, Bill asked me out. Whenever he walked behind me, he pinched my ass and said, "I'm takin' bacon." It made me feel like I was his prize. He wanted us to be a secret because he had a girlfriend. He said that any one of his friends could tell her and she would come after me.

He showed me how to give him a blow job. I pretended not to know what to do. He sat on his double bed with his back against the wall, spreading his legs. I slipped between them, my stomach pressing on the blue satin sheets, nipples touching his hip bones. He put my hand on his sleepy penis, left his hand on top of mine and guided me up and down.

My body tensed.

He placed his hand in back of my neck and pushed my face forward. My mouth covered the slit in the head of his cock. His dick pushed my lips further apart and slid across my tongue. I pressed my lips against it squeezing hard. In my mind I saw my stepbrother's stringy brown hair hanging over me. I slid out from between Bill's legs and sat on the edge of the bed with my back to him.

"Hey," he said.

I hung my head.

"You okay?" he asked.

"My stepbrother . . . "

Bill and Mark went to junior high together. They were in the same grade. "If I'd known what that loser was doing to you, I would've kicked his ass."

I cracked open another beer.

I saw my stepbrother's face in my mind every time I gave Bill head. To this day I still sometimes see Mark's face when I'm having sex. I forced myself to keep going, sometimes crying quietly until he came. When he noticed my wet eyes and asked if those were tears, I said no. And when he asked if I was forgetting to breathe, I said maybe. And every time he laughed and said, "You've gotta breathe."

I had sex with him for the first time two months before turning sixteen. I didn't want to do it. Vicki said it was painful when boys popped your cherry. Sometimes you bled. I didn't want pain and the sight of my own blood made me queasy. I wanted to stay a virgin until I got married. Whenever I told Betty this she called me Puritanical like it was a bad thing. Bill kept pressuring me and I was afraid of losing him. So, I took three Valiums before calling him and saying, "I'm ready."

Bill went to San Francisco for a couple of weeks. He asked me if I wanted to go but I thought Betty wouldn't let me, so I didn't ask. I thought I would have to tell her I'd had sex. I wanted to believe she'd get mad. Which was pretty ridiculous since she was always encouraging me to explore my sexuality. Still, I told Bill I couldn't go.

I went to the Mulholland Fountain and met my friends before going to that weekend's parties. I drank Seagram's, Michelob, Bacardi 151, tequila, and vodka. I took a few hits off a joint. I fell face first countless times. Friends picked me up and took me home. I staggered into the apartment. I braced myself against the wall. I took a step and knocked the lamp over. I crashed into the arm of the couch. Betty came charging out of her bedroom.

"You're drunk," she said.

She wiped the blood off my face.

She walked me to the dining room table and helped me sit in a chair. She sat next to me, lit herself a Viceroy. "I'm not going to live with any more alcoholics. If you don't stop drinking, you're going to have to move out."

Through my tears I blurted out the excuses for my drunkenness. "I had sex with Bill and then he wanted me to go to San Francisco with him, but I told him I couldn't go . . . "

Having lost my virginity seemed to make my mother understand why I had gotten so drunk.

In the morning when I woke, I saw the black eye and fat lip I'd gotten the night before. The black skirt with the white flowers I'd worn was on the floor. On top of it was the black tank top I'd worn with it. There was a tear in the skirt hem. Deep down I knew I was an alcoholic. But I was only fifteen. Too young. I'd have to slow down a little. Maybe not drink tequila. Maybe drinking Bacardi 151 straight out of the pint bottle wasn't such a good idea either. Maybe I should start using a glass and mixing in some Tab. I didn't want to be an alcoholic. I looked at the skirt on the floor and blamed it for giving me a black eye. It was bad luck. I put it on a hanger, hung it in my closet, way in the back.

On December 9, 1977, Ward killed himself. Betty told Julie over dinner like it was a story she'd heard on the evening news.

Vicki came over with a bottle of pills she'd taken from her mother's medicine cabinet. We took three each and pilfered wine from Betty's jug of Almaden she kept under the kitchen sink. We sat on my bed drinking and waiting for the pills to make our brains fuzzy.

Before going out Vicki made me pretty. She blow-dried my hair and made it feather perfectly. She put blush on my cheeks, mascara on my lashes, and pink lipstick on my lips.

She told me to wear my pink dress with the ruffled hem and my platform sandals.

She was wearing all black; a low-cut leotard, wrap-around skirt, and black espadrilles that laced around her ankles. She looked like a Spanish princess. She was so beautiful.

"Feel better?" she asked.

I nodded. I always did when I was with her.

We took the bus to a club on the Sunset Strip we knew wouldn't card. We had rules about hitchhiking only during the day. I followed her inside past the bar and into the dining room. We walked past the tables and caught the eyes of all the Rod Stewart wannabes and waited for one of them to ask us to join them. Vicki tilted her head slightly to the left so that her velvety black hair fell over her right eye. I did, too. Two of the lookalikes smiled.

"Want to sit?" asked the one with the darker yellow hair.

"Sure," Vicki said, and we slid into the black leather booth.

"I'm Bob. This is Rob."

"This is Fawn and I'm Dawn," Vicki held out her hand. "Nice to meet you."

"Likewise," Rob said.

"So, what brings you ladies out?" Bob asked.

Vicki looked at me and grinned mischievously. "Looking for a good time."

We giggled. She slid her hand under the table and squeezed my thigh. I laid my fingers over hers.

"All right," Rob and Bob said.

Rob waved to the waiter. "What are you girls drinking?"

"Gin and tonic," Vicki answered.

Vicki moved in closer to Rob. My hand fell off her thigh. Bob's skin-tight velour shirt rubbed against my arm. His breath was hot in my ear. My toes curled under. The drinks came and Vicki made a toast, "To good times ahead."

"All right," the boys said, and then Rob took a gram of cocaine out of his red leather jacket pocket. He held the vile under the table and Vicki lowered her head. He dipped the spoon into the powder and brought it to her nose. She was inhaling as she rose. Rob dipped the spoon into the powder again and I leaned across Vicki's lap and inhaled the coke. Then came Rob's turn. He took two snorts for our one and passed the vial to Bob who kept it under the table but raised the spoon to his nose without lowering his face. Like Rob he took two snorts. Vicki and I finished our drinks while waiting for more coke.

"The next snort's going to cost you a kiss," Bob said.

The boys leaned into our mouths and french-kissed us.

Rob scooped more coke onto the spoon and Vicki lowered her face to the edge of the table and inhaled the white powder. I moved closer to her and Rob dug the spoon into the vial once again and put my right nostril into the cocaine. Bob ordered four gin and tonics. We snorted, we drank, we french-kissed. Snorted, drank, french-kissed. Snorted, drank. When Bob's hand slid into my crotch, I grabbed Vicki's thigh. Rob saw and must've thought it was orgy time because he said, "What about going back to my place?"

I knew what an orgy was. I walked in on one night when I woke up thirsty and went into the kitchen to get a glass of diet soda. I heard sex sounds and looked into the living room. Betty was on the mattress with two men and a woman and my mother was kissing the lady. All of their eyes were closed. All of them were naked.

"Where's your house?" Vicki answered.

"Not far," Bob replied.

"Okay," she said. "We've gotta go to the bathroom first."

"How do you know Fawn's gotta go?"

"I know everything about her." She kissed my lips.

Vicki and I walked toward the bathroom hand in hand and ran out of the club.

"I thought for a second you were serious about going home with them," I said.

"I'll kiss a loser for his drugs but he's gotta be ten times foxier before I sleep with him. Besides those two were fucking cheap. We would've had to spend three days with them to finish that gram."

The next time we went to that club we went straight upstairs to the disco. Older men with orange tans watched us dance. They invited us to sit with them. They ordered us Vodka gimlets and drew lines of coke on the tabletop. I tried not to notice the creepy way they were leering at us.

"Do you girls want to be in the movies?" they asked.

"You make movies?" I asked.

I wanted to believe they weren't pornographers, but they were. Rumor was that the club was a hangout for men working in the porn industry. It was why girls got in for free. It was why the doormen never carded. Vicki said it wasn't anything to worry about as long as you remembered to get away from the men before they got you too fucked up.

"I'm a producer," one of the men said.

"My brother's a producer. Tony Ray? Know him?"

"Heard of him," one of the men said.

"Small world," Vicki said.

"Real small," they said.

Vicki and I laughed, and the men got up from the table. We stared at our empty cocktail glasses.

"Maybe next time you should wait until we've gotten a little higher before using your brother's name," she sighed.

I was relieved when Betty told me the ABC offices were moving from West Hollywood to Century City. I was embarrassed to go to school on Mondays because I couldn't remember what I'd done at the parties over the weekend. Whenever a guy said hello to me, I filled with dread. Had I fooled around with him on the hillside next to the party house? I'd come out of blackouts a couple of times where I was making out with a boy from my high school. I practically begged Betty to move. I'd been wishing to get away from myself for at least six months. I honestly thought that if I lived closer to the Pacific Ocean, I would stop being so promiscuous.

Rent on the Westside of town was more expensive than in Los Feliz. The only apartment Betty could afford was in a building next to a bank parking lot right off of Santa Monica Boulevard near the Nuart Theater. My new high school was a rich kid's school. The first questions I was asked were, "How old are you? What kind of car do you drive? What do your parents do?" My answers to their questions were, "Sixteen, I don't, I don't know." Instead of my new neighborhood and school making me feel better about myself it made me feel poor, like my face was pressed against the glass of a candy store.

The summer before I turned seventeen, Vicki introduced me to Bryce and Glen. They were in their thirties. They lived in the Pacific Palisades. They had endless supplies of ketamine, a powder they just called "green." I snorted it even though I didn't know what it was. It made my eyes close but stay open at the same time. Made the ground slide out from under my feet but wouldn't make me fall. Robbed me of my motor skills without making me pass out.

Bryce was thin and tan. Glen had a beard, a beer belly, a hairy chest, and a tan. At first, I didn't have to fuck them. They were worried I might flip out on them and cry rape, which would've been a serious charge considering my jailbait status. But then they told Vicki not to bring me over anymore because they didn't think it was fair I was getting all the drugs for free. I didn't want to lose out on the drugs. So, weekend after weekend I participated in their orgies.

I looked for Vicki's hand. She was riding Bryce. Up and down. I closed my eyes and saw us, two girls on a carousel. My horse was brown with a crown made out of gold and ruby red jewels. Vicki's horse was beige with a thick brown tail and a sapphire studded head. We were bouncing up and down, the merry-go-round moving in circles, cotton candy in hand.

Then the merry-go-round stopped, the horses disappeared, and the bouncing ended. My eyes opened. Glen was moving me so that he was on top and I was on the bottom. He pounded into me. I couldn't see Vicki anywhere. All I saw was this gorilla man of a hairy chest. I finally found Vicki's face. Bryce's arms were wrapped around her round breasts. He was fucking her from behind. Her big brown eyes were staring into mine. We held each other's hands, moved our bodies closer. Her nipple skimmed my rib cage. Her lips fell on mine. Our mouths opened. Gorilla man disappeared.

Then Bryce pulled her away and gorilla man returned. His big chest was crushing me. I had to stop fucking. I squirmed. He asked what the matter was. I said I didn't know. He grabbed the jar of amyl nitrite they kept on a shelf above the bed and held it under my nose. The fumes turned my mind into a fun house mirror. It made the sex look like it was happening to another person, in another place.

Vicki introduced me to Stan, who she met at that club on Sunset. He introduced us to rich men who wore suits and ties and drove Rolls Royces, Porsches, Jaguars, and Mercedes. In exchange for sex they got us high on massive amounts of coke. I never admitted to myself that I was turning tricks for drugs. I went to their houses in the hills above Sunset Boulevard. They gave me cocaine and I gave them my sixteen-year-old body.

When I was in bed with the men I was sexy, I was wanted, I was loved. When I was coming down off the coke, I saw them, their wrinkled skin, and gray hair. I begged them for more drugs. Sometimes they gave me what I asked for. Other times they were coming down too, and saw me, an underaged girl in their bed, and they just wanted me to get the hell out of their house.

The name of one of the men was written on the side of a building on the Sunset Strip. Every time I passed by it, I shuddered. I think he said he made movies. I don't know if he knew I was my father's daughter.

Stan arranged for Vicki and me to meet some famous rock stars that were staying at a house in Malibu. It was one of those rare weekends Betty didn't go to Sandstone, the free love club in Topanga Canyon. I was putting on my pink halter dress when she walked into my room.

"Where are you going?" she asked.

"Me and Vicki are going to meet these famous . . . I mean, we're going to a party."

"Famous who?"

"Musicians."

"And how do you know them?"

"This guy Vicki knows."

"And what is this 'guy's' name?"

"Stan."

"And how does Vicki know Stan?"

"I know him, too."

"How?"

"We met him at a club."

"And what does Stan do?"

I shrugged.

"Nicca. What does Stan do?"

"He introduces us to people."

"To what kind of people?"

"I don't know. Guys?"

"And what are you going to do with these 'guys'?"

"Hang out."

"And why would they want to hang out with you?"

"Because I'm pretty?"

"If they're famous don't you think they already know a lot of pretty women?"

"Maybe Stan told them something nice about me. Maybe they want to make me famous, too."

"He's prostituting you."

"Just because someone wants to help me get famous, he's got to be prostituting me?"

She grabbed a chunk of my hair, dragged me across the room, and pushed me onto my bed.

"You are not going. Do you hear me? You're not leaving this house. If I have to sit on top of you to stop you from going, I will. And I don't want you seeing Vicki anymore. I should've put my foot down long ago and forbid you to see that girl."

"What are you talking about?"

"She might not care that she's prostituting herself, but you are my daughter, my baby girl, and I will not let you leave this house."

She dragged me into the living room, grabbed the phone, shoving the receiver into my hand.

"You're going to call her right now."

"No."

"Do it, Nicca, or you'll be sorry."

"Be sorry? What are you going to do to me?"

"Whatever I have to."

"Can I at least be alone with her when I do it?"

"No."

I wanted to tell Vicki I was sorry. I wanted to tell her I loved her. When we kissed and our naked bodies touched it made the orgies bearable. She was the only girl I wanted sexually.

She was the only person I wanted to say I love you to.

"Vicki? It's me."

"What's wrong?"

"I can't go."

"Don't cry."

"I'm sorry."

"Are you all right?" she asked.

"My mother says we're prostituting ourselves."

"She's fucking nuts."

"She won't let me see you anymore."

"What?"

Betty grabbed the receiver from my hand, and said, "I mean it, Vicki. You leave my daughter alone."

I stormed off to my bedroom, put on my headphones and sang along to the Doors. Hunger. I had it. I craved for everything. Why couldn't I be Jim Morrison carousing through the Hollywood streets, bottle of gin in tow, kissing girls and kissing boys and singing on the top of my drunken lungs?

Well, for one thing, Morrison was dead.

Break Your Plans Because I Have Five Minutes to Give You

Pierre Cottrell, a French producer who also worked putting subtitles on films, had done the subtitles for Wim Wenders' film *Kings of the Road* and was producing Wenders' *The American Friend*, based on the Patricia Highsmith novel *Ripley's Game*. *The American Friend* starred Bruno Ganz and Dennis Hopper and featured Sam Fuller. Originally Wenders wanted Jack Nicholson to play the part of Ripley, but Nicholson's scheduling conflicts wouldn't permit him to, so Nicholson suggested Wenders cast Dennis Hopper as Ripley. Hopper arrived on the Hamburg set from the Philippines jungle, fresh off the *Apocalypse Now* shoot.

"He was scarily wild. Reckless and irresponsible. On every drug in the book. He took everything at the same time. He was clearly suicidal. After shooting the first few days I told Dennis, 'I don't want you to die on my set. If you continue like this I will have to recast your part.' I told him in no uncertain terms that I couldn't work with somebody who didn't even know who he was or why he was there. Dennis really sobered up. He decided he wanted to live after all. He always referred to *American Friend* as the film that saved his life. He called me his St. Bernard dog who found him in the avalanche," Wenders said.

Nick, who had finally dried out, was sober a couple of months when *The American Friend* production moved from Hamburg to New York City to shoot the scenes featuring Sam

Fuller. Fuller was delayed getting to the set and in those several days of waiting for his arrival, Pierre Cottrell introduced Wim Wenders to Nick. Wenders saw that Nick was in financial need and offered him a part in *American Friend,* figuring they could shoot new scenes while waiting for Fuller.

Wenders thought Derwatt, a character who appeared in earlier Ripley novels, but not in *Ripley's Game,* would appeal to Nick.

In the background of the Patricia Highsmith stories there were forged paintings. Wim Wenders came up with the idea of including Derwatt, the painter of those forgeries in his film.

"I don't remember if Nick was familiar with the work of Patricia Highsmith, but I told him about the character of a painter who is believed to be dead and is now forging his own paintings. Nick was immediately attracted to the idea of the dead painter continuing to produce. He related to the character in a deep way. Maybe because of his own biography. Nick in a strange way, in terms of his filmmaking career, was like a dead master himself at that time," Wenders said.

In his personal life Nick was taking stock of how much he had lost because of alcohol. Maybe that's why Nick showed up unexpectedly during the summer of 1977. He didn't reek of booze or walk around our apartment in leopard print bikini briefs. His drug dealer, Arthur, wasn't with him. He came to our apartment alone. He was tall. He stared at me with piercing blue eyes. He wasn't wearing his eyepatch. I wouldn't give him a chance to get close to me. I was mad at him because I was forced to cancel a date with David. Why should I have to cancel my plans for my father? He never canceled his plans for me. He took Betty and I to a restaurant in Beverly Hills that had burgundy leather booths. I sat across from them. I wouldn't open my menu. I refused to talk. They ordered me lobster. I didn't know how to eat it. Nick demonstrated how. I ignored him. That night he slept over. In the morning when I woke he was gone but he had slipped a letter under my door.

It read:

> Sometimes we resent criticism because we know it is unjust. We know there is a bad or mean purpose behind it. Sometimes we resent criticism because we suspect we deserve it, and may be correct but we haven't yet taken the time to figure it out for ourselves and it makes us uncomfortable. It irritates us, we resent it, it makes us angry because we fear it may be true. We nearly always fear that which is unknown to us so the logical, simplest thing for us to do is to take the time alone, or with someone we trust and find out about it. Sometimes we feel more comfortable if we do it alone because then nobody else can see how difficult it is to be honest with ourselves but eventually we learn that nearly everybody else has the same problem. When we learn that, or find it to be true of somebody else we've usually started the foundation of a friendship because we have found something real to talk about and have talked about it.
>
> First. I have resented criticism. Most when I have been criticized for something I know is justified; and especially when I have been trying to correct my faults without anybody having had to tell me. This is when I'm in danger. Then I think, I know nobody understands me. Nobody cared enough about me to notice how hard I've been trying then I say to hell with it. I may as well hang on to my faults. Not only that I'll make my fault bigger. And when I do that it makes them pay attention, or even hurts them, and I'll be even with them, etc. etc. But does it hurt them? Did it? Maybe it did, a little if they truly cared for me. But who did it hurt the most? The longest? When I'm honest

about it to myself I know it is I who was damaged the most and what is so terrible is that I didn't have to get even or show anybody in the first place. What could I have done? What should I have done instead of saying to hell with it?

I'll do the same fault over and over again. I'll make it a habit and really be a loner. I'll be the best bastard loner in the whole miserable lot of loners. I'll be the most wasted of the wasted, the orneriest of the ornery, the loudest of the loud, the sloppiest of the sloppy, the most sullen of the sullen and the angriest of the angry. How could I have avoided all that misery?

For one thing, I could have talked to someone I trusted. I could have told her or him that I thought I was making some mistakes and maybe doing some things wrong but I was trying to correct those things. What's more, I could have asked that person to help me a little bit, or even a lot, just by letting me talk about it sometimes. And maybe just trying to correct my own faults was too much in my head and I wasn't really doing anything about it. But if I had just let somebody know I was trying to do something and already knew I had to do something then I wouldn't have been misunderstood in the first place. At least not by everybody. So maybe I wouldn't have had to go through all that misery.

At least not alone.

And *whoosh*. Nick was gone.

Dear Darling, I've Come
to Say Goodbye

Nick called Betty on a Saturday afternoon in February of 1978 and asked her to bring me to John Houseman's house on the Malibu Colony, where he was staying. I had switched off the fuck you Nick voice in my head and switched on the voice that said, I need to see Nick more than I need anything else in my life. I'd started believing that Nick understood me better than Betty ever would. I based this on two things. One was reading in a book that Nicholas Ray understood teenage angst and juvenile delinquency. The second was based on that letter he had slipped under my bedroom door.

I could not wait to go. He was going to be the person I could trust with my innermost secrets. He was the one person who was going to make me feel less alone. I knew it. Because when he had written that letter to me, he knew who he was speaking to. He knew the kinds of things I was thinking about while Betty never asked me what I was thinking about.

In February 1978, Nick had just finished filming Miloš Forman's *Hair,* based on the popular sixties play of the same name, at a military camp in Barstow, California, a town in the desert. Forman had cast Nick as the general on the recommendation of his screenwriter, Michael Weller, who played in a weekly poker game with Nick on the Lower East Side. Originally, Nick was contracted for one week, but, because it was evident that Nick needed money, Forman let Nick stay on the payroll for two weeks. No one on set was aware that Nick had been diagnosed with cancer just two months before.

I learned from my stepmother Susan's book, *I Was Inter-rupted*, that doctors found a tumor in Nick's right lung, in November of 1977. On December 14, Nick entered Roosevelt hospital. The next day Nick had a liver and brain scan. The surgeon was optimistic. On December 23, after a three-hour operation, the doctors decided to leave the tumor inside. Once they opened Nick up, they discovered his condition was much worse than they'd thought.

In 2007, I was talking to Miloš Forman and learned that he was mortified to think that the smoke machines used during the scene in the movie, *Hair*, where Nick is talking to the troops, were any way connected to Nick's imminent death. "Only later did I find out he was in the final stage of lung cancer. For me, I was, 'My God.' I felt like I had contributed to killing him. Nobody had told me he was sick. And I had exposed him to the smoke," Forman said.

In February 1978, Betty and I were going about our Saturday routine. She was putting away the groceries and I was listening to Van Halen's latest record, *Van Halen*. We were living in an apartment on Butler Avenue between Santa Monica Boulevard and Ohio Street. It was on the ground floor of a nondescript brown building across the street from a Bank of America. The apartment wasn't much, but it meant more to me than anything my mother had ever bought me, because I had begged her to move to the west side of town. I had wanted a new neighbor-hood and a new school to bring about change in me.

This time when Nick called out of the blue, Betty certainly wasn't singing "Lovesick Lady" anymore. She was furious with him for expecting her to drop everything so that she could drive me to Malibu. "I just hated it when Nick would bolt into town and play Hollywood with the kids. Bringing Nicca to Houseman's! Why would he bring her there? Houseman had never been a part of her life," Betty said.

I'll tell you why he couldn't come to us. Where he was staying, at Houseman's Malibu Colony cottage, was far superior to the no frills one-bedroom apartment we were living in. It was like living in a box. There were only two windows, one in my bedroom, and one in the kitchen.

Neither looked out onto anything interesting. All Betty and I could offer Nick was a view of the parking lot for the Bank of America that was across the street.

In 1978, Nick's only connection to Hollywood was the past. And the only person from that period of Nick's life who remained was Houseman. They had been inseparable from 1943, when Houseman hired Nick to be in charge of the Folk Music Division of the Voice of America, to 1947, the year Houseman produced *They Live by Night*, Nick's first feature.

In 1978, when Nick called asking Betty to drive me to Houseman's house in Malibu, she flat out refused. Even when he said the reason he wanted to see me was so he could tell me in person that he was dying. He could have asked her to tell me, but he insisted on telling me himself.

Because Nick wasn't concerned with our comfort, he was concerned with his own. Not to mention how much more dramatic it was for him to have the waves of the Pacific Ocean crashing against the shore as his backdrop as he told me of his impending death.

"I found it so yucky," Betty said.

I was standing in my bedroom doorway listening to Betty tell Nick, "If you want to see your daughter you find a way to get her there."

She hung up before he had a chance to answer.

At the time, I thought she was being cruel. How could she not take me to see my father? It was as if I had forgotten what a disappointment he had been. I wasn't even mad that once again he was calling and expecting me to drop whatever plans

I had, because he wanted to see me. Granted, I had moved away from the neighborhood I had grown up in and was having a difficult time making friends in my new neighborhood, so my social calendar wasn't exactly full. Suddenly, seeing Nick was the moment I had been waiting for all of my life. And Betty was going to keep me from him.

"Why can't you take me?" I asked.

"I'm not going to drop whatever I'm doing for him."

"But you're the only one with a car," I said.

"Don't start."

"I'm not starting. Fuck."

I stormed into my bedroom and started changing into my favorite outfit: A three-tiered drawstring white skirt with a red flowered print that fell to midcalf and a matching bikini top. Years later, when I was twenty-seven, I shared with my therapist how that day I had dressed as if I were dressing for a date and felt sickened by the realization.

Nick called again. This time, to say he had arranged for Tim to pick me up.

Houseman answered the door wearing gray trousers and a powdered blue pullover. He was distant. The way he said hello and walked me to the outside deck where Nick was waiting, was more like the way a host in a fine dining restaurant kindly greets a customer before showing them to a table. I wasn't expecting him to be or act like anything. At sixteen, I had no idea what his relationship to my father was or that he was my godfather.

Nick was sitting in an Adirondack chair at the far end of the patio. He smiled the kind of smile my grandmother used to give me when she was drunk and her dentures were losing their grip. Whenever my grandmother smiled like that I had to look away. I couldn't exactly stop looking at my father. Who knew when I'd see him again? Not that I knew he was dying in that moment. I didn't. My insecurity about when I would see him again stemmed from having only seen him three times from the time I was twelve until that very moment.

Nick gestured to the matching chair across from him.

And I sat.

He was skin and bones, which made him look like he was seven feet tall. His gaunt face and sunken cheeks made his nose look long. He started coughing for what felt like a half an hour. The waves were crashing, and we were so close to the water that the whitewash mist sprayed our skin. I counted the wood planks and watched the seagulls flying over the whitewash.

My father wasted no time in telling me, "I have cancer."

When he told me he was dying, I stopped breathing. When I came home from seeing Nick at Houseman's, in 1978, I went straight to my bedroom, and shut the door behind me. Betty didn't pry. I stared in the full-length mirror and brushed my hair, then wrote in my journal, "I saw Daddy today. I need a new hairbrush."

I was checking out, splitting off, fragmenting, using the survival skills I'd been mastering all of my life, so that I could stay alive one more day. It makes me really sad. All of these years, I've read and reread that one particular journal entry, and not understood why I hadn't written more about what it was like seeing my father for the last time.

The last months of Nick's life, Betty and I were living with Roberta, my mother's best friend since taking dance classes and dancing with Jimmy Durante. We lived in a three-bedroom apartment on La Grange and Overland not far from the Mormon Temple on Santa Monica Boulevard. We'd moved in the summer before I started twelfth grade. Roberta worked with Betty at ABC and was having a difficult time after her two children went off to college. Betty couldn't afford the rents on the West side herself and wanted a nicer apartment for us. Renting an apartment together saved both Betty and Roberta. And me too in a way. There was a 7-11 store in the strip mall on the corner where if I needed alcohol and couldn't find any in the house, I would buy NyQuil and drink that instead.

My boyfriend during my senior year of high school was the school's coke dealer. He didn't fit the profile of a drug dealer you'd see on the cop shows *Kojak* and *Baretta*. He was from a well-to-do family, a jock, and a good student with plans to go to college. He shielded me from my sadness over the impending loss of my father by treating me like a princess. He showed his love for me through his generosity. I was given everything I could possibly want. We went to every concert. We ate at the finest restaurants. He even gave me a sapphire and diamond ring. I thought that I'd finally become the good girl I'd always wanted to be because he surrounded me with the finest things.

It took looking through the journals I was keeping during those months to remember that I was acutely aware of Nick's impending death. My constant cocaine high helped me remove myself from whatever it was I was feeling about losing the father I never knew.

March 24, 1978: "Talked to Daddy. Daddy sounds okay. I hope he doesn't die. He won't. He won't."

September 28, 1978: "Daddy's going back into the hospital. He doesn't have any tumors, but he's been fainting and stuff. They are going to send money to us so we can see him before he dies."

October 11, 1978: "My father has cancer again and this time I really think he's had it. He is going back into the hospital. He doesn't have any tumors but he is fainting. I just want to see him before he dies. What a morbid thought. Why does life have to include death? It's just so unfair. Especially when there's not enough time. I don't think I will ever get to know my father the way I wanted. I'm sad about it. I know he loves me in his own special way. That's what I've got to keep thinking. I was looking at those old pictures of my mom's and came across that letter daddy wrote me where he wanted to tell me of love and was having trouble. It's all so heavy I keep crying. I'm not going to get drunk for a long, long time. I get so plastered, sick, and fuck. I hate alcohol. I hate it. I hate being an alcoholic."

October 27, 1978: "Rolling Stones. My papa is a rolling stone. My papa's dying. At this point I don't think I'll ever have the talk with him that I've always wanted to have. Dreams that are most wanted never seem to come true. Ah shit. I'm crying."

December 28, 1978: "I'm going to Palm Springs and New York. I'm positive about Palm Springs but New York I'm not so sure. I'm hesitant about seeing Daddy for a whole week. I'm afraid I'll run out of things to say. But that's nonsense. There's a whole seventeen years I have to tell him about. And a whole sixty-eight years for him to tell me about."

I never made it to New York. If I had would he have started the conversation, or would I have? My tongue gets tied and my eyes well up just thinking about what I would've said. I miss you don't leave me come back. I'm sorry I hate you don't go. I don't know what to do with my life come back don't go. Why did you tell me I never had to worry about loving or being loved?

Daddy?

Have you seen the things I've done?

The Call

We waited for the phone to ring. When it did, Julie answered. We were sitting on our mother's bed watching television.

She heard Susan on the other end of the line.

"Julie? Your father's dead."

Julie dropped the receiver.

"Mom. Telephone. Daddy's dead." And she ran outside onto Overland Avenue.

"I ran outside because I didn't want them to see I wasn't crying. I was relieved."

Betty ran after her.

I felt the ground slipping out from under my feet. Believing that Nick could save me from Betty may have been fantasy I'd harbored since 1970 when my mother married Ward, but believing that he could help me escape the emotional paralysis I felt and show me how to live an adventurous life had been my secret hope.

On June 17, 1979 I wrote: "Daddy died yesterday and I'm in a state of shock. I feel hurt and empty. The one thing I wanted was to have him get to know me and I never had the chance. I don't know how to handle death. My father's especially. I'm just shocked. I can feel something inside of me changing. I have a feeling when I'm in New York I will hear stories about my father that will enable me to understand and know him better. I see similar characteristics in us. The urge to do what we want.

The importance of being an individual. I am not going to allow society to structure me or make me go along with the way of others. I'll do what I want, be whom I want to be, and act the way I want. Daddy's death brings these needs to me in a much stronger way."

The next day Chris Sievernich, the producer of *Lightning Over Water,* the docudrama Nick spent the last weeks of his life making with Wim Wenders, picked Julie and me up and flew with us to New York City because there was going to be a memorial for Nick at Lincoln Center. We stayed with Susan, Nick's last wife, in the loft on Spring Street they'd shared since 1976, and where *Lightning Over Water* had been filmed. There was still camera and lighting equipment in the loft when my sister and I arrived. *Lightning Over Water* chronicled Nick's last days dying of cancer. It was hard for me, at seventeen, to reconcile how my father had chosen making a film in his last days over spending time with me.

"*Lightning Over Water* was the way he wanted to die. As he said, 'I don't give a fuck what I'm shooting on. Cardboard, celluloid. Give me anything. I'll shoot the film," Chris Sievernich said.

I don't remember if I had known that Nick was making a movie while he was dying. "Nick felt making the film would protect him not so much from dying—Nick was pretty fearless. He wasn't afraid of dying. But protect him from a hole he might fall into. And protect him from regretting his own history," Wim Wenders said.

Critics of the film saw it as exploiting Nick but the cinematographer, Ed Lachman, said it best when he told me, "Nick exploited the audience because he wanted to make this film. He wanted to participate."

When Betty was dying of cancer in 2016, she had wanted to be a participant in her death as well. She asked the chaplain what she could do, how she could be a part of it. In her last days she was as engaged with life as she was with her own death. I sat with her in a room full of people when she announced that she was dying. There was no self-pity involved and no fear.

This was her next adventure and we were all invited to be a part of it. Nick and Betty were alike in this way.

When I arrived in New York City in 1979, I met some of the people who had been involved in making *Lightning Over Water*. I was confused that Nick had chosen to spend his time with them and not me. It was the first time I heard people who were not his children saying that he had been a father to them. I know they didn't say this to hurt me. That Nick was more of a father to these people than he was to his children is something I have had to accept. I ask myself, won't it set me free to be as cavalier as Pierre Cottrell, when he says, "Who cares if he was a father to us."

I have suffered a crippling resentment over how easily being a surrogate father came to Nick. Being a surrogate mother came just as easily to Betty. Spending the last months of her life with her and watching her engage with the younger women she counted as daughters and seeing how much they gave to her life and her to theirs helped me to look at my father's ability to be there as a father for everyone except his children. I don't know that any one of his kids would have been on the *Lightning Over Water* film shoot. I say this and then I remember that Tim was there. He was working as one of the cameramen, along with Ed Lachman. Tim was helping to chronicle our father's last days. At seventeen there was no way I could have been a part of that. I had no relationship with Nick except for my fantasies of what may have been or could be. When I took care of my mother as she was dying from throat cancer, I used up all of my energies just so she could enjoy and endure and be present for the last days of her life.

My mother needed to be surrounded by friends up until her last hours. Nick needed to be surrounded by a film crew.

I can see now how resenting the young people he chose to be around instead of me only kept me from seeing what Nick Ray gave to them.

"We were all aware that Nick was thriving on having a working crew around him. I once said, too, that we would have done it without film in the cameras just to accompany Nick but as we knew he was expecting the cameras were running for real, we were doing it for real. We all knew, all of us behind the camera, that the stakes were really high, that we were treading on very touchy grounds and that we were part of a therapy or some sort of life-saving procedure that was extremely unusual, to say the least, where the realities of life and death were by far stronger than in any fiction we had ever been involved in. Every single one of us on the set knew this, felt this, lived with this, and dreamed of this," Wim Wenders said.

In 2016, when I was taking care of Betty during the last weeks of her life, I stepped back and put what I thought I needed from her aside. Those weeks weren't about me. They were about making her as comfortable as possible so that she could enjoy what time she had left. My mother loved people and she needed them around her at all times. It was one of the things about her that made me feel I didn't matter. She had so many "adopted" daughters, as she would call the young women who followed her every word, that I felt like I was never enough. In those last weeks I watched how much joy these women gave her, and I also saw how much hope she gave them.

What Nick and Betty did in their last weeks was show us how we didn't need to fear death. We don't have to stop living because we are dying.

In 1979, when Nick died, Susan asked if the *Lightning Over Water* production could cover the cost of flying Julie and I to

New York. Betty flew out a few days later and stayed in Princeton with her brother, David.

It was the first time I'd met Susan. She was ten years and one month older than I was. She was small in height and size. She wore a perfectly pressed white linen dress. Her dark hair was tied back in a loose ponytail. She sat on a stool at the butcher-block counter, talking on the phone, and organizing the memorial. She smoked Marlboros. She brewed coffee in a silver pot.

She showed me photographs of Nick taken in the months prior to his death.

He looked like a newborn bird, fuzzy headed, unsteady, and fragile. He was pale with faded red lips. All of his features were pronounced. His ears, jaw, and nose were too big. His cheekbones and eyes were sunken in.

On June 19, 1979, I wrote, "When I close my eyes, I visualize Daddy walking towards me and he disappears into blackness. It's always black. This happens every time I close my eyes. I still cry whenever I talk about him. I feel a hollow pit of emptiness in my stomach every time I think about him. I saw some recent pictures of him. Just before he died. His head was shaven. He was extremely thin. I choked up. I feel so solemn. Serious. I may be serious for a while. I'm trying to get my head together but I'm not going to press it."

There was a constant stream of people, friends and fans of Nick's, coming in and out of the loft.

"I just wanted a little bit of privacy. There were twenty people just crashing there and I'm like just let me use the bathroom and please don't open the door. Our father had just died, and it was like a party," Julie said.

Tim's best friend from his Switzerland boarding school days, Harry Bromley-Davenport, swaggered into the loft looking like a cross between Tiny Tim and someone who should've played with the Velvet Underground. He hit it off with Sherry Nelson-McClean, the Anne Francis lookalike from Texas who met Nick in San Francisco. They snuck off into the bedroom that was behind two large sheets of sheetrock. Even Arthur was there pouring pure white mescaline powder into a punch bowl for everyone's pleasure including mine.

"I was like, 'Here Nicca, take some more of this. It'll make you feel better.' If we do more drugs it'll make us feel better. It was my remedy all of the time," Julie said.

I got strep throat my third day there. Getting sick had been my way of dealing with stress since I was eight and Betty married Ward.

"All the people were talking about Nick with this nostalgia. I thought they were full of shit. They were talking about this man who was in his leopard print underwear, a complete fucking mess. He couldn't even support himself. They didn't want anything to do with Nicca or I. We were inconsequential. I didn't understand why I was even there," Julie said.

One night, Arthur gave Julie and I each a gram of pure mescaline, and Chris Sievernich dropped us off at the disco New York, New York. We hadn't even gotten to the dance floor when two middle aged businessmen asked us to join them at the bar. They each moved down a seat so that the two stools between them were free for us to sit in. They ordered me a gin and tonic and Julie a Kahlúa and milk.

"So, where are you girls from?"

"L.A."

"So ah, what brought you to New York?" they asked.

"Our father died."

As soon as we said those words we bowled over in uncontrollable laughter. We were keeling over, holding our guts, practically peeing in our pants. Much to their relief we excused ourselves and ran into the bathroom where we squeezed into one stall and proceeded to finish what was left of our mescaline.

"Nicca and I were having so much fun that week. We both wanted to live in New York. We tried to get out of the loft as much as possible. We thought Susan was cool for having put all of this together and having drugs in her loft. She told us that Nick loved us very much and I thought, Ummm. Nicca and I talked about what a mess he was. She remembered him at that point, and we were both, 'Oh yeah, our father, whatever,'" Julie said.

I remembered Nick at that point? I talked about what a mess he was? Then why have I told myself since I was eighteen that I wanted to live with him after I graduated from high school, but he died and left me feeling like I had nowhere to go? Was this a lie I told myself so I could justifiably drink and do drugs with reckless abandon or was my wanting to live with him once I graduated high school really a secret wish I harbored for years? Am I deceptive? Do I present myself one way when in truth I am not that way at all? The writer, Joan Didion, says we tell ourselves stories in order to live. Do we tell ourselves lies in order to survive? Could my father's abandonment have crushed me that much that my entire life I've been lying to myself about what he meant to me?

What if he meant nothing to me?

Have I spent all of these years since 1999 looking for reasons he did matter?

He had to have mattered.

He was my father.

I am his namesake.

He was my father.

The day of Nick's memorial Betty took an early morning train into the city from Princeton, where she was staying with David. She met Julie and me at the loft and together, with Arthur, we headed to Lincoln Center.

"When we got there, we didn't know exactly where to go. We wound up going underground and were trapped in what felt like a vault," Betty said.

We got lost. It reminded me of how when I was a kid my mother always got lost going to the Los Angeles International Airport. She never drove the freeways, so we took the surface streets from Los Feliz to Westchester and every time we ended up in Manhattan Beach instead of at the TWA terminal. Entering Lincoln Center, we were instructed to go to the performers entrance, which I remember being like a series of hallways that led to the backstage area. So, we were in this tunnel and my mother "didn't know how to get out. I get terrified when I don't know where I am. Arthur—I loved that guy. I really did. He hurled his body against this door and unlocked it. And we scrambled out of there."

"Mom was horrified with the memorial. She told me it was absolutely macabre. She thought Nick would have hated it. She didn't think anyone there got him at all. She was telling me she thought it was so full of shit and I kept saying, 'Yeah, yeah, yeah Mom. Daddy would have hated it," Julie said.

My mother was basing her opinion on who Nick had been twenty-two years earlier.

"There were hundreds of people at the memorial," Julie said.

There were people in attendance who were much more qualified to talk about Nick than either Julie or me. Like Elia Kazan who was sitting in the back with Tony. Or even Nick's wives, Jean, Betty, and Gloria.

Betty thought it was a hoot that Gloria Grahame was sitting two seats away from her. "I looked down in front of me and there's Gloria sitting with Tim. And she turned around and she said, 'Oh, Betty, what are *you* doing here?' And I said, 'Touche, Gloria.' I loved her. And then I looked around for Jean, and she was at the other end of the auditorium sitting with Tony."

I don't remember if, before we'd left L.A., Susan had warned Julie and me that we would be speaking at our father's memorial but she must have because I brought the letter he'd written to me about sharing our secrets with someone we trusted, the one he had slipped under my door when I was fifteen. Why else would I have brought that letter with me if not to read it at the memorial? When I showed it to Susan, she said it was perfect thing to share. She said he never spoke to people in that way. Regardless of whether that was true or not, her saying that made me feel special.

I wanted to wear a slinky lavender disco dress that I brought with me, but Susan said it was inappropriate. She suggested I wear one of her dresses instead. It was rust with a cinched waist that buttoned to the neck. The skirt was pleated and fell mid-calf. It reminded me of the dresses girls wore on the TV show *Little House on the Prairie*. It was a size too small so I had to hold my breath to make sure the buttons wouldn't pop open. On top of being uncomfortable because the dress was too tight, I was still sick with strep and finding it painful to talk.

Alan Lomax opened the memorial by saying, "My name is Alan Lomax and I'm greatly honored to be given the privilege to be talking here tonight about one of my oldest and most beloved friends, Nicholas Ray, and to be with you all here in remembering him."

He stood at the podium looking like a bear. The second he started speaking I dug my toes into the stage floor.

Lomax continued, "Many people all over the world are with us this evening thinking about the man that we all loved so much and admired so much, this great creative American, Nicholas Ray. His admirers are legion. His friends are scattered all across America and not all of them can be with us in this theater. But they all share with us our love and belief in this remarkable man, and in our grief over his painful end. Nicholas Ray was more fortunate than most artists. He communicated greatly in his own time. He changed and bettered the world he lived in, and he was loved and rewarded and revered in the time that he lived. He was loved by women and he was the father of beautiful children who look like him and are like him in his charms and talent and gifts and good looks. These children are Anthony Ray, Timothy Ray, Julie Ray, and Nicca Ray. They're with us here tonight."

He called Julie to the microphone and all she said was, "Everyone knows Nick was a great man, but he was also really difficult."

Everyone laughed.

She was so poised, so less emotional, so much more approachable than me.

I walked to the podium and read from the three-page letter he had slipped under my bedroom door.

As soon as I said the words, "Sometimes we resent criticism because we know it is unjust . . . " I burst into tears.

"I couldn't understand why she was crying. We had had such a fun week," Julie said.

In spite of my sobbing I continued to read.

"It was just heartbreaking," Betty said.

Harry Bromley-Davenport said watching me on stage was horrifying.

I saw my mother leaving.

"I was feeling very uncomfortable. So, I went outside for a smoke," Betty said.

When I finished reading it was so quiet you could hear a pin drop.

What I had just shared was the most personal encounter I'd ever had with my father. Granted, we'd never discussed the contents of the letter, but in it he had spoken to me like no one else ever had. I had felt a connection with him. I had felt like he had seen me. He had targeted much of what had been troubling me without us ever talking about any of it. He *knew* me. That's what I needed acknowledged. I thought everyone sitting in that auditorium would stand up and cheer. Or give me a hug. Or say, 'You really are your father's daughter.' Instead I stood in front of everyone crying and the room stood still.

The isolation was excruciating.

I could never really talk about how lonely I'd felt up on that stage. After the memorial Betty hogged the conversation with a story about what had happened to her when she'd gone out for a smoke. She said, "Down the street I see this real long bicycle with a tall black man pedaling. I mean, he was like out of *King Solomon's Mines*. He had all kinds of stuff on this bike. Feathers and tambourines and all kinds of stuff. I'm smoking this cigarette and watching this apparition come toward me and his feet sidled down on the pavement and he looked up at me and said, 'What's going on today?' I said, 'A memorial for my children's father.' He said, 'Oh, he taught you how to kick ass. Now it's your turn.' And he pedaled off. And I thought, perfect epitaph for Nick."

My mother always took center stage and people *loved* listening to her. I just started feeling invisible. It was easier to go inward than it was to articulate what my father's death meant to me. I couldn't make small talk. I couldn't sum up who he was in a couple of palatable sentences. I couldn't hide my anguish. It was better for me, and everyone around me, if I just stayed quiet.

Back at the loft, Arthur poured more pure mescaline into the punch bowl, and I did what I always did when I was out of sorts, I got high.

Abandon

When I went back to Los Angeles after the memorial, I started having a recurring dream. It went like this: My father was staying at the Century City Plaza Hotel because he wanted to be close to his family. I was sitting on a bench outside of Judy's clothing store in the Century City Mall and got the feeling he was dead. I was running to the hotel and my back went out. I couldn't run anymore. I saw Val, my childhood best friend, and wanted her to help me get to my father but she said she never liked his most famous film, *Rebel Without a Cause*. I screamed at her, "I never want to see you again." I ran to the hotel with my back hunched over. Guards were blocking the entrance to his room. I told them who I was, but they didn't believe me. I begged them to please let me see him, please. My mother appeared. She was screaming at me, "You're too late. Too late."

That summer of 1979, I was waking every morning with a head full of father, seeing the pictures Susan had shown me, the ones of Nick without hair, gaunt face. He was tall and thin, barely any flesh left on his bone. In some of the pictures he had this look in his eyes, like he was alerting us: Death was coming.

Relief came when I met Jeffrey Jolson-Colburn at an afternoon pool party in Beverly Hills. He was related somehow to Al Jolson, but I never could figure out how. He was lying out by the pool. His slinky body was propped up on his left elbow. He wore a watch with a thick gold band around his wrist. Tan trunks fitted, but not tight. Smooth olive skin with a sprinkle of hair on his chest. Gold chain around his neck. His features were delicate, brown eyes, curly brown hair just covering his ears. We spent the afternoons sipping Piña Coladas. I concentrated on drinking slow but the minute my concentration slipped I lost control.

Jeffrey's roommate Ruben Blue had a *Rebel Without a Cause* poster hanging in his bedroom. It was the one where James Dean leans against the wall. I thought it was a sign from my father. Jeffrey was going to be good for me. I pointed at the poster. "My father directed that."

"Yeah?" he said.

"He just died."

"I heard."

"You did?"

"It was in the papers . . . "

"Oh, yeah."

"I'm sorry," he said.

"It's not your fault."

"I know, but to lose your father . . . "

I was the stem of the champagne glass slipping and shattering across the floor. As long as I kept drinking, as long as I kept to myself, kept soaking up the sun, floating on rafts from one end of the pool to the other, as long as I smiled when Jeffrey smiled, as long as I let him light my cigarettes, as long as I inhaled the nitrous oxide from the tanks his friend stole from his father's dentist office, as long as I kept smiling no one would know I was losing my grip.

At night we went to Jeffrey's house and smoked so much coke I went from wearing a size eight to a size four in two months. I sat on his bed and he sat at his desk, cutting the coke with the razor blade. Freebasing was a long process.

"Is it ready?" I asked.

"Almost."

"Faster . . . "

"Cooking . . . "

"Hurry."

We passed the pipe. We flicked the Bic. We inhaled. We held our chests to keep our hearts from jumping out. Flicking flicking flicking making our speeches about who we were going to become.

I got really attached to Jeffrey and his cocaine. He made me feel safe. He kept my mind off serious things. In the mornings we took a few hits off the pipe and went to the beach. We spent the afternoons swimming in pools with underwater sound systems. At night we cut more coke and danced at the Odyssey, a disco in West Hollywood.

"Who loves you?" he would ask.

"You do?" I was afraid it was a trick question.

Sometimes he couldn't have sex because of all of the coke, and he would stick my toes into his mouth. I liked it because it was naughty in a harmless way. I felt so comfortable around him. Like I could be all fucked up and sad—if that's the way I was that day—just needing to escape.

That summer of 1979 we went to see the English punk band, 999, at the Hong Kong Café. It was my first official punk rock show. I dressed wrong, in tight jeans, a low-cut t-shirt, and Candies, the slip on high heeled sandals that were all the rage. Jeffrey and I were at the bar getting drinks and two girls wearing black lace-up boots, fishnets, and spiked collars pushed into me. He put his arm around me, and we moved closer to the stage, which wasn't very close because the club was jammed. The band played their instruments fast and sang their songs quick and the crowd jumped up and down and I did too. It reminded me of the way the Peanuts characters danced. I was jumping up and down and swinging my arms over my head and for a moment I felt like I was living in a comic strip and that was great; to be a comic strip, not to be real.

I went to my next punk rock show by myself. The Bags at the Hong Kong Cafe. I took the bus from Overland Avenue and Santa Monica Boulevard to Chinatown, near downtown Los Angeles. I'd read in *The Los Angeles Reader*, a weekly newspaper, that they were playing with Nervous Gender, also a band I'd never seen or heard. It was the band's name, Nervous Gender, that enticed me to take a bus alone from Westwood to Chinatown. I didn't know how to drive and hadn't met anyone on the punk rock scene at that point who could take me.

On stage, Alice Bag, a striking Hispanic woman dressed in a tight-fitting knee length raspberry colored dress, stared out at the crowd while the band played. Her thick black eyeliner dramatically extended past her eyelids to her temples. It reminded me of how the toughest cholas in junior high did their eye makeup, only she had added a beatnik edge to her application. I'd never seen anyone apply makeup like that. It was fierce just like the fierceness she projected on stage. It had nothing to do with accentuating eye color and cheekbones. She defied what the fashion magazines were teaching girls to be. We were supposed to be sunshine and happiness.

We were all supposed to want to look like Farrah Fawcett. Well, I wanted to look like Alice Bag. Then she sang, and her words cut into the air, like nothing I'd ever heard before. Her songs had a guttural anger that perfectly expressed the way I was feeling. Fast. Snap. Jab. For me, watching her performance was a revolution in what it meant to be a girl. I didn't have to present a happy disposition. I could present myself as the angry, sad, hopeless girl I was inside.

Jeffrey's other roommate, a model named Marie, introduced me to Chris Ashford. He had put out the seven-inch "Forming/ Sexboy" Germs single on his What? record label in 1977. One night at Chris's Brentwood home we played a drunk game of poker with the Germs guitarist Pat Smear (I'd be surprised if he remembered me) and his girlfriend and fellow band mate, Lorna Doom. I was wearing a sleeveless black and white striped romper with a low back that I bought at The Village Mews, a New-Wave clothing store in Westwood. I drank too much straight whiskey and passed out. When I came to the words *Nicca-is-a-fucking-whore* were scrawled across my legs and arms in black Sharpie. I thought I'd made it into punk-rock-dom.

Later that night Chris was driving Pat, Lorna, and I home and Pat threw up all over the front seat of the car. Chris peeved but laughing pulled over. He found some rags in his trunk and handed one to each of us. We were diligently wiping when Pat threw his puke-covered rag at me. I threw mine at him. He threw it back at me. Vomit rained over us all. Flecks of puke stuck to the words fucking whore. I was in heaven.

Pat Smear, who went on to play with Nirvana (and later The Foo Fighters) listened to Public Image Ltd every day all day long for seven days. He told me this one day, in 1980, when a group of us, including him, thought we should go to college and enrolled at Santa Monica Community College. We all had to take the same classes because we were punks and back then punk rockers in certain parts of Los Angeles got beat up for looking weird. Pat Smear told me he listened to PiL every day all day long when we were sitting in his living room. He lived in a house next to a Pup 'N' Taco fast food restaurant. He owned a lot of birds, too, big ones, little ones, I don't know which kinds. He fascinated me. Shortly thereafter I stopped going to college because I was too busy sleeping all day. Next time I saw him we were in the Licorice Pizza parking lot across the street from the Whisky a Go Go on the Sunset Strip. I was having trouble walking because I was so drunk and there was blood red paint smeared across my forehead because I wanted strangers to know my brain was bleeding. He was horrified not because of the fake blood but because I was so drunk I could barely stand up. I remembered this a few afternoons ago when I was listening to a dead boy sing. If he were alive today would there be track marks on his arms? I'm talking about Jefferey Lee Pierce the singer of The Gun Club, not Kurt Cobain. In 1993, Kurt Cobain performed Lead Belly's song, "In the Pines," on *MTV Unplugged.*

I had just started college at the New School University. I still didn't know much about Nick, let alone his relationship with Alan Lomax, or that Lead Belly used to cook them rice and beans at the house in Arlington, Virginia. If Kurt Cobain had ever seen any of my father's films, had he liked them? I bet anything if Nick had been alive in 1993 his mouth would have dropped watching Cobain performing "In the Pines."

Nearly a year after Nick died, I got a job at Julian's, a store on Sunset Boulevard in Silverlake, that sold jewelry, socks, and vintage dresses. Julian was one of the neighborhood's more eccentric small business owners. He was a fast-talking, chain-smoking designer, of what, I can't remember. His design studio was on the second floor of the store. It was also where he lived. He was thin with shaggy black hair and wore glasses with large round black frames. He liked wearing kimonos and silk blouses with long belled sleeves. He also liked going out for Japanese food, drinking bottles of Sake, and doing nose dives into plates of sticky rice. I had first worked for him in October 1977, at a Pumpkin Festival where he operated a stand that sold lemonade and ice cream. I ran into him again during the summer of 1980, at a party hosted by *Slash Magazine*, a punk fanzine that included a 45 rpm record of a local underground band in each issue. When Julian offered me a job working at his store I jumped at the chance. After working there for a few weeks, Marcello, a tall, thin Argentine boy with jet-black spiky hair, big brown eyes, long eyelashes, and nectarine lips walked in. He was one of the prettiest boys I'd ever seen. He leaned on the glass case and pointed to a black pin with a red "A" on it.

"How much is it?" he asked.

I took it off the shelf. "You can have it if you tell me what it means."

"Anarchy."

I knew the word from the Sex Pistols song, "Anarchy in the UK," but I had no clue what the word anarchy actually meant.

"Oh." I smiled and handed him the pin.

Marcello lived off Sunset, around the block from the store, in a one-room guesthouse with a kitchen and bathroom. He had a roommate, David, who told me that everyone said he looked like Sal Mineo. David was average height, had short black hair, plump cheeks, olive skin, and black doe-ish eyes. I had no idea who Sal Mineo was, let alone that he was one of the three leads in *Rebel Without a Cause*. David also told me, "He was murdered. I've had a premonition. I'm going to be stabbed to death, too."

I don't exactly know why David believed he was going to be stabbed just because he looked like him and was gay, but I was intrigued that he wasn't afraid to die. He was just as okay with dying as I was. I had started resigning myself to the fact that I was going to be dead soon. I know now that it is common for victims of incest to suffer from suicidal thoughts. David was not the least bit fazed by my death wish. We were both going to die and that was fine. I only hoped I wasn't with him when he got butchered with a knife, like Mineo.

Shortly after I met Marcello and David they asked if I wanted to move into a bigger house with them. I had pretty much moved into the one room guesthouse they were renting. It's not like my living with them had been planned. I was just that girl from the store on Sunset who came over one night and never left.

Marcello found a three-bedroom, one story house with brown shingles on a tree-lined street. He dreamed of turning it into a real home. You know, with living room furniture, a dining room table, and a kitchen where pancakes were flipped on Sunday mornings. I just needed somewhere to live. In order to move in we had to come up with $1,600. I had saved $400 working the graveyard shift at Dolores's, before getting the job at Julian's. I didn't tell Marcello that Julian paid me in cocaine instead of cash.

It turned out that Marcello and David's friend, Libby, needed a place to live, too. She was kicked out of her apartment across from the Whisky a Go Go after a group of us threw eggs from her balcony at the crowd of people standing in a line across the street to see the band, X, play, and her landlord got wind of how the Whisky management called the police on her and her delinquent friends.

Libby worked for outcall services, a sort-of temp agency for sex workers, if you will, and made a lot of money. She put up the $600 we needed, and on August 1, 1980, the four of us moved in together.

A couple of weeks after becoming roommates, I was driving with Libby in her root beer-colored Dodge Dart that she'd spray painted the words "Reagan Sucks" all over. We were traveling five miles per hour through the dregs of East Hollywood on Santa Monica Boulevard because she was looking for new outcall services with better paying clients. She slammed on the brakes at each corner where there were kiosks carrying *The Los Angeles Free Press* along with other throwaway newspapers that advertised sex for pay. At one of the corners was a kiosk that wouldn't open, so she kicked it with the toe of her black motorcycle boot, until the door came off its hinges. She grabbed the entire stack of throwaways and jumped into the car with a smile so big you would have thought she'd won the Powerball. I'd never met anyone like her. She was fearless. She would go to the homes and hotel rooms of these anonymous men, take money, get undressed, fuck, and leave without ever being harmed. She always appeared in control.

It wasn't long before Libby offered to take me with her on a date with two overweight Russian brothers who lived on Curson Street off of Santa Monica Boulevard, in the Little Russia section of Hollywood.

On the drive over Libby coached me, "The faster we make them come, the quicker we're done. Just follow my lead."

The fatter brother answered the door wearing a loosely tied gray terrycloth robe. It parted as he stepped aside to let us in. I caught a glimpse of his hairy groin. For a second I debated walking back out the door. Before following the brothers into the bedroom, Libby politely asked to be paid upfront. The skinnier brother, who was also wearing a gray terrycloth robe (only his was tightly tied), took a couple of hundred-dollar bills from his pocket and put them in Libby's hand. She, then, dropped them in her black patent leather purse, and we followed the brothers into a sparsely furnished bedroom. Above the king-sized bed was a sliding glass window covered with a beige Venetian blind. On the dark wood bedside table was a quart of Smirnoff and four rocks glasses. The skinnier brother poured. We toasted "to good time." The brothers untied their robes and let them fall onto the blue shag carpeting. I drank the rest of my straight Smirnoff down. Libby took my black t-shirt off and ran her hand over my breasts. She tweaked my nipple, then slid her hand down my stomach, and unbuttoned my tight, black jeans. The skinnier brother helped me take my pants off. The fatter brother unzipped Libby's black dress. I unhooked her black lace bra. The brothers slid our black panties down our legs with their teeth.

Libby and I lay in the middle of the bed. The brothers lay on either side, looking like two cherubs, watching as we fulfilled their girl-on-girl fantasy. No one brought out condoms. No one knew about AIDS yet. Libby put her finger in my mouth, and I sucked on it like it was a rattle.

The skinnier brother was pounding into me. "Like that? Like that, baby?"

I just wanted it to be over. I wanted everything to be over and then I started thinking about the hundred-dollars I was going to get and the Quaaludes I could buy and I started moaning, "Ooooo baby, c'mon, fuck me harder, you can do it harder than that."

The next day they called Libby, asking her if they could pay me $500 a week to be their personal whore. Would I come to their apartment whenever they called? I could have used the money. Julian had never paid me cash. I'd gotten a job at a restaurant in downtown Los Angeles, but the owner would only let me work in the take-out department because of my spiked hair, safety-pinned-together clothes, and spiked bracelets running up and down my arms. I only lasted at the job a few weeks. When I met the Russian brothers my only source of income was panhandling. I could have really used that $500 a week. But, in my mind, saying yes would mean I was really a prostitute. I justified turning the occasional trick as meaning I was having sex for pocket money.

Libby wasn't the only girl I knew who was having sex for pay. I had a friend whose sister lived with a sugar daddy in the hills above the Sunset Strip. Through her I met a man who paid $100 just to spend an hour rubbing cream on his privates. He was fat. I mean, FAT, rolls of blubber, fat. Like, how could you find his penis under that mass of skin? You had to dig. But, for $100 and no penetration, I could dig through his excavation site. Especially, if beforehand, I took a couple of Quaaludes or drank a 40-ounce of malt liquor.

The one trick that horrified me beyond belief was a trick I never actually turned. Libby took me to the Century City condominium of a short, dark haired man, who wanted to have sex with a sixteen-year-old. I was eighteen but Libby was positive I would be able to pass for a teenager. I wore a short black dress, knee socks, and Mary Janes, very little makeup, and combed the spike out of my hair so what little hair I had rested flat on top of my head. Libby came with me to the trick's apartment. When he answered the door, he took one look at me and said, "She's too old." He was shutting the door. Libby pushed her way halfway inside the doorway using her torso as a doorstop and screamed, "You don't know who she is. She is Nicholas Ray's daughter. She is not too old! Her father directed *Rebel Without a Cause.*"

"Get out of here," he said. "Now. Before I call the police."

"You can't call the police. You're the one who wanted to pay for sex with an underage girl."

The next day when I woke up, I was filled with a remorse so deep I could not imagine ever living out another day. I'd regretted getting too drunk before, kissing someone I shouldn't have kissed, passing out backstage, starting fights, falling down flights of stairs, spilling alcohol all over myself. That kind of regretful behavior could be forgotten by getting drunk again. Being introduced to a potential trick as Nicholas Ray's daughter? I needed to disappear.

Libby's boyfriend, Joe Blow, loved the band FEAR, whose song "I Don't Care About You (So Fuck You)" was the mantra of all of my friends. Joe Blow was a punk from the Masque days, a club founded by Brendan Mullen in 1977. Mullen was the first club owner in Los Angeles to book bands like The Germs, The Controllers, The Skulls, and The Weirdos. I had never gone there.

I did not hear about the Masque until I moved in with Libby, David, and Marcello. The people who had gone there were considered first generation punks. They had punk rock credibility I would never have.

Joe Blow started a band called the Strap on Dicks, with the intention of never playing a show. There wasn't really a band. He just liked shouting, "Come see the Strap on Dicks," wherever there was a crowd gathering, just to get a rise out of them. One afternoon, Joe Blow knocked on the window of the den that I made my bedroom and woke me up. He was dressed in camouflage and army boots. I had no idea he had really been in the Army before landing in the basement of the building that housed the Masque. Standing under the tree next to him was a chubby girl wearing a leopard print slip skirt and a white t-shirt with the print of a newspaper headline that read, "I Want Justice for my Sid," with a photograph of Sid Vicious below. I crawled out of bed and opened the front door. No one else was home. I was still wearing the black jeans and wife beater T-shirt I'd worn the night before. "Hey, can we use your kitchen?" he'd asked. "Sure," I'd said.

That was the day I met Anndoll, the person who was going to save me. Libby must have told Joe Blow I hadn't paid rent and was getting the boot. Why else would he have known to introduce me to my future roommate? Joe Blow and Anndoll had known each other for three years, since the Masque days. She had just gotten back from living in London, where she'd spent six months seeing bands, sleeping in abandoned buildings called squats, and sniffing glue. Joe Blow and Anndoll had just scored Dilaudid, an opioid in the same class as Oxycodone and morphine and used for post-operative pain, from a nearby dealer, and needed to get high quick. So, Joe Blow asked if they could shoot up in our kitchen.

Joe Blow broke off the filter from a Marlboro and rolled it into a tiny ball while Anndoll held a lit book of matches under a teaspoon to melt the two Dilaudid pills. The pills melted and Anndoll dropped the rolled-up cotton cigarette filter into the liquid. I watched as Joe Blow drew the Dilaudid up through the cotton and tapped the needle until the bubbles in the cylinder rose. He pushed the plunger up and pushed the bubbles out then stuck the point of the syringe into a vein in the crux of his arm. Anndoll followed suit, using the same needle.

She asked me if I wanted to get high.

"I'm afraid of needles. I always faint when doctors take blood."

"Oh, Nicca, one day you'll see how great it is."

Anndoll held court wherever she went. She was the punk rock queen. We went to shows every night there was a gig. We saw Eddie and the Subtitles, The Angry Samoans, Black Flag, The Castration Squad, D.O.A., The Gears, Redd Kross, The Alley Cats, Mau Maus, UXA, FEAR, The Circle Jerks, Flipper, Saccharine Trust, Wasted Youth, Mad Society, The Mentors, Channel 3, The Plugz, and on and on. She did Mae West impressions to get us backstage. She'd put her hand on her hip, a lit Benson and Hedges in her mouth, and look the bouncer up and down. Then she'd take a hit off her cigarette and say, "I generally avoid temptation unless I can't resist."

I became her giggling sidekick.

That fall of 1980, the Darby Crash band played at the Starwood. I was still living with Libby, Marcello, and David in a house on Hampton Drive in West Hollywood. Anndoll and I had shared a pint of Myers's Rum before going to the club and I'd blacked out during the show. I came out of it sitting in the living room of my house next to Brian Redz, the bass player from The Gears. We had been flirting with each other for a few weeks so when I came out of my blackout and saw his arm was around me, I figured I was his girlfriend now. It wasn't long before Redz noticed I never went to bed without a beer and started taking the bottles out of my hand before we went to sleep each night. He would gently say, "Can't you be with me without it?"

I was too scared to be sober around him. I wasn't sure exactly what he saw in me. He had red hair and blue eyes and was really cute. He didn't shoot drugs like Anndoll. He was tall and liked playing basketball. His band and his friends were the people in the bands who made the scene and there were always girls in pretty dresses with perfectly combed hair hanging around backstage flirting with him. I, on the other hand, looked like a big fat fuck you.

He was always trying to get me to be more introspective asking me questions like, why did I like slam dancing when I bruised my whole body doing it? Why do I dye my hair? Why didn't I want to be myself? He was the first person who saw I wasn't the hardcore terror I pretended to be. He wanted me to get back to whoever I'd been before, but he didn't understand that I didn't remember who that was. One night we were at the park on Robertson Boulevard between Santa Monica and Melrose, in West Hollywood, and he said to me, "I like you better sober than drunk." He was the first boy—the first person—who ever said that to me. His words really sunk in deep, but I couldn't stop drinking no matter how hard I tried and he was getting fed up.

I knew he was going to break up with me. It became evident on the night The Gears opened for the band X at the Santa Monica Civic. Redz hadn't asked me to come. My half-brother Tim had been hired to take pictures of X and invited me to come with him. I took a few Quaaludes before getting there and was standing backstage talking to Redz and drinking a beer. Everything was fine for a minute but then my beer slid out of my hands and Redz saw that I was really high. He rolled his eyes and walked away from me. I started crying.

Tim told me I was an alcoholic. I'd known that since I was fifteen. The next day he introduced me to a group of people who wanted to help me get sober. Betty agreed to let me move back home as long as I didn't drink or do any drugs. We treated my withdrawals like they were the flu.

Once I stopped withdrawing, I got a job waitressing at The International House of Pancakes on Sepulveda Boulevard in West Los Angeles. The uniform was a blue polyester dress with a full skirt and peasant-style top. Wearing it made me feel like the girl on the Swiss Miss hot chocolate packets. Still, the job gave me a chance to get my life on track. But then I saw *Lightning Over Water*, the jarring film documenting Nick's physical disintegration from cancer. Chris Sievernich called my mother and invited us to see it at a small screening room in a building near Doheny Drive and Sunset Boulevard. I didn't know what to expect but I must have had some idea that watching the movie was going to upset me. When I went to the screening, I wore thick black tights held together with tiny gold safety pins, a plain black cotton dress, motorcycle boots with chains wrapped around the ankle, and a black leather jacket covered in spikes. I thought looking tough on the outside would make me tough on the inside.

When I first saw my dying father on the screen I was startled, to say the least. It was almost as if in my wasted haze I'd forgotten he had died. I had never seen anyone dying of cancer. I hadn't visited my father in the hospital. I wasn't prepared to see him sitting on the edge of his bed, half naked, and so skinny it looked like he had knuckles up and down his spine. His skin was sallow, his eyes were sunken, his scalp was covered in peach fuzz. He was tall, gaunt, brittle. A six foot two inch radiation marker.

In the film Nick wakes up to the sound of the Mickey Mouse alarm clock. On the bedside table are a Jack in the Box, pill bottles, an almost empty glass of orange juice, a pack of cigarettes, and a full ashtray. Watching him sit up in bed is frightful. He is too thin, the bones in his neck stand out the way my grandmother's used to when she would lift her head up off the pillow she had been resting on all day. He's wearing a red long-sleeved t-shirt and no pants. Not even any underwear. He's got an old person's ass.

On screen, Wim Wenders says, "I wanted to talk to you, Nick."

"About what? Dying?"

After I moved back into my mother's apartment, Libby moved out of the house on Hampton Street, too, and into a one-bedroom apartment on Larrabee Street, off the Sunset Strip. I went to visit her the night of the screening of *Lightning Over Water*. I arrived holding a six-pack of Schlitz Malt Liquor I'd gotten the cab driver to buy for me at the 7-Eleven on the corner of Overland and Little Santa Monica Boulevard, down the street from my mother's apartment. Libby was sitting in the living room with a couple of friends, listening to Joy Division. They'd just finished painting a spider's web on her ceiling. They'd also just scored some Demerol. Libby shot me up.

After getting high we went to the Starwood on Santa Monica Boulevard and I was on the sidelines of the moshpit watching the band playing fast 1-2-3-4, and the stage divers flying off the second story bannister onto the stage below. The Demerol and hardcore rituals weren't mixing so well. I felt like I was a cardboard paper doll cut out of a book. The bodies swerving and the shaved heads moving up and down looked like people bobbing for apples. I didn't blend. I was on the outside looking in.

I was standing in the parking lot behind the fence guarded by bouncers. All I wanted was a vanilla milk shake from the donut store in the strip mall across the street. But if I left the premises, I wouldn't be allowed back in. I wanted the shake more and convinced a friend of mine to leave with me and drive me home to my mother's. We drove the scenic route through Beverly Hills where the wide streets were decorated with maple trees that looked like giant green puffs of cotton candy.

When I closed my eyes that night my mind became empty space, a sheet of black velvet, a blank sugar-coated space. Those emaciated images of my father without hair, not from balding naturally, but from clumps falling out, evaporated, and he turned into a blank slate.

The next day, I moved out of my mother's without telling her I was going to. I threw what few belongings I had into a Hefty trash bag and took the bus to Anndoll's one-room cockroach infested apartment on Highland Avenue, in a building two doors down from the parking lot of the Hollywood Bowl.

I had never seen so many roaches living in one place. They crawled up the walls. They raced over the carpet. They stood on top of the numbers inside the clock radio. They swam in the toilet bowl and hung from the toothbrush holder. If we forgot to leave the light on in the kitchen and went in there at night, a sea of roaches would be flittering across the floor.

A black lace curtain covered the only window, and punk rock fliers that had been taped to the neighborhood lampposts were now taped to the closet doors. Anndoll's oil paintings covered the walls. One, a portrait of Johnny Rotten, painted prior to his performance with PiL at the Olympic Auditorium in 1979, hung on the wall between the window and the kitchen doorway.

He had even signed it.

On the evening of the PiL concert, Anndoll had found out which hotel Johnny Rotten was staying at and hung out in the parking lot until he arrived. She held the painting up for him to see. First, he signed it, and then he invited her to his room, where they spent hours talking and doing drugs. I would never have had the guts to wait in a hotel parking lot like she had. I was in awe of her. As for the Johnny Rotten painting, it haunted me. He was always staring at me with his startled amped-up eyes.

We didn't have a phone. Ashtrays were never emptied, because we saved cigarette butts. We didn't buy tampons, we used toilet paper because we needed our money for Thunderbird wine and cheap speed like black beauties. We didn't wash our clothes even though there was a laundry in the building. We rarely bathed. We had a coffee maker and a toaster oven. We ate bread that tasted like cardboard. We cooked Top Ramen noodles in the toaster oven because we couldn't use the stove since we never paid the gas bill. We hung 8-by-10 glossies of our mothers on the bathroom wall. Underneath the pictures we wrote in red paint, MOTHER'S REVENGE I CAN FEEL IT AGAIN AND IT'S AWFUL.

We blamed our unhappiness on our mothers. Anndoll's mother, Hexie, was certified insane by the State. She was paranoid and delusional. She would come over, frantic, in the middle of the night, convinced there was someone stalking her. We would have to take her back home and stay with her for as long as it took to convince there was no one watching her through the windows. Whenever Hexie wasn't asking Anndoll to protect her, she was lashing out at her, and calling her a waste. All Anndoll wanted was for her mother to be okay . . . to be sane . . . to be a mom. But, Hexie was incapable of nurturing, and, at twenty-one, Anndoll was too young to fully comprehend the seriousness of her mother's mental illness.

Both Anndoll and I were furious at our mothers for not being the protectors, nurturers, guidance counselors, or mentors that we wanted them to be. We spewed our grievances and with much bravado claimed not to want or need them in our lives. But we did need them. That was the mother's revenge.

We spray-painted a green syringe on our bathroom door. Beside it we wrote, METH MONSTERS. Crystal methadrine was everywhere.

Our friend, Animal, shot water into the veins in his neck if he didn't have any drugs to shoot. He shaved his head and tattooed the word *lobotomy* on the side of his skull. When he wore camouflage pants, he painted his face to match. He liked the band FEAR and every time he did too much speed he'd yell out "1-2-3-4 FEAR!" at the top of his lungs. Our friend, Nanette, was in love with him and carved his name up and down her arms.

The L.A.P.D. had caught Nanette with works and she was waiting for her court date. In the meantime, her mother flew in from New Jersey in hopes of establishing a curfew, but it didn't work. Nothing could stop her from shooting drugs or drinking. Not even time spent in a "psycho-ward." That's what she called it. "When my mother made me do time in that psycho-ward," she would say, rolling her eyes.

I would come home from my job at the IHOP and find Anndoll carving the words Sid Lives into her stomach with a razor blade. I wasn't slitting my skin. I was throwing red crazy color dye on the back of my head so it looked like my head had just exploded.

There was something mentally and physically wrong with me. My urine was a burnt yellow-red and my liver always hurt. I was fantasizing about being institutionalized, thinking if I lived inside a padded cell I wouldn't have to worry about feeding, bathing, or dressing myself. I could just be a body without a soul.

Weeks later I woke to the syringe on the bathroom door staring me in the face and I thought staying on Highland another night would lead to twenty-thousand more nights, and twenty-thousand more nights were going to kill me.

It's one thing to romanticize death, it's another to feel it. My side was hurting badly, my skin was yellow-gray, my eyes were puffy and dull, my stomach bloated, my breath sour.

I went to the payphone that was in a small park across the street from our apartment building and called my sister in New York City, collect. It had been months since we'd spoken.

"Julie?"

"Nee?"

"There's something wrong with me."

"Have you called Mom?"

I started crying. "I can't."

"Nee. You have to call her. You've got to go to the doctor. You've got to get help. She'll help you. She loves you. You're her daughter."

"But I've made a mess of everything."

"It's okay. We love you. Now call her and then call me back."

"Julie? I have to get away from punk rock. Can I come live with you?"

"Yes. But first call Mom. And get out of that place you're living. I love you."

I called my mother at her ABC-TV office in Century City.

"Mommy?"

She came and got me that night. The next day the doctor told me I had hepatitis. He said I couldn't drink or do drugs anymore. I knew I wouldn't be able to do that if I stayed in Los Angeles so I convinced my mother to buy me a one-way ticket to New York.

After a few weeks of sleeping fifteen hours a day in Julie's apartment in Hoboken, New Jersey, I was feeling better. I called Nanette. Her mother had dragged her off the streets of Hollywood and back home to New Jersey. We got drunk and went to a club on Avenue A called the A7. The club was across the street from Tompkins Square Park, which was pretty much abandoned and dark and overrun with rats. We cut through it to get to the alphabet streets, to where we copped drugs. I knew I shouldn't be getting loaded but justified it by panhandling enough money to buy myself jars of red cabbage. Someone told me it was good for the liver.

One night at the A7, I picked up a guy with dark hair and eyes and went to his apartment. In the middle of sex, I told him I had hepatitis. He jumped off the bed, grabbed my clothes off the floor, threw them into the hallway, and pushed me out after them.

"Where am I going to go?" I asked.

"That's your fucking problem." He slammed the door.

The neighbor cracked his door to see what the fuss was about. He saw me standing there naked. Just a girl in distress, no danger to him. He shut the door.

It was 3 a.m. and I was wandering the streets with bra in hand asking strangers for help.

When no one laid out a hand I hailed a cab.

"Where to, miss?" the cabbie asked.

"Do you know where that store Steve of SoHo is?" I knew Nick and Susan lived across the street from the store because I owned a sweater with a Steve of SoHo tag that had belonged to my father.

"I remember where the store used to be."

I had no idea whether or not Susan still lived there. The cab driver stopped in front 167 Spring Street. I got out of the cab and rang Susan's bell. The driver waited because he needed to get paid and I didn't have any money.

Susan ran down the one flight of stairs and opened the glass lobby door. She was wearing white cotton pajamas, her dark hair in a ponytail. The last time she'd seen me was at Nick's memorial in 1979, two years earlier. I'd had a tan and long blonde hair. Now my skin was gray, and my hair was pink, blue, and green.

"Can I help you?" she asked.

"Susan?"

"Who are you?"

"Nicca."

"Oh my God."

She told the cabdriver to hang on she was going upstairs to get money to pay him. After she paid, we went inside to her loft and sat at the butcher block counter near the kitchen. She perched herself on a barstool across from me. She poured two glasses of San Pellegrino water and lit us each a cigarette.

"What's happened to you?" she asked.

I sobbed.

She reached across the counter and took my hand gently. "You can stay here tonight. Take a shower. We'll get some sleep and talk more in the morning."

It was early afternoon when I woke up. I had to pee. This time it was easy. For a second I thought the hepatitis might be gone. But then I looked into the toilet bowl and saw the burnt yellow urine.

Susan heard me come out of the bathroom. "Morning."

"Morning," I said.

"Join me."

I walked to the far end of the loft and sat in the orange rocking chair next to her bed. On one of the walls hung a poster that was kind of like the flyers bands used to tack onto signposts so that people would know they had an upcoming show or a record coming out. This particular flyer caught my eye because it was for the band, Television, and quoted my dad calling them, "Four Cats with a Passion." I loved Television, and I especially loved their original bassist and songwriter Richard Hell and his song "Blank Generation." Knowing that Nick knew the person who wrote those lyrics made me feel like I was connected to my father.

I needed that.

I needed that so much.

My father was my lifeline.

In Your End Is My Beginning

Many nights my father blew through the loft like a wind. Susan felt him, too. I could feel his spirit standing at the foot of my bed, watching me, breathing life into me. He was everywhere. The books he'd read were on the bookshelf, the records he'd listened to were on the turntable, the cups he'd drank out of were on the shelf, the forks he'd eaten with were in the silverware drawer, the blankets he'd slept under on the beds, some of them covering me. Susan gave me a daily meditation book that had once belonged to him. On the page before the title page he had written, "I am not here to die. I am here to get well and healthy."

I read his words every day and repeated them like a mantra.

On June 16, 1981, the second anniversary of Nick's death, I wrote:

> Talk about anguish, feel about love, think about friends, change and place. Talk about a lie, a hurt, a fear. The anniversary of my father's death. Two years. Today. Full moon. Daddy's dead. Whirlwinds. Whirlwinds. Blizzard brain. Quaaludes. Valium, heroin, heroin, go away.
>
> Needles, death, go away. Anger, restless. Battle, silent. Scream, yell, hit, whine, cry. Music.
>
> Relief. Dance. Fight. Release. Mind works. Bang bang. Shut up, shut up, shut up, shut up. Frustration.

Rebel. Rebel. Rebel rebel. Punk rock. Hardcore.
Drinking drinking shooting madness. Forget it or
blame it to forget it. Hostility. Mother's revenge.
Tears. Where'd I go?

My name is Nicca. New York, tall frightening, big
town. Little girl. Opportunity. Life. Forgiving my dad
for dying, forgiving myself for self-destruction and
not having the control I'd like to have over it. It happens sometimes, subconsciously . . . when death seems
so far, the wanting is greater. I want death more.
When death is so close, I am threatened and cheated
because I've just begun to live. I've died already or
played with the thought too much. To throw away life
because there's loss of hope is too passive. Why die
here when there is every bit of a chance to live? Death
holds such a serenity, but I don't want death anymore.
Death being the purpose of life is so true. Without
death there is no life."

I thought I was turning over a new leaf where dying wouldn't
be in the forefront. But, then Anndoll got work as a featured
extra in a movie and made enough money to come to New York.
I loved her. I couldn't say no. Susan let her stay in the loft.

Before going to clubs like the Peppermint Lounge, we
would drink liquid acid from the jar Susan's roommate, a
science major at New York University, made and stored in
the refrigerator. Sometimes we wanted to pretend we were
normal, so we went to the club without spiking our hair or
putting on too much makeup. When we got to the club no
one noticed us, so we went to the bathroom and spiked our
hair with the dispenser soap. Anndoll liked wrapping a piece
of cellophane into a huge bow on the top of her head. The
bow shone like a rainbow underneath the lights. With her
green roots and thick spiked hair, she looked like she stepped
out of a cartoon.

Susan knew I was doing drugs, but she didn't have it in her heart to make me leave. She hired Anndoll and I to work as production assistants on a documentary about Tiny Tim she was producing. He was famous for singing "Tiptoe Through the Tulips," in a high screeching voice, and getting married to his girlfriend, Miss Vicki, on *The Tonight Show* starring Johnny Carson. Susan was trying to find someone to play the part of Miss Vicki. The part required rubbing Tiny Tim's body with lotion. Lotion was his fetish. In the middle of his apartment there was a long table filled with hundreds of bottles. I shouldn't have been surprised that Tiny Tim wanted me to play the part of Miss Vicki. Thank God Susan was there to stand up for me and say no. Left to my own devices I would've said okay just because I didn't know I could say no. I was twenty-seven before I learned that I could say no to someone who was sexually attracted to me.

Saying no to Tiny Tim got me banned from having anything to do with the production. When filming ended Susan told me to tell Anndoll she had to move out. We were standing underneath the arch in Washington Square Park when I finally mustered up the courage to do it.

"Susan doesn't want a lot of people living there," I explained.

"Why do you get to stay?"

I shrugged.

"I don't think it's good for you to live there. There's so much stuff about your father. Let's me and you get a place on the Lower East Side. Come on. We'll live on Avenue D and 4th Street. In the heroin district."

"I don't know."

"Why doesn't Susan tell me herself I have to go? Why is she making you her mouthpiece?"

"I'm not her mouthpiece."

"I can't believe you didn't stick up for me. I can't believe you didn't say, 'If she has to go then I have to go.' I would've done that for you."

I hated telling her she had to go but my hepatitis wasn't gone and I was still getting loaded and I knew I needed to stop. But it took a few more times before I pulled myself away completely.

Anndoll moved into a five-story walk-up on 11th Street between First and Avenue A. The apartment belonged to DeDe Troit, the singer for the early punk band, UXA. We knew her from Los Angeles. As I recall she wasn't living in the apartment at the time. Black Randy, a singer for the sort of psychedelic punk band Black Randy and the Metro Squad was living there, though. Anndoll and I would shoot drugs with him using the same needle. They'd both tell me they better not catch my hepatitis and I would remain silent.

It was a crowded two-room railroad with slanted wood floors, a bathtub in the kitchen, and no exposure to the sun. A year earlier I would've left the loft and moved in with her. I would've told myself Susan was taking away my freedom by threatening to kick me out if I did drugs in her house. I would've marched across Third Avenue carrying my belongings in a black Hefty trash bag and woken the next day in the same bed as Anndoll, used cottons and dirty spoons on the floor, and thought I was home.

The thing about being drunk or high all of the time was that I kept coming out of blackouts and landing back in my life. I never saw how I got from here to there. I never claimed responsibility. Landing on Susan's doorstep changed that. I began realizing I was responsible for my life. I couldn't just get fucked up and land anymore.

Two weeks after turning twenty I got sober.

Lightning Over Water was having its premiere at The Public Theater on Lafayette Street. I was worried about what would happen to me if I saw the movie again. If I would cop dope or not. I was walking home from a dinner with a group of new friends in Greenwich Village, walking downtown on Sixth Avenue, debating with myself whether or not I was strong enough to see Nick live and die again on screen.

At dinner my friends told me I could put the film and my father on the shelf. They explained how the shelf is an imaginary place, like an attic in your heart or mind, where you can store the subject until you are strong enough to face it.

I wasn't ready to face my father. I put him on the shelf.

It was night, not too late. The sun had only been down a few hours. The air smelled like rain and I was feeling in awe of the moment, noticing how the streetlights and the moon and the car headlights worked together to light up the evening. I was in awe of life, of having made it.

Bring It On Home

Wim Wenders said that when he thought of Nick he pictured "that one eye that was like an eagle's eye. One seeing eye that could see through everything."

He could see through bullshit, especially his own. He saw himself. Some of the people I met along the way of this journey believed Nick was a man without conscience: someone who could move through people, wreak havoc on their lives and not blink an eye. If this is true, explain to me the tear drop stain on the stationary addressed, "Dear Betty, Julie, Nicca."

I'm not defending his tormented and sometimes cruel character. God, I used to hate it when people would describe him as tormented. It was a way his admirers absolved him from having to take responsibility for his actions. He was, though, a man riddled with torment who lashed out at those he loved with crushing results.

He had to wake up one afternoon and find himself with nothing but a masterpiece film to use as his calling card.

Yes, he resorted to conning people out of money to make the next great movie. Like any good junkie, he was a scammer. I haven't known any drug addicts or alcoholics who awaken proud of their previous day's intoxicated actions. The only remedy for the guilt and shame (aside from a commitment to sobriety) is to imbibe again, with more fervor than the day before, until the cycle is the quicksand that pulls you under. He removed himself from my sister and my life because he convinced himself he could bring nothing of value to the table.

I spent years listening to what stories those who knew him had to share. I read and reread the transcripts of the interviews with a microscopic eye. I wanted my own concrete assessment of my father. Sometimes the truths left me debilitated for a day or two, but I never considered getting drunk or high, though I did eat too much ice cream sometimes. Hell, a girl's gotta do what a girl's gotta do.

Betty used to say, "I don't believe in labels," whenever I asked her questions about Nick's psychological diagnosis. After she died, I threw away those labels, too, and looked at Nick with nonjudgmental eyes, setting aside anger, fantasy, hope, love, hate, desperation, pride, and shame. I had to look at the whole picture of who he had been as a father, husband, and film director with forgiveness.

It was ultimately by forgiving his (and my mother's) trespasses and taking responsibility for and forgiving my own that I was able to come to terms with the person he was: grand, intuitive, sensitive, genius, cruel, too many men living inside one body.

He was too much to contain and restrain. His attempts at self-restraint came by way of self-destruction. In death his mania could be stopped. Self-knowing, self-revelatory. Romantic and brutal, defined and undefinable, a walking contradiction, no ordinary man.

I say this without daydreamy glaze or fantasy attached.

When I talked to renowned film historian Jeanine Basinger, she said Nick "was from another planet."

Had he been an average man he would not have made movies that have stood the test of time. If he had not used film to understand the human condition, and in turn himself, we would not have Bowie in *They Live by Night,* Dix Steele in *In a Lonely Place,* Jeff McCloud in *The Lusty Men,* Jim Wilson in *On Dangerous Ground,* or Plato, James Stark, and Judy in *Rebel Without a Cause.*

When I close my eyes, I see Nick, an electric current, a white bolt shooting out of the sky.

I pray he is not forgotten.

Sources

All interviews conducted with the help of Stacey Asip.

TINKERBELL BETTY.

All Betty quotes from interview.

"Nick Ray emerged . . . " Houseman, John, *Front and Center*, Simon and Schuster, 1979.

"You propose to have a group . . . " Eisenschitz, Bernard, *Nicholas Ray: An American Journey*, Faber and Faber, 1990.

FOR LOVE AND THEATER.

All Tony quotes from interview.

Jean Evans, "She sort of kept an open house . . . " Eisenschitz, Bernard, *Nicholas Ray: An American Journey*, Faber and Faber, 1990.

Jean Evans, "We were rebelling . . . " Eisenschitz, Bernard, *Nicholas Ray: An American Journey*, Faber and Faber, 1990.

Jean Evans, "We had a . . . " Eisenschitz, Bernard, *Nicholas Ray: An American Journey*, Faber and Faber, 1990.

Edgar Tafel, "What happens when the corners . . . " Tafel, Edgar, *Apprentice to Genius: Years with Frank Lloyd Wright*, McGraw-Hill Book Company, 1979.

Nick said, "The most obvious influence . . . " Hillier, Jim editor, "Charles Bitsch: Interview with Nicholas Ray," *Cahiers du Cinema 89, November 1958*, reprinted in *Cahiers du Cinema: The 1950s-Neo-Realism, Hollywood, New Wave*, Harvard University Press, 1985.

"tempestuous," Henry Schubert quote, Eisenschitz, Bernard, *Nicholas Ray: An American Journey*, Faber and Faber, 1990.

"I have felt the hand of . . . " Eisenschitz, Bernard, *Nicholas Ray: An American Journey*, Faber and Faber, 1990.

Stanislavski, "What we are undertaking . . . " Braun, Edward, *Meyerhold: A Revolution in Theatre*, Methuan Publishing Ltd., 1995.

Harold Clurman, "had not blood relationship . . . " Clurman, Harold, *The Fervent Years*: *The Group Theatre and the Thirties*, Da Capo Press, 1975.

Harold Clurman, "to establish . . . " Clurman, Harold, *The Fervent Years*: *The Group Theatre and the Thirties*, Da Capo Press, 1975.

Harold Clurman, "basic struggle . . . " Clurman, Harold, *The Fervent Years*: *The Group Theatre and the Thirties*, Da Capo Press, 1975.

Kazan, "what I wanted . . . " Kazan, Elia, *Elia Kazan: A Life*, Alfred A. Knopf, Inc., 1988.

"words are decorations," Kazan, Elia, *Elia Kazan: A Life*, Alfred A. Knopf, Inc., 1988.

"The Group Theatre brought . . . " Norman Lloyd interview.

"recalling the circumstances," Kazan, Elia, *Elia Kazan: A Life*, Alfred A. Knopf, Inc., 1988.

"We believed every word . . . " Perry Bruskin interview.

"They did something . . . " Kazan, Elia, *Elia Kazan: A Life*, Alfred A. Knopf, Inc., 1988.

Jean Evans, "The only people . . . " Eisenschitz, Bernard, *Nicholas Ray: An American Journey*, Faber and Faber, 1990.

Nick, "The great thing about the theater . . . " Speaking to San Francisco theater company The Stage Group on July 15, 1977 courtesy of Bernard Eisenschitz archive.

Nick, "Kazan and I became friends . . . " Ray, Susan, *I Was Interrupted: Nicholas Ray on Making Movies,* University of California Press, 1993.

"Kazan was made of iron," Eisenschitz, Bernard, *Nicholas Ray: An American Journey*, Faber and Faber, 1990.

"more alert . . . " Ray, Susan, *I Was Interrupted: Nicholas Ray on Making Movies*, University of California Press, 1993.

"Nick and I were much . . . " Kazan, Elia, *Elia Kazan: A Life*, Alfred A. Knopf, Inc., 1988.

"In other words," Norman Lloyd interview.

"The show was quite complicated . . . " Norman Lloyd interview.

Earl Robinson, "We worked with . . . " Eisenschitz, Bernard, *Nicholas Ray: An American Journey*, Faber and Faber, 1990.

FOR LOVE AND MUSIC.

Alan Lomax, "Nick was certainly . . . " Eisenschitz, Bernard, *Nicholas Ray: An American Journey*, Faber and Faber, 1990.

"ramshackle church," Lomax, Alan, *The Land Where the Blues Began*, A Delta Book published by Dell Publishing, a division of Bantam Doubleday Dell Publishing Group, Inc., 1993.

Lomax to Charles Kuralt, Alan Lomax Archive, YouTube, December 7, 2012.

Lomax, "Nick was a searcher . . . " Transcripts from Nicholas Ray's Memorial Service, courtesy of Chris and Lilyan Sievernich.

"I had thousands of records, some of the first that were ever made," Bernard Eisenschitz Archive. Interview with Alan Lomax.

Pete Seeger, "driving up to Connecticut . . . " Pete Seeger interview.

"Dick Clarke on acid," Real Don Steele Collection Gallery: RDS . . . Reel Radio, www.reelradio.com.

Lomax, "Young people of the world . . . " Lomax to Charles Kuralt, Alan Lomax Archive, YouTube, December 7, 2012.

Lomax, "Nick was a very bad singer . . . " Bernard Eisenschitz Archives courtesy Bernard Eisenschitz. Eisenschitz interview with Alan Lomax.

Betty, "*Back Where I Come From* . . . " Betty interview.

"the avenging angel," Klein, Joe, *Woody Guthrie: A Life*, A Delta Book published by Dell Publishing a division of Random House, Inc., 1980.

THE DARKNESS.

Gretchen Horner, "Lena wanted nothing . . . " Gretchen Horner interview.

"She led me to a hotel room . . . " Eisenschitz, Bernard, *Nicholas Ray: An American Journey*, Faber and Faber, 1990.

Gretchen Horner, "I never saw . . . " Gretchen Horner interview.

"I was reading . . . " Letter to me from Barbara Price.

"Oh yeah, she was . . . " Gretchen Horner interview.

"She slumped . . . " Fairweather-Kemp, Karen, *Patterns*, Winepress Publishing, 2001.

Gretchen Horner, "She was bound . . . " Gretchen Horner interview.

Gretchen Horner, "porcupines . . . " Gretchen Horner interview.

Betty, "had never experienced . . . " Betty interview.

"I was born . . . " Nick's journal, 1968.

"I wanted to make it . . . " Nick's journal, 1968.

BE FREE.

"It was very idealistic . . . " Betty interview.

"like coming from hell . . . " Betty interview.

"Before I could go back . . . " Betty interview.

"respectable family man," Lewis-Herman, Judith, *Father Daughter Incest*, Harvard University Press, 1981.

STATES OF MIND.

"We discovered that folk music . . . " Houseman, John, *Front and Center*, Simon and Schuster, 1979.

"There was a good deal . . . " Houseman, John, *Front and Center*, Simon and Schuster, 1979.

"the most successful instance . . . " Houseman, John, *Front and Center*, Simon and Schuster, 1979.

"I saw what drew him . . . " Houseman, John, *Front and Center*, Simon and Schuster, 1979.

"is likely to emerge . . . " RKO inter-office memo . . . RKO archives at UCLA.

"the cop is . . . " Houseman, John, *Front and Center*, Simon and Schuster, 1979.

"He and Nick seemed . . . " Houseman, John, *Front and Center*, Simon and Schuster, 1979.

"revoke the assignment . . . " Eisenschitz, Bernard, *Nicholas Ray: An American Journey*, Faber and Faber, 1990.

"The character played by . . . " Eisenschitz, Bernard, *Nicholas Ray: An American Journey*, Faber and Faber, 1990.

"He is a man . . . " Bernard Eisenschitz Archive. Courtesy Bernard Eisenschitz. Notes compiled by Aideen Whitten for Film Buff Series, Whitten credits *Sight and Sound*, Autumn, 1961, and *Underworld USA* by Colin McArthur as her sources.

"We had two pictures . . . " Houseman, John, *Front and Center*, Simon and Schuster, 1979.

"A treadmill of stumbling . . . " Eisenschitz, Bernard, *Nicholas Ray: An American Journey*, Faber and Faber, 1990.

New York Times review, "For all of Nick's . . . " courtesy Motion Picture Library.

Hollywood Reporter review, "a good sound story . . . " courtesy Motion Picture Library.

"But it is the kind of failure . . . " Wilmington, Mike, "Nicholas Ray: The Years at RKO, Part Two." *The Velvet Light Trap*, #11 Winter 1974.

"What happens in . . . " Jeanine Basinger interview.

FOR LOVE AND HOLLYWOOD.

"It was like two magnets . . . " Eisenschitz, Bernard, *Nicholas Ray: An American Journey*, Faber and Faber, 1990.

"At four or five . . . " Eisenschitz, Bernard, *Nicholas Ray: An American Journey*, Faber and Faber, 1990.

"You must remember when all things . . . " Schary, Dore, *Heyday*, Little Brown, 1979.

"Jesus, how am I going to direct her . . . " Eisenschitz, Bernard, *Nicholas Ray: An American Journey*, Faber and Faber, 1990.

"The atrocity . . . " Eisenschitz, Bernard, *Nicholas Ray: An American Journey*, Faber and Faber, 1990.

"I did the film because I got a call that Cagney . . . " Goodwin, Michael and Wise, Naomi, "Nicholas Ray: Rebel!" *Take One*.

"he needed time to form . . . " Eisenschitz, Bernard, *Nicholas Ray: An American Journey*, Faber and Faber, 1990.

"something new and . . . " Eisenschitz, Bernard, *Nicholas Ray: An American Journey*, Faber and Faber, 1990.

"Like James Dean . . . " Stewart Stern interview.

"Nick felt Jimmy was his possession . . . " Stewart Stern interview.

"He was wary and hard to catch . . . " Nick's journal, 1968.

BIGGER THAN LIFE.

"Thank God you're here . . . " Lambert, Gavin, *Mainly About Lindsay Anderson*, Knopf, 2000.

"saw this tall . . . " Gavin Lambert interview.

"I knew . . . " Gavin Lambert interview.

"I'm a new . . . " Gavin Lambert interview.

"You can imagine . . . " Gavin Lambert interview.

"So how did you like . . . " to "Just like me . . . " Gavin Lambert interview.

"Possibly that he . . . " to "Like a car . . . " Ed Lachman interview.

"I think the European . . . " "Making Deals and Matching Actions: An Interview with Ed Lachman," *Wide Angle*, 1983.

"Thirty-one . . . " to "Old enough . . . " to "Three men . . . " to "astonishment and accept . . . " Lambert, Gavin, *Mainly About Lindsay Anderson*, Knopf, 2000.

"Butch handshake . . . " Lambert, Gavin, *Mainly About Lindsay Anderson*, Knopf, 2000.

"scared about his career . . . " Lambert, Gavin, *Mainly About Lindsay Anderson*, Knopf, 2000.

"Officially you belong . . . " Lambert, Gavin, *Mainly About Lindsay Anderson*, Knopf, 2000.

"Nick expected me to take him . . . " Gavin Lambert interview.

"There were times . . . " Lambert, Gavin, *Mainly About Lindsay Anderson*, Knopf, 2000.

"Dr. Siegal. He gave everybody shots . . . " Barbara Rush interview.

"Nick was this lovely . . . " Barbara Rush interview.

"He was this kind of person . . . " and "He was a mimic . . . " Barbara Rush interview.

Gavin Lambert's description of *Bitter Victory*, "a story of betrayal . . . " *Mainly About Lindsay Anderson*, Knopf, 2000.

"a heroin addict . . . " *Mainly About Lindsay Anderson*, Knopf, 2000.

"What's this . . . " conversation with Nick in hotel room from Budd Schulberg interview.

"Nick, Nick don't leave me," to "Jesus Christ . . . .she never stopped," Budd Schulberg interview.

"Where's Nick getting heroin . . . " Eisenschitz, Bernard, *Nicholas Ray: An American Journey*, Faber and Faber, 1990.

"He would come out late . . . " Budd Schulberg interview.

"You do realize . . . " Eisenschitz, Bernard, *Nicholas Ray: An American Journey*, Faber and Faber, 1990.

"It is the story of . . . " Budd Schulberg interview.

IN A LONELY PLACE.

"In my capacity . . . " Curtis Hanson interview.

"This movie . . . " *The New York Times*.

"I don't know how this film developed . . . " Curtis Hanson interview.

"I hate a script . . . " Ray, Susan, *I was Interrupted: Nicholas Ray on Making Movies*, University of California Press, 1995.

"Intimacy in film . . . " Bernard Eisenschitz interview.

"I was having them look . . . " Curtis Hanson interview.

"You think about *In a Lonely Place*," Curtis Hanson interview.

Hollywood Reporter and *Motion Picture Daily* reviews courtesy Motion Picture Library.

Account of Gloria Grahame's seduction of Tony and Nick's response are used with permission from Tony Ray and taken from his unpublished manuscript.

"I don't know how to approach . . . " Tony Ray interview.

BETTY.

All quotes from Betty are from Betty interview.

"Nick's medicine cabinet . . . " Gavin Lambert interview.

"I did see Nick . . . " Norman Lloyd interview.

"He'd come to my house . . . " Eisenschitz, Bernard, *Nicholas Ray: An American Journey*, Faber and Faber, 1990.

"We'd all go smoke . . . " Dennis Hopper interview.

REBEL WITHOUT A CAUSE.

"James Dean ate Nicholas Ray . . . " Charles Bitsch interview.

NEAR DEATH PARTY GIRL EXPERIENCE.

All quotes from Betty are from Betty interview.

All quotes from Tony are from Tony interview.

"In the *Savage Innocents* . . . " Bernard Eisenschitz Archive. Courtesy Bernard Eisenschitz. *Toronto Film Society Screening Notes*, R.R. Anger, February 26, 1968.

BABIES, SPEED AND MUSIC.

All quotes from Betty are from Betty interview.

All quotes from Gretchen Horner are from Gretchen Horner interview.

All quotes from Tony are from Tony Ray interview.

All quotes from Tim are from Tim Ray interview.

"I feel rather poetic . . . " Ray, Susan, *I Was Interrupted: Nicholas Ray on Making Movies*, University of California Press, 1993.

"It was a very interesting time because people . . . " Beverly Pepper interview.

"I was with *Newsweek* . . . " Bill Pepper interview.

"The choice we faced was between . . . " Navasky, Victor S., *Naming Names*, Farrar, Straus & Giroux, 1980/2003.

"They were all refugees . . . " Beverly Pepper interview.

"My guilt is what we did to the Czechs . . . " Navasky, Victor S., *Naming Names*, Farrar, Straus & Giroux, 1980/2003.

"Must every film . . . " Heston, Charlton, *The Actor's Life: Journals 1956-1976*, A Henry Robbins Book, E.P. Dutton, 1976.

"It was my feeling from the very beginning . . . " Bernard Gordon, Eisenschitz, Bernard, *Nicholas Ray: An American Journey*, Faber and Faber, 1990.

Bernard Gordon, "He was working the foreground . . . " Eisenschitz, Bernard, *Nicholas Ray: An American Journey*, Faber and Faber, 1990.

Manuel Mamposo, "Ray told me the eyes of the Empress . . . " Eisenschitz, Bernard, *Nicholas Ray: An American Journey*, Faber and Faber, 1990.

Charlton Heston, "most impressive . . . " Heston, Charlton, *The Actor's Life: Journals 1956-1976*, A Henry Robbins Book, E.P. Dutton, 1976.

Charlton Heston, "was surely one of the best directors . . . " Heston, Charlton, *The Actor's Life: Journals 1956-1976*, A Henry Robbins Book, E.P. Dutton, 1976.

"Nick Ray was theater," Stewart Stern interview.

Phil Yordan, "He had no heart attack," Eisenschitz, Bernard, *Nicholas Ray: An American Journey*, Faber and Faber, 1990.

"Barrington Cooper seemed to be able to . . . " Gavrik Losey interview.

"I wouldn't make him out to be the devil . . . " Beverly Pepper interview.

"He was fairly unorthodox . . . " Gavrik Losey interview.

"She was hysterical . . . " Gavin Lambert interview.

A DOG DOES NOT A FATHER MAKE.

All quotes from Julie are from Julie interview.

All quotes from Betty are from Betty interview.

"photos and would say, 'Look, . . . " Barbet Schroeder interview.

Letter from Paul Kohner courtesy Motion Picture Library.

Ellen Ray, "a film about . . . " Eisenschitz, Bernard, *Nicholas Ray: An American Journey*, Faber and Faber, 1990.

"Langlois said, 'Well you know there's this American filmmaker . . . " Ellen Ray interview.

"looking like he was on his last legs . . . " Ellen Ray interview.

"came from the drug culture . . . " Ellen Ray interview.

"I think it just blew him away . . . " Ellen Ray interview.

"believed it was his documentary . . . " Ellen Ray interview.

"He had no idea that the . . . " Eisenschitz, Bernard, *Nicholas Ray: An American Journey*, Faber and Faber, 1990.

"living in a . . . " Tim Ray interview.

FAMILY TIES.

All quotes from Tim Ray are from Tim Ray interview.

All quotes from Betty are from Betty interview.

All quotes from Tony are from Tony Ray interview.

All quotes from Julie are from Julie interview.

"As occupational therapy . . . " Eisenschitz, Bernard, *Nicholas Ray: An American Journey*, Faber and Faber, 1990.

"The first sign when I realized . . . " Eisenschitz, Bernard, *Nicholas Ray: An American Journey*, Faber and Faber, 1990.

"He had no idea where reality . . . " Gore Vidal interview.

IDENTITY LAPSE.

All quotes from Betty are from Betty interview.

All quotes from Julie are from Julie interview.

All quotes from Arthur Whittal are from Arthur Whittal interview.

All quotes from Tim are from Tim Ray interview.

All quotes from Phyllis are from Phyllis Stewart Smith interview.

All quotes from Tom Farrell are from Tom Farrell interview.

All quotes from Richie Bock are from Richie Bock interview.

All quotes from Gene Stavis are from Gene Stavis interview.

Nick "a ninety minute feature film where we . . . " From *We Can't Go Home Again* story by Nick Ray courtesy of Bernard Eisenschitz archive.

"We never shot improvisation . . . " Leslie Levinson interview.

"For three weeks after he got back . . . " Greenberg, Jeff, "Nicholas Ray Today," *Filmmakers Newsletter* Volume 6 #3 February 6, 1973.

"I prefer the outlaw . . . "Lecture for the American Film Institute held at Cal Arts.

HOMECOMING.

All quotes from Bernardo Bertolucci are from Bernardo Bertolucci interview.

All quotes from Tom Luddy are from Tom Luddy interview.

"I remember coming in one morning and . . . " Phil Kaufman interview.

"Peter called me and said . . . " Steve Wax interview.

"It was late at night . . . " Steve Wax interview.

"I'm looking at the footage . . . " Peter Gessner interview.

"Peter and I—our eyes . . . " Steve Wax interview.

"His students struck us . . . " Steve Wax interview.

"Nick was just another part . . . " Peter Gessner interview.

"He looked like a death mask . . . " Rob Niilson interview.

All quotes from Betty are from Betty interview.

All quotes from Julie are from Julie interview.

BREAK YOUR PLANS BECAUSE I HAVE FIVE MINUTES TO GIVE YOU.

"He was scarily . . . " Wim Wenders interview.

"I don't remember if Nick was familiar . . . " Wim Wenders interview.

DEAR DARLING, I'VE COME TO SAY GOODBYE.

All quotes from Betty are from Betty interview.

"Only later did I find out . . . " Miloš Forman interview.

The Call.

All quotes from Julie are from Julie interview.

All quotes from Betty are from Betty interview.

"*Lightning Over Water* was the way he wanted to die . . . " Chris Sievernich interview.

"Nick felt making the film would protect . . . " Wim Wenders interview.

"Nick exploited . . . " Ed Lachman interview.

"Who cares if he is a father to us," Pierre Cottrell interview.

"We were all aware . . . " Wim Wenders interview.

"My name is Alan Lomax . . . " Transcripts from Nicholas Ray's Memorial Service, courtesy of Chris and Lilyan Sievernich.

INTERVIEWS.

Gretchen Horner, Barbara Price, Perry Bruskin, Norman Lloyd, Peggy Lloyd, Pete Seeger, Farley Granger, Curtis Hanson, David Thomson, Dennis Hopper, Jeanine Basinger, Gavin Lambert, Stewart Stern, Charles Bitsch, Bernard Eisenschitz, Barbara Rush, Budd Schulberg, Gore Vidal, Bill and Beverly Pepper, Gavrik Losey, Ellen Ray, Myron Meisel, Barbet Schroeder, Stephane Tchlajeff, Harry Bromley-Davenport, Pierre Cottrell, Michou, Arthur Whittal, Phyliss Stewart Smith, Tom Farrell, Richie Bock, Leslie Levinson, Ken Jacobs, Gene Stavis, Bernardo Bertolucci, Tom Luddy, Phil Kaufman, Sheri Nelson-McLean, Peter Gessner, Steve Wax, Rob Nilsson, Maila Nurmi, Frank Mazzola, Wim Wenders, Chris Sievernich, Gerry Bamman, Dan Edelman, Miloš Forman, Annie Golden, Jon Jost, Ed Lachman, Corey Allen. And my family, Betty Meltzer, Tony Ray, Julie Ray, Tim Ray.

NICHOLAS RAY

JANUARY22, 64
Avenida America 31
Madrid—Spain

CURRENT address ON ENVELOPE: LV. FOE Paris (2) Munich(2)

I had a message from the bank this morning.
Yesterday mornig in the morning. Not like now
When it's just A. M.

The message was "we regret that due to absence of
funds we are cancelling your order to send
$ _____ x _____ each month to Mrs. E. Ray.   Est 1, 1157

Betty darling — since then I've received
your letter of panic and I've sent off
cables for loans — calls have been made —
the little — the big — who mount to dozens
who owe me. No response. Not yet. People
know I'm in trouble. (I always thought that was
when the effort to give was to be made).

I don't know how I've kept out of jail
or how I've managed to keep working and
fighting and keeping hope and confidence
and all that shit — but I do —

I even hope to be able to send an invitation
to you and the kids to come for the summer.
But first — bread for tomorrow — am trying —

Letter from Nicholas Ray to Betty; January 22, 1964

317

7ᵗʰ Auqust 1966

NICHOLAS RAY

To

Elizabeth

It is possible that I will be in California for
two days between now and the first week in August.

Mike has written me that you have an attorney - so
if you wish to have any papers signed relative to
divorce, perhaps he could have them prepared and
leave them with Mike for me to read and sign if
necessary.

To be consistent it is best that Nicca and Julie
do not know I am there - if I get there - any more
than they should be reminded of me at any time.
With the possible exception of Tim, I love them beyond
any other humans (including myself) I have ever known,
and earnestly desire never to have to prove it.

You, certainly more than anyone else, can appreciate
what I mean by that. By now, a unity in your family
should have begun to show strongly regardless of any
internal squabbles or intrusions from the outside.
The resultant security and stability coming from that
can only be threatened or weakened by the children
having recourse to an object which divides their
loyalties and disturbs their daily concerns with living.

Whatever form that "object" takes; - a postcard, a
picture, a gift, (Tim & Sumner both violated my
instructions) a flashy visit, a promise which can or
cannot be kept; is, in my probably unorthodox and
unacceptable opinion, both harmful and disturbing.
Certainly the sentimentalized "awareness" of being
loved by an "absent one" cannot be beneficial.

Nor do I give a damn how long the list of "Uncles"
becomes. Neither the occasional visitor nor the legal
division of authority will do anything the girls own
fantasies won't rationalize according to the character
they already have.

Letter from Nicholas Ray to Betty (Elizabeth); August 7, 1966, page 1

318

NICHOLAS RAY

-2-

This arrogant, unsolicited and unscientific opinion
became a decision on the day I finally conceded to
send the girls from Madrid to you. I have encountered
nothing to make me change the decision, and if it
reflects confidence in you, it is intentional.

Should you marry again, and I hope you do happily,
there will be no disturbing "third man" image for them
to cope with. Should there ever be need beyond your
ability to cope - it will be met - but I will not be.

Nich

I have had no address for you until
Now, when I am about to leave.
I understand there has been no
money from the bank. Enclosed
you will find ~~a check~~ cash.

It is regrettable if some park of the
above sound self-ennobling or such.

Letter from Nicholas Ray to Betty (Elizabeth); August 7, 1966, page 2

```
322P PDT AUG 22 66 LC251
L CDU366 26 PD INTL CD WESTERLAND VIA WUI 22 1655
LT RAY
  4311 MELBOURNE HOLLYWOOD (CALIF)
AM AT HAUS WEISENHOF KAMPENSYLT GERMANY NEXT TEN DAY  DOES
NICCA HAV DOG KISS JULIE THIRLLING TO SEE YOU LOVE

  NICK.
```

Telegram from Nicholas Ray to Betty; August 22, 1966

620 Eucalyptus Lane
Mill Valley, California 94941

1 August 1974

Dearest Betty,

I learned from Tim, with considerable dismay, that your last marriage has, at least temporarily, gone sour. I don't know why, nor do I have any intention of asking why. As I tried to explain to you at our last and most fulfilling encounter - the most dangerous part of my decision not to see Nicca and Julie again lay in the hope that any image of me would disappear, and I was happy they were in Mexico with your brother when we last met. The risk I was taking was that there would be no feedback from them - that their father had rejected them, didn't love them. My darling Betty, the only photographs I carry with me, daily, are those I have of Julie, Nicca and you, and the three of you are and have always been my only loves.

I, in my unmailed letters, told them that I would either write or send them one of my obituaries which would declare, if any did, my undying love for them. Not having had the chance to write my own obituary, except in this film when I say, "I was interrupted", I doubt if any cinema history or gossip columnist would include it. But, "I was interrupted" has as much to do, or more, perhaps, with my resolution to see the three of you again and setting the record of love straight than any other personal statement I have been able to make in any of my films. As an actor, swinging in a barn with a noose accidentally slipped around his neck, and which his weakened arms could not release -- the only "adjustment" I could take for that scene was that I hadn't, as yet, faced up to the responsibility I feared would come from my decision not to be a weekend father who could not keep his promises. Deeply, I think I was right. As deeply, I think I was wrong.

I was going to include two separate letters to Nicca and Julie, just letters of my reasoning and life-lasting love for them - as for you. Perhaps it is not necessary, if you think you can share this letter with them.

I leave here in a week for a lecture in Virginia; will return to California - Hollywood, this time - to fight C.F.I. and get a proper print of our film. I would be grateful to hear from you regarding how I can be of help to you and the girls, if at all, before I leave)(332-9701 - studio, or 388-5574 - house.)

Nick

Letter from Nicholas Ray to Betty; August 1, 1974

NICHOLAS RAY

Avenida America 31
Madrid—Spain

BETTY - JULIE - NICCA:

You are dreams - beautiful dreams
to me - NOT FANTASIES. And this is no time for me to
set xxwxix bang— I cracked my head on the
typewriter. I cant stay awake any
longer but I have to —

Look darling, your letter
saying & implying a lack in reality
on my part because I "have removed
myself from you for my own convenience"
or because I don't send money, has
a significance to you, mostly. It has
to me too but on a more practical
level, I think. If that sounds contradict-
ory to your financial condition which is
dramatic and tough — I beg you to
hold on until I can send some good
news — after that the hell part
won't be so difficult to talk about.
That's why I haven't written, mostly.
But now! among other things, Cooper
has admitted his expense account to

Letter from Nicholas Ray to Betty, Julie, and Nicca; Date unknown, page 1

Emerald Films contained the double
charges which my accountant and I
knew. Maybe this will begin to break
a part of the small freeze.
I will be living (am) at a new address
until May 1ˢᵗ - it is:

LITHLANDHOF
KAMPEN AUF/SYLT
Germ

Happy Easter! - but like Happy
last Valentines + Happy Lost Xmas
I too am eating grass - When nobody's
looking. By the way - be cautious
of the tax forms or any injuries sent
to you about a company called
Carousel etc — all my real love
is with you —

Letter from Nicholas Ray to Betty, Julie, and Nicca; Date unknown, page 2

11/6/74

Dear Betty:

It is imperative to me to try to make myself clear - or clearer to yourself than you think you are about me, therefore, I must think it is to you benefit as well as mine that you understand some of these things with an insight somewhat bolder than that which has given you such magnificent recovery and exterior control.

I did not come to this unspeakable chunk of land and people to take anything from you. I need not go into Tim's call for me regarding you and I asked for a few days to deliberate. Ten years of keeping one's opinion, and acting on it rightly or wrongly could very well lead that person towards an easy touch. I did not take or come to take from you. Immodestly, I viewed my action in coming here in two ways (to be of help - for Tim had somewhat overdramatized, I think) and secondly to take selfish satisfaction from a rationale provided for me to abate the long large hunger for the sight and sound and touch of you, Julie and Nicca. I did not come to take from you. The purpose of the coming was to give what I could and expect nothing in return. Before entering the apartment I was hesitant and

Letter from Nicholas Ray to Betty; November 6, 1974, page 1

afraid. I still am. And I would ask none
of you to do for me what I wouldn't try to do for you.
No longer an I one to be lived with.

When we met so briefly in '66 you remarked that you couldn't remember the
first three years of our marriage.. Yet,
you do – some things at least, or have begun
to. But I do not expect your insight
can or should be bold enough for you ever
to permit your suspicion of me to disappear
or a forced evasion to be appraised as
less than dishonesty.

Perhaps it would have been best for me
to permit the "legend" to reach the highest
cloud of absurdity and somehow disappeared
within it. Should such a phenomena
occur I will be seeing the three of you.

For practical reasons – many of them,
it is best I live apart from you
and our children – but above all others I
can bring you no joy.

Ciao –

N

Letter from Nicholas Ray to Betty; November 6, 1974, page 2

Aug. 1, 77.

Dear Nicca:

Thanks for your letter. I suppose that that moment on Sunday morning was about the warmest we've had together. At least it is one both of us can remember.

I can think of things I'd like you to have but either I can't afford them or can't be certain you'd like them, so use the enclosed as you wish. Only please don't buy any more gaucho pants, hunh?

Love you,

Dad

Letter from Nicholas Ray to Nicca; August 1, 1977

Acknowledgments

First and foremost I want to thank these two women:

Gillian McCain: My undying gratitude. Without you this book would not be.

Stacey Asip: Where do I even begin? San Francisco, Paris, Los Angeles. Those big tape recorders . . . Your flawless journalism skills. Your tenacity. Your guidance. I learned so much from you and am forever grateful for the time and energy you put into making sure no stone was left unturned. This book would not be without you.

Jesse McCloskey: How does a girl get so lucky to find someone like you? Thank you for never letting me quit. Eddie and Sisu forever.

Barbara Hroza and John Rukavina for being my family for the last thirty-seven years.

Peter Trachtenberg for telling me, years ago, I knew how to write this book. Your friendship and support throughout the years has given me the strength to keep on going. I love you.

The women who have helped keep my foundation strong: Ayn Plant, Ilene Waterstone, Maria McCabe, Elizabeth Hershon, Lexie Montgomery, Alison Cunningham-Goldberg, Victoria Allen, Jen Haus, Lynn Blumenfeld, Emily Jane Corbett, Gillian Welles, Isabelle Holland (RIP), Gloria Pochner (RIP).

My lifelong friends, Valerie Tremaine, Debi Squires, Nicole Heinmets, Alysa Johnson.

My Writer's Asylum crew, Lee, Michelle, Kate, and Anne.

Puma Perl, Tammy Faye, Donna Lee, Sara Glasser Havens, Elizabeth Kresch.

Pete Pavia who introduced me to Legs McNeil who connected me to Gillian McCain.

Daisy Wake, the transcribing queen.

Charles Silver and Josh Siegal.

Leith Adams for introducing me to Frank Mazzola and Catherine Hader.

The librarians at the Warner Bros. Archives at USC, The Margaret Herrick Motion Picture Library, UCLA Film and Television Archive, American Film Institute Library . . . I cannot remember all of your names, but your assistance opened my world immensely.

Bernard Eisenschitz for making your archive available to me. And for taking me to see *The Lusty Men* at the Bleecker Street Theater many moons ago. My gratitude for all of your hard work and generosity knows no bounds.

Chris and Lilyan Sievernich for your generosity and support.

Julie White, Tim Ray, Tony Ray (RIP), and the Fabulous Betty (RIP): Thank you for your bravery in opening up to me about Nick. I love my family.

Some of the people I interviewed for this book gave me the support and encouragement I needed to keep persevering by something they said during our interviews or by calling me every so often to check up on me and my progress. These people are Gavin Lambert, Curtis Hanson, Frank Mazzola, Dennis Hopper, and Jack Larson. May they all rest in peace.

And lastly, Peter Carlaftes, Kat Georges, and Mary Rose Manspeaker, my heart explodes.

About the Author

Nicca Ray was raised in Los Angeles, not far from the Griffith Park Planetarium where scenes from her father, Nicholas Ray's, most famous film, *Rebel Without a Cause*, were shot. First inspired by the New York Dolls performing on the *Real Don Steele Show*, she started going to clubs on the Sunset Strip when she was fifteen, and became heavily involved in the L.A. punk scene when she was seventeen. At age twenty, she began work on getting sober, and shortly after, moved to New York, where, in her early thirties, was accepted into the New School University. While a student she published short stories in various journals, made two short films—including one that screened at the New York Underground Film Festival—and starred in *Cutting Moments*, the first film in the underground gore classic series, *Family Portraits: A Trilogy of America*, directed by Douglas Buck. After graduating in 1999, at thirty-eight years old, she devoted her life to researching and interviewing people about her father's life, for which *Ray by Ray* is a culmination. She currently lives in New York City.

Recent and Forthcoming Books from Three Rooms Press

FICTION

Rishab Borah
The Door to Inferna

Meagan Brothers
Weird Girl and What's His Name

Christopher Chambers
Scavenger

Ron Dakron
Hello Devilfish!

Robert Duncan
Loudmouth

Michael T. Fournier
Hidden Wheel
Swing State

William Least Heat-Moon
Celestial Mechanics

Aimee Herman
Everything Grows

Eamon Loingsigh
Light of the Diddicoy
Exile on Bridge Street

John Marshall
The Greenfather

Aram Saroyan
Still Night in L.A.

Richard Vetere
The Writers Afterlife
Champagne and Cocaine

Julia Watts
Quiver

MEMOIR & BIOGRAPHY

Nassrine Azimi and Michel Wasserman
Last Boat to Yokohama: The Life and Legacy of Beate Sirota Gordon

William S. Burroughs & Allen Ginsberg
Don't Hide the Madness:
William S. Burroughs in Conversation with Allen Ginsberg
edited by Steven Taylor

James Carr
BAD: The Autobiography of James Carr

Richard Katrovas
Raising Girls in Bohemia:
Meditations of an American Father

Judith Malina
Full Moon Stages:
Personal Notes from
50 Years of The Living Theatre

Phil Marcade
Punk Avenue: Inside the New York City Underground, 1972–1982

Alvin Orloff
Disasterama! Adventures in the Queer Underground 1977–1997

Nicca Ray
Ray by Ray: A Daughter's Take on the Legend of Nicholas Ray

Stephen Spotte
My Watery Self:
Memoirs of a Marine Scientist

PHOTOGRAPHY-MEMOIR

Mike Watt
On & Off Bass

SHORT STORY ANTHOLOGIES

SINGLE AUTHOR

The Alien Archives: Stories
by Robert Silverberg

First-Person Singularities: Stories
by Robert Silverberg
with an introduction by John Scalzi

Tales from the Eternal Café: Stories
by Janet Hamill, with an introduction
by Patti Smith

Time and Time Again:
Sixteen Trips in Time
by Robert Silverberg

MULTI-AUTHOR

Crime + Music: Twenty Stories
of Music-Themed Noir
edited by Jim Fusilli

Dark City Lights: New York Stories
edited by Lawrence Block

The Faking of the President: Twenty
Stories of White House Noir
edited by Peter Carlaftes

Florida Happens:
Bouchercon 2018 Anthology
edited by Greg Herren

Have a NYC I, II & III:
New York Short Stories;
edited by Peter Carlaftes
& Kat Georges

Songs of My Selfie:
An Anthology of Millennial Stories
edited by Constance Renfrow

The Obama Inheritance:
15 Stories of Conspiracy Noir
edited by Gary Phillips

This Way to the End Times:
Classic and New Stories of
the Apocalypse
edited by Robert Silverberg

MIXED MEDIA

John S. Paul
Sign Language: A Painter's Notebook
(photography, poetry and prose)

FILM & PLAYS

Israel Horovitz
My Old Lady: Complete Stage Play
and Screenplay with an Essay on
Adaptation

Peter Carlaftes
Triumph For Rent (3 Plays)
Teatrophy (3 More Plays)

Kat Georges
Three Somebodies: Plays about
Notorious Dissidents

DADA

Maintenant: A Journal of
Contemporary Dada Writing & Art
(Annual, since 2008)

TRANSLATIONS

Thomas Bernhard
On Earth and in Hell
(poems of Thomas Bernhard
with English translations by
Peter Waugh)

Patrizia Gattaceca
Isula d'Anima / Soul Island
(poems by the author
in Corsican with English
translations)

César Vallejo | Gerard Malanga
Malanga Chasing Vallejo
(selected poems of César Vallejo
with English translations
and additional notes by
Gerard Malanga)

George Wallace
EOS: Abductor of Men
(selected poems in Greek & English)

ESSAYS

Womentality: Thirteen Empowering Stories
by Everyday Women Who Said Goodbye to
the Workplace and Hello to Their Lives
edited by Erin Wildermuth

HUMOR

Peter Carlaftes
A Year on Facebook

POETRY COLLECTIONS

Hala Alyan
Atrium

Peter Carlaftes
DrunkYard Dog
I Fold with the Hand I Was Dealt

Thomas Fucaloro
It Starts from the Belly and Blooms
Inheriting Craziness is Like
a Soft Halo of Light

Kat Georges
Our Lady of the Hunger

Robert Gibbons
Close to the Tree

Israel Horovitz
Heaven and Other Poems

David Lawton
Sharp Blue Stream

Jane LeCroy
Signature Play

Philip Meersman
This is Belgian Chocolate

Jane Ormerod
Recreational Vehicles on Fire
Welcome to the Museum of Cattle

Lisa Panepinto
On This Borrowed Bike

George Wallace
Poppin' Johnny

Three Rooms Press | New York, NY | Current Catalog: www.threeroomspress.com
Three Rooms Press books are distributed by PGW/Ingram: www.pgw.com